THE LANFRANC BOYS

The story of the Holtaheia
plane crash in Norway

Rosalind Jones

Commemorating all those who died
on Holtaheia, August 9th 1961.

This book is dedicated to the families and friends
of those who died and to all those involved
in the rescue, especially the
Stavanger Red Cross Hjelpekorps.

All proceeds from this book will go to the
Stavanger Branch of the Norwegian Red Cross
to assist with their International Aid Work.

THE LANFRANC BOYS

ISBN 978-0-9531890-3-8

Published by Craigmore Publications,
Blanchards, Les Monts, Avernes-s-Exmes,
61310, Normandy, France.
www.craigmore-publications.co.uk

In association with Filament Publishing.

Filament Publishing

www.FilamentPublishing.com

Author Rosalind Jones.

Book designed by Susan MacKinnon,
CGL (Oban) Ltd.

This book is translated into Norwegian under the Norwegian title 'Flystyrten i Holtaheia.'

All rights reserved. No part of this publication may be reproduced, stored in a retrievable system or transmitted, in any form or by any means, electronic, mechanical, photocopying, recording or otherwise, without the prior permission of the publisher.

FOREWORD

by Sir Michael Parkinson

Certain stories stick in the mind. I had covered disasters before but the Lanfranc air crash, involving as it did so many young people, was particularly poignant and has remained in my memory ever since.

I remember the meeting with Rosalind Jones if only because she was a direct and articulate witness to a terrible tragedy. Her family had phoned the Daily Express so the access we were granted was free of the normal gamble of finding people willing to talk about such a tragedy. Her book is the story of a terrible disaster and the ripple effect it had on all the families of the victims. No-one involved at the time, including those journalists who covered it, will have forgotten the events of that terrible day. I certainly haven't and I thank Rosalind Jones for her moving account of this awful tragedy.

Daily Express
10th August 1961.

AUTHOR'S PREFACE

'The Lanfranc Boys' chronicles the worst tragedy to overtake a British school in peacetime. It happened in August 1961 and deeply affected the population of Croydon in South London and also of Stavanger in south-western Norway.

It tells of the ill-fated flight of Cunard Eagle's Viking 'Papa Mike', which crashed 20 miles off course, into Holtaheia, a low mountain, killing all 39 on board. At that time it was Norway's worst aviation accident. Those who died were 34 teenage boys and two masters from Lanfranc Secondary Modern Boys School in Croydon, and three Cunard Eagle Airways crew.

The book, in a diary of events, shows the victims as they were, vivacious and with bright futures ahead of them. It details the history of Papa Mike's last flight and its crash in mysterious circumstances. It links personal memories of what happened to the families and friends of the victims, and also the rescuers. It includes some thought-provoking stories. The positive effect of visiting Holtaheia, the scene of the disaster is seen through my eyes as a 16 year old, analysed with the wisdom of hindsight. Premonitions of the disaster are reviewed, whilst a recent discussion by Norwegian aviation personnel involved at the time give new insights as to what may have happened to cause the crash. Relatives and friends have supplied memories of those who died. Fifty years on, the Lanfranc Boys are not forgotten.

The fresh content of this book is owed entirely to the wealth of individual contributors who contacted me through newspaper articles published on both sides of The North Sea. Monica Porter's popular column 'Missing and Found' featured in The Daily Mail brought in the majority of British contacts worldwide; articles by Tor Inge Jøssang of Stavanger Aftenblad provided me with wonderful Norwegian contacts, whilst articles by Aline Nassif and Ian Austen of The Croydon Advertiser supplied the majority of Croydon contacts.

Notices left in Croydon's libraries, Croydon Cemetery, Crystal Palace Football Club and other websites brought me others, whilst word of mouth and serendipity provided the rest. I was amazed at the response. None had forgotten August 1961. All wanted the tragedy to be remembered. Much graphic additional information was provided by newspaper reports and archival material both from Norway and Britain, and from personal archives.

The Lanfranc disaster had an effect analogous to a boulder dropped into a millpond. Shock waves created propagated ever outwards, picking up and irrevocably carrying away flotsam in their wake. It was a disaster that totally changed and re-ordered the lives of those involved, and its effects live on today. Numerous personal stories have come to light. Some have been sealed away for years, buried deep, too traumatic to bear scrutiny. For many, sharing their memories has been a painful process. I thank everyone, sincerely, for their courage and altruism in re-opening painful scars. Whilst the majority have been pleased that their relative or friend will be remembered, a handful wished never to be reminded of those dreadful days. It is entirely thanks to the combined help, input, and encouragement of families, friends, rescuers, helpers, or even bystanders who never forgot their experiences, that a more complete account of the Lanfranc Air Crash can be told. They are all acknowledged and thanked.

'The Lanfranc Boys' is dedicated to the families and friends of those who died and to all the rescue workers, especially those members of the Stavanger branch of the Norwegian Red Cross Hjelpekorps who rescued the crash victims. The book commemorates the people of Stavanger and Strand who showed such compassion to strangers from the town of Croydon. In recognition of this, all royalties from this book will be donated to the Stavanger Red Cross to help with their International Aid Work, so that others suffering and in need, may benefit and be able to rebuild their lives – as we did.

Rosalind Jones, 2011

THE LANFRANC BOYS

INTRODUCTION

"The Toss of a Coin"

An innocent gamble, the tossing of a coin, changed my life and that of my family, completely, utterly, and forever. As a result my carefree childhood ended and I suddenly grew up, whilst my family's happiness and close-knit structure was shattered. It was in August 1961 that it happened, yet I can remember the details vividly even now – so deeply were they etched in my heart and mind at the time.

I was just fifteen and part of a large happy family. I had four brothers, Tony and Martyn older than me, and Quentin and Nigel younger. I was the only girl sandwiched between. It was Quentin, my junior by a year, whom I was closest to. Though small for his age, Quentin was very distinctive, having mahogany red hair, green eyes, and rosy cheeks. His dynamic character made him the equal of his friends who nick-named him 'Greenfly' and 'Kew Green'. A pupil at Lanfranc Secondary Modern Boys School in Croydon (now named Archbishop Lanfranc School) he was, out of school, head chorister at church, a keen cyclist, cricketer, and a newspaper round boy. We always spent our free time together.

I met him on his way home from school that fateful day and I remember our conversation well. He had come home from school very excited the previous afternoon, telling my parents that there was one spare place suddenly available on the school holiday to Norway. Quentin had had the chance to sign up for the trip but preferred to have a new bike. Now a boy had pulled out and Quentin and another boy both wanted to go. My father who had never been further than the Isle of Wight was keen that each of his children should travel abroad, so he agreed Quentin could try for the last place – on the condition that if he went then he must pay back for his bike from his earnings as a paper boy.

When I saw Quentin I asked 'What happened about the Norway trip Quentin?'

'We had to toss for it' he replied.

I knew he always called 'Heads' when a coin was tossed whereas I always called 'Tails'.

'Guess what?' he said.

'You lost!' I replied, for his face was dead pan.

'No! I WON!' Quentin whooped – his face transformed, delighted that he'd fooled me.

But Quentin had LOST. He lost and we lost, and we all paid a very high price for that small gamble.

The day came in August when Quentin was to go. It was August 9th, Quentin was still thirteen. He would have been fourteen on August 21st but he will always be thirteen in my memory. Unlucky 13. I was still in bed when he came to say goodbye early that morning. As teenagers we'd stopped giving each other kisses, but this morning I grabbed his hand and said 'Kiss me goodbye Quentin.'

'Oh *no* Ros…' he replied,pulling away.

'*Please* kiss me goodbye Quentin' I urged, suddenly aware that a voice inside me was crying out for me to say *'I'll never see you again.'* I was amazed. What was happening? I knew I couldn't say what had come into my head yet somehow I felt impelled, so I consciously modified the unnerving message and said instead *'I may never see you again…'*

'Oh don't be so morbid Ros' he laughed. Then he gave me a fleeting peck on the cheek and was gone.

But the voice inside my head was right. As he closed my bedroom door that *was* the last time I ever saw him.

It was a fine August day in England and my mother and I, in the garden after lunch, imagined Quentin commencing his 'adventure holiday' in Norway together with his school friends. My mother (who used to be the school secretary at Lanfranc) was telling me about Mr Beacham and Mr Budd, the teachers leading the trip whom she knew and admired, when I heard the telephone ring. I dashed to answer it in case the caller rang off. It was Quentin.

'Quentin! Why are you calling from Norway?'

'I'm still at London Airport. The plane has had engine trouble but they're putting it right. We are going to fly out soon.'

He wasn't there yet! I wanted to shout 'DON'T GO!' into the receiver but how could I? I felt confused. My stomach churned. What was going on? Was I crazy?

My mother spoke to him, and when Quentin said goodbye, simultaneously we said 'Goodbye Quentin, God Bless you.' My mother now shared my unease but reassured me by saying that she had taken Quentin for a blessing at church the morning before. I tried to be rational; of course I was being silly, I was always too imaginative, *nothing* would happen to Quentin. Nothing would happen to *our* family, dreadful things only happened to *other* people I thought, not us. My mother immediately telephoned my father in London to say that the plane hadn't left yet. My father's response was to insure Quentin at the last moment. It was uncanny. We all felt a sense of foreboding but we didn't *believe* our sixth sense because we had never experienced it before. My mother and I pushed our fears aside because as Christians we believed that 'God would protect'. My father believed that by taking out insurance Quentin would undoubtedly be fine whilst he would simply lose the insurance premium, which was a price worth paying for peace of mind. It was surreal. We couldn't have stopped Quentin from going because like his 33 school friends and their masters he was looking forward to a fantastic adventure holiday – in far off Norway!

The hours passed and assuming the party had arrived safely, that evening I was away from home with my parents looking at a folding caravan for our family camping holidays. We returned home after nine o'clock to find my eldest brother Tony hovering anxiously by the front door. He ran to meet the car, breathless.

'Where in Norway was Quentin going? What was the name of the place?'

'Stavanger I think. Why?' asked my father.

'Oh God NO!' said Tony, suddenly ashen. 'The nine o'clock news announced that a plane from London Airport to Stavanger, with an 'all male' passenger list is missing!'

Fear and disbelief clutched at my heart. My head was numb with terror as my father phoned London Airport. Our worst fears were confirmed. It *was* the Lanfranc School party. We glued ourselves to the radio for the next news, hearing the official statement. 'A plane which took off from London to Stavanger in Norway is missing. The plane, a Vickers Viking, code name Papa Mike has an all male passenger list, but no details can be given until all next of kin have been informed.'

No one knew that it was Lanfranc School from Croydon. No one knew that it was a plane full of school boys! A strong journalistic streak made my mother realise the importance of this as a story. The public should know, not be kept in the dark. Powerless to do anything practical to help, all she could do in the terrible vacuum was to inform a national daily newspaper. My father 'phoned the Daily Express and within half an hour two young men were with us taking the story about the school holiday to Norway. Everything felt unreal. Time moved slowly. My senses seemed more acute. Earnestly I told my story to the main journalist who fired questions at me. He was a young man with attractive craggy features, straight dark brown hair, and a Yorkshire accent. I remember his alert directness. It felt like a dream yet the clawing pain in my stomach and the panic in my heart told me it was *real*. The men raced back to Fleet Street taking away a school badge, a recent photo of Quentin (ominously looking skywards) pleased with the story angle they'd learned from me about Quentin winning the last place on the plane on 'the toss of a coin'.

Unknown to me then the young reporter was Michael Parkinson – one day to become internationally famous as 'Sir Parky'.

Alone again we tried to dismiss the awful possibilities. Despite my forebodings I attempted to be optimistic – what did I know about Norway? I'd learnt about the country in geography lessons at school – it had lots of long fjords I told my parents. The plane might have come down in a fjord and planes could float…

couldn't they? And Quentin could swim, although not far… We imagined the boys climbing out on to the wings of the aircraft and clung to the hope that Quentin and his friends were alive. My parents insisted I went to bed whilst they remained anxiously waiting for news. My father and mother hopefully envisaged Quentin and his friends wandering around, lost in the dark somewhere. Perhaps some were injured but surely they'd be found as soon as it was light. The truth was that we had very little idea of what Norway was like at all. I couldn't sleep for recalling that I'd also learnt that fjords are very, very deep. What if the plane had sunk without trace? I also remembered a music lesson when Grieg's sombre 'Hall of the Mountain King' had been played – but I tried to cast out such black thoughts and finally slept.

When I awoke early the next day for a blissful few seconds it felt like any other morning until realisation sucked me back to reality. Quentin's plane was missing! I rushed to find my parents to ask if there was any news – but there wasn't any. Stationed by the radio in our kitchen my elder brothers and I waited in a state of fearful hope. My weary parents walked arms about each other, round and round the central rose bed in our drive when a news flash came through. 'The plane missing near Stavanger in Norway has been found crashed in the mountains. There are no survivors.' An invisible spear plunged into my heart. Tony and Martyn were speechless with misery, six year old Nigel didn't understand. When my parents walked back in shortly after, I knew that I must be the one to tell them. Eyes brilliant with tears I forced myself to speak.

'The news says they've found the plane…' my voice choked on the lump in my throat '…and there are no survivors.'

'There are *nine* survivors?' said my father mishearing me, clutching at a straw.

'No Daddy!' I said blinking back my tears 'there are NO survivors…'

I threw my arms around them both to comfort and be comforted as my tears fell. We were all stunned. The unbelievable had happened. A nightmare had begun, but not just for us. For all thirty six families of boys and masters in Croydon and for the three families of the air crew the news was as though a guillotine had fallen. Once compos mentis heads felt separated from bodies, unable to take in the enormity or finality of what had happened. Normality had ceased to exist. It was impossible to take in 'NO survivors' when only yesterday our loved ones had been alive and so full of life!

My mother, a small lady with a strong faith, already used to tragedy, bravely accepted the news. Stoically and silently she handed her young son 'back to God' believing that children were given to parents in trust only. Quentin she believed was with his heavenly father and she was comforted by her sure and certain belief in everlasting life. It was her strength that sustained me and my brothers. My tall professional father could not accept this philosophy.

We did not have much time to think about anything, for the day suddenly became not only the most momentous but also the busiest of my young life. The telephone kept ringing, hordes of reporters turned up or telephoned to take our story, bunches of flowers arrived and numerous well-wishers called. We were just sitting down to a very late lunch of sorts when the doorbell rang again. 'I'll take it' I said seeing the care-worn expressions on my parent's sad faces. I opened the front door and looking out into the sunlight I saw a man I knew from television appearances standing on our doorstep. The sun shining behind him lit up his fluffy blonde hair instantly reminding me of yellow duckling down. His soft-skinned baby-pink face wore a deeply sympathetic look.

'Good afternoon' he said looking down at me benignly, 'I'm sorry to disturb you, but I'm Godfrey Winn.'

'Yes I know you are' I said numbly, adding, surprised at my rudeness, 'Please come in'.

He stayed with us for a couple of hours talking about Quentin. He had already seen another family with the same surname as us who had lost their son. The long article he wrote was published the following day and in it he said that he'd come with the intention of comforting us but instead had gone away comforted. He had been particularly impressed by my mother, whilst my father had shown him his rose garden. During Godfrey Winn's visit we had all managed to control the depths on our grief.

My childhood ended on August 9th. Before that day my life had been secure and my happy family had seemed invulnerable. Now our family circle was rent and my favourite brother gone. I had never heard my father cry, but he did the night of August 10th. Once all our sympathetic visitors had departed I heard a terrible noise I'd never heard before. At first I couldn't think what it was. When I realised, it tore at my heartstrings. It was the worst sound I had ever heard. My father, who hadn't cried since he was a little boy, was howling with grief; able at last to give vent to his pent up agony. His son was dead and as head of the family he blamed himself for letting Quentin go.

Spread throughout Croydon the 35 other families spent their own unforgettably horrendous day. It is true to say that everyone in Croydon felt shocked and horrified by the news as almost everybody knew a family involved. Elsewhere in England the families of the three air crew were also prostrate with grief.

'The Toss of a Coin' is my own particular memory but my brother Quentin was just *one* boy out of 34 boys, two masters, and three crew, whose families had their own stories. Over the years I have been able to trace back everything that has happened to me since to that one defining moment when my brother called 'Heads' and my world and that of my family changed forever. I have often wondered what happened to the lucky boy who called 'Tails' and lost the toss but won his life. My research unearthed many surprises.

Rosalind Jones

THE LANFRANC BOYS

CROYDON IN 1960

'The Lanfranc Boys', both those who died and those who went on to live their lives, were born as the Second World War ended and peacetime began. Raised on frugal post-war rationing, they grew into fit, energetic lads, who with 1950's austerity behind them looked forward to a bright future in the 60's. They all lived in the go-ahead, Surrey market town of Croydon, ten miles south of London.

Croydon was famous for its international airport, London's first official airport with an iconic purpose built terminal. Charles Lindbergh, Amy Johnson, and Winston Churchill had all piloted planes from Croydon, and it had served as an RAF station during WWII. Croydon suffered much wartime bombing, but post-war urban encroachment sadly forced the airport's closure in 1959 – disappointing its populace, especially its boys who 'spotted' the planes flying in and taxiing up to its famous flat roofed buildings. The Lanfranc boys would have enjoyed, for a decade of more, the excitement of watching planes that swooped down from the blue, or took off, engines roaring, into the open sky. The thrills of seeing close to, the activity at Croydon Airport from Purley Way, the road that ran next to it, was like a virus that aviation-mad boys couldn't eradicate. It was a very sad day when Croydon Airport closed.

Despite the airport's closure, Croydon retained its commercial importance because of excellent shops and light industries. Croydon's George Street almost rivalled London's Oxford Street with three department stores, Allders, Grants, and Kennards, plus Marks and Spencers, C&A, and British Home Stores, and it boasted Surrey Street Market. There were numerous prospering service industries offering apprenticeships and varied job prospects. Croydon was a proud County Borough with an active Council, and by 1960 had new Technology and Art colleges, with 'The Fairfield Halls' theatre complex under construction. Modern architecture sat alongside Medieval; Whitgift Alms

Houses (built 1596) occupied the corner of George Street and presented a peaceful haven amidst a busy town centre. 1960 was a momentous year because Croydon celebrated one thousand years – having been chronicled in Saxon times as 'Croindene' in 960 – named for its crocus flowers. All 'Croydonians' nurtured high expectations for their municipality – in its 'New Millennium'.

Croydon is a large borough, elongate north-south, consisting at that time of 14 wards, and unusually, Lanfranc boys lived in almost every one of them. In the north the leafy suburbs of Norbury and Upper Norwood, then southwards the terraced streets of Thornton Heath, West Croydon, South Norwood, Selhurst, and Woodside. In the centre the light-industrial districts of Broad Green and retail districts of Croydon, residential Waddon, and East Croydon. Addiscombe, South Croydon, and hilly Shirley comprised the southeast. Sixteen railway stations made Croydon convenient for commuting to London. It was a town 'on the up' and by 1960 it showed few of its wartime scars.

The post-war baby boom, plus the raising of the school leaving age, meant that during the 1950's Croydon's schools underwent rapid growth and development. They had to because demobbed servicemen had celebrated their return to wife and home, resulting in a bumper crop of babies 'found under the gooseberry bush'. Britain's population growth bulged in 1947, when the birth rate doubled. Croydon Education Committee rose to this demographic challenge by extending old schools and building new ones, including a modern complex for Lanfranc Boys.

LANFRANC
A Rough Tough School

Lanfranc School was an educational 'guinea pig', being the first Croydon school to have a vocational bias towards mechanical trades. Emphasising technology, the curriculum was widened to provide better educated practical workers for the new, free world. Established in 1931, it was in 1947 that Mr. A. T. Fowle became its second headmaster. In 1956 'Lanfranc Secondary Modern School for Boys' moved from Rosecourt Road, the short distance to Mitcham Road, on

Croydon's northwest boundary. Its scholastic intake was from a pool of boys not offered places in any of Croydon's Public, Grammar, Technical, or academic streams in Modern Schools, who collectively 'creamed off' the academic best. Lanfranc boys were judged as 'bottom of the barrel' from their marks in the competitive 11+ exam. There were other Secondary Modern schools in Croydon besides Lanfranc, but discerning parents wanted their children to benefit from a place at this newly built experimental school with a reputedly excellent headmaster. As a result Lanfranc's pupils lived throughout Croydon and whilst most were within walking or cycling distance, others had lengthy bus journeys to school.

The new Lanfranc school was built where fragrant 'Mitcham Mint and Lavender' had historically grown. When gravel was discovered, extraction left a 15 acre pit that in time was filled with bomb rubble and post-war waste. Adjacent to Croydon Cemetery and Mitcham Common, the landfill site was deemed ripe for development when Croydon Education Committee searched for a suitable school location to accommodate some baby-boomers. The landfill site was literally ripe because the infill wasn't consolidated, so Croydon Education Committee's architects decided to build on piled foundations sunk into the landfill. Lanfranc's bright modern school was erected on top of a slowly subsiding cavern of wartime waste.

Conceptually futuristic the layout was limited by the most economic usage of the costly piles, so a compact rectangular plan for the school was used. An Assembly Hall formed its core around which practical rooms for metal work, wood work, and science, then classrooms, gymnasium, library, dining room, kitchen, administrative rooms, and cloakrooms were built. Surrounding land was rolled and seeded to provide extensive (but initially hazardous) playing fields for football, rugby, and cricket. When building work finished, because Lanfranc was named after the 1st Norman Archbishop of Canterbury, the 99th Archbishop of Canterbury, Dr Geoffrey Fisher, was invited to officially open the school in 1956. Did His Grace notice an unpleasant whiff on his visit? The new school atop its piles sometimes smelt of methane, whilst nearby light industry added their own chemical perfume. On windless days pupils and staff kept the windows closed.

Lanfranc had a 'Rough and Tough' reputation but the roll of over 600 boys, many of whom felt doomed to be 'factory fodder', were lads with unproved potential, ready to be shaped and moulded by their teachers. Most came from caring middle and working class families, others from less happy backgrounds including broken homes. Some lived in pleasant neighbourhoods with back gardens, whilst a few still lived in old houses with gas lighting, outside toilets and tin baths hanging on their back walls. Most boys played football and cricket in the streets. Class didn't matter at Lanfranc where all were treated equally, nevertheless boys were 'streetwise' and classes were large, so discipline was strict to deter cheeky lads from disrupting lessons. The slipper (a P.T. plimsoll), and in extremis the cane, helped maintain order, the rationale being that pupils were at school to be *educated* and the place to release exuberance and aggression was on the playing fields or in the boxing ring! Croydon Education Committee monitored its schools and Lanfranc was expected to meet or exceed their standards. Mr Fowle didn't like using the cane but he knew that to 'spare the rod' was to 'spoil the child', so strict fair discipline was the status quo. Most boys accepted this cheerfully – they were happy to 'toe the line', but a few rebels hated it.

In 1960 foundation piles emerged as the landfill subsided, leading to jokes that Lanfranc was built on stilts! Adventurous boys discovered they could crawl underneath the main building from the playground at the back to the school entrance at the front. None dared emerge because Lanfranc's frontage, for staff and visitors only, was out of bounds. Boys had their own side entrance at the back of the school, near the school garden and playgrounds. Many took a short cut to school through Croydon Cemetery, saving valuable time, whilst late arrivals slipped through unfinished boundaries avoiding prefects on duty detailed to report them – or risk paying a shilling fine *not* to report them!

Lanfranc had a hierarchy, from new intakes in the first year (who unless they had an elder brother to protect them were at the mercy of the older boys), through second, third, and fourth years, to the prefects and leavers in the fifth year. Lanfranc's echelon consisted of mainly ex-service teachers and headmaster.

Lanfranc Secondary Modern Boys School, 1960.

*The Headmaster of Lanfranc.
Mr A. T. Fowle*

The school badge.

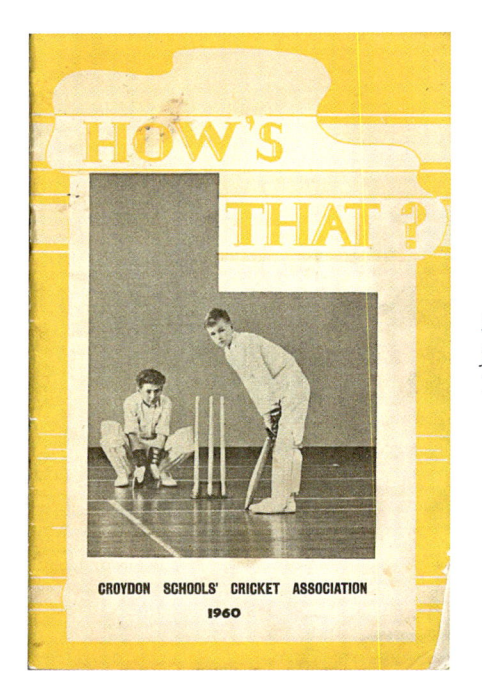

How's That? magazine featured Wicket Keeper Trevor Condell.

Lanfranc Under 15 football team 1961, Geoffrey Green 6th from left top row, John Wells 3rd from left bottom row.

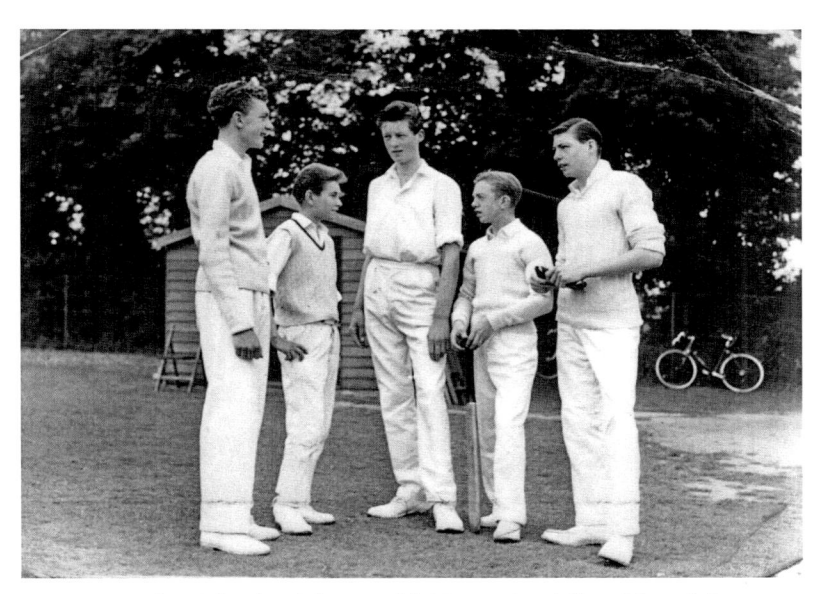

Croydon Schools cricketers with Trevor Condell 2nd from left.

*Over 15 football team. Reggie Chapple and David Hendley top row.
Peter Boyes and John Bradbery bottom row.*

*Boy Scout camp.
Brian Mitchell
2nd from left.*

*A Youth Club outing.
Derek Goddard
2nd from right.*

*The 5th
East Surrey
Company of
The Boy's
Brigade.
Eddie Prosper
is in the
group photo.*

School trip en route to Calais in train carriage with teacher Harry Barlow. George Budd looking through window.

School trip to Bolzano, Italy, Brian Mitchell 2nd from right.

Guide with George Budd and Harry Barlow in Austria.

Mr. Naish, John Beacham, George Budd on the Bruges trip.

Lanfranc's Headmaster and Staff

Mr. A.T. Fowle was known as 'Tommy Fowle' to staff, and *'Mister Fowle'* to pupils. Universally respected for his vision, ambition, dedication and strict discipline, everyone sensed his underlying kindness. Awesomely judge-like, he was also a father-like headmaster whom the boys looked up to. They hated to be sent to Mr. Fowle for misdemeanours but all knew that if they got caned – they deserved it. Short, robustly built, charismatic, Tommy Fowle ran a tight ship with his loyal staff of 30 almost exclusively male teachers who respected his energy and diligence. His finger firmly on Lanfranc's pulse, he made twice-daily tours of the school, morning and afternoon – and woe-betide any boy he found standing *outside* the classroom for bad behaviour! Having the slipper for disrupting lessons was bearable but being sent *outside* knowing that at any moment grey-haired, rosy faced Mr. Fowle might appear in the corridor was *unbearable*. To be discovered by him was bad, but to be sent to his study was worse. Miscreants thought the wait outside felt like a condemned man awaiting execution at Tyburn. Yet they all felt he hated having to administer the punishment – which was duly registered in the school's punishment book. It hurt their pride more than anything else as the boys knew they'd let him down, the result being they strived never to be sent a second time. Punishment was salutary… but the upside was it gave the boys street cred with their peers, whilst their parents almost invariably thought if their son had got the cane then he must have deserved it. Some parents brought in truanting sons to receive 'proper' punishment from him knowing their son must be corrected. Convinced that distinctions between 'right' and 'wrong' could only be made to stick *with* the stick, corporal punishment was applied. Not 'Six of the best' as in 'Whacko' and 'Billy Bunter' – popular T.V. programs then, but salutary stings to keep them on the straight and narrow. Many of these Lanfranc boys today swear it was the making of them.

Having received primary education at one of Croydon's many Junior Schools, Lanfranc's pupils anticipated a minimum of four years, and if unlucky, possibly five years glued to their desks before they were free to start earning money! Keeping a lid on simmering ambition to get out into the world called for passionate teachers to instil knowledge and control the steam of their pupils. Lanfranc was blessed with many.

Ron Cox, Head of Social Studies, disliked corporal punishment, so maintained order by strategy. Refusing boisterous juniors admission into his classroom until he arrived, he researched potential trouble-makers in advance and allocated them permanent places next to a quiet boy, whilst exhibitionists were seated at the back, and devious boys at the front of his classes. 'Lines' were a punishment his pupils hated because they had to perfectly copy a page from a book, magazine, or newspaper. Many boys preferred the slipper as writing was a chore and Mr Cox always asked questions, which meant they had to remember what they'd copied. Yet the boys liked Ron Cox because he injected humour into his lessons whilst history tests were highly competitive, based on chance, and fun.

John Beacham taught Geography and Religious Knowledge. Still building a personal reputation at Lanfranc, John was much stricter. Not only had he the biggest plimsoll the boys had ever seen but he also kept six dowel rods numbered 1-6 for a sporting punishment. Placing these up his sleeve with the ends sticking out, anyone misbehaving gambled for their deserved punishment – to the rapt attention of the rest of the class who regarded 'Billy Beacham's' punishments as entertainment. The dowel selected might elicit one stroke, or, if very unlucky, six! About to administer, he always asked, 'Do you want it hard or soft?' They knew that it they replied 'Soft' they were whacked hard, so wise boys answered 'I suppose I deserve it Sir – so it had better be hard.' Then they got it 'soft'. It was an acceptable game – the boys took the discipline, learned from his lessons and idolised 'Billy Beacham' – who with his big dark-rimmed glasses and wavy black hair looked uncannily like their late lamented pop idol Buddy Holly. This didn't stop them playfully cheeking him, entering his classroom muttering just loud enough for him to hear *'Beacham's Powders do the trick. Yes they do they make you sick!'* The boys particularly liked him because, aged 31, he was younger than many other masters and he took them on camping trips with his dog Rusty and also on school holidays. During rehearsals for the school play (invariably by Shakespeare), he would dramatically greet his form '2B' at registration time with the immortal words 'To be…? Or not, to be…?' There was no question about it. They thought 'Billy Beacham' was a 'lovely fellow' and admired him!

Another teacher they loved was Head of Science George Budd. Ex-R.A.F. quiet, unflappable George, known as 'Buddy' to the boys, never resorted to corporal punishment. For many boys science was conceptually difficult but they were enthralled not only by George's relaxed style but by his enthusiasm for Chemistry and Biology. They liked seeing sodium pellets whizz around in a bowl of water, and magnesium burning incandescently, but best of all they loved nickel plating pennies – and after school trying to fob them off as half crowns on the buses! Always hard to anger, and rarely cross, this father of two sons bantered with the boys; was always amiable, and never sarcastic. Stout and balding, he had a booming voice that carried right across the playground but his kind smile transformed him, so some thought him the nicest master in the school and worked hard for him – because they wanted to. George ran a Stamp Club after school and also kept a menagerie of school animals. Volunteers looked after rabbits, rats, mice, and guinea-pigs, in school and holiday times because they liked 'Buddy'. (And they liked the animals.)

The Physics teacher had a different approach. Jokingly nick-named 'Mighty Mouse' because of his ability to bring tears to the eyes of the toughest bullies, tweed-suited Mr Taylor educated with the aid of a metre rule. Holding this over the head of a pupil, thin side down, he fired questions in his Yorkshire accent, and if the pupil got it wrong a whack on the head painfully instilled the fact! Mr Taylor was considered even by other staff to be a 'hard man' but future events were to reveal that his tough carapace concealed a sympathetic heart.

Lanfranc's staff included many senior teachers whose reputations went before them. Syd Gubby taught woodwork and instigated sensible rules because boys were handling hammers and chisels. Each year every form created a carved wooden Totem Pole in his class. Syd was a master craftsman, his stock phrase to his pupils being 'Come on boys! Go and mark out the wood and let me check it!' He instructed rigidly and had a quick temper if his pupils did anything wrong but they felt very pleased if they received a compliment from him for their handiwork. Contrastingly his colleague Neville Mearns wore a lab coat full of holes because it had been nailed to the bench so often by the boys, who got up to tricks whenever possible. Neville took a cynical view of his charges. Other teachers found themselves the butt of the boy's jokes almost to the point of paranoia. Each classroom had an integral store room off-limits to boys. Craft teacher Mr Bonaud had a class of lively lads including one who haunted him by persistently pinning (with a school pen nib), amusing messages inside its door, signed *'The phantom strikes again!'*

Most teachers taught a sport and were as 'sport-mad' as the boys. Welsh biologist, Peter Funning, coached rugby, taught his teams to do the Maori Haka, and dreamt of taking the school fifteen to Wales for a *real* game – in the Valleys! English teacher Norman Patterson, a fine club cricketer but 'control freak' in the classroom, instilled his love of cricket into his charges. Maths teacher Norman Cook also taught Physical Education and coached football. An exception to the testosterone-fuelled staff was lone female, art mistress Diana Jones. Miss Jones, 'Dai' to her colleagues, was a respected focus of attention – especially to the older boys.

The dynamics of Lanfranc worked well and gave rise to a happy, balanced, enterprising school the boys were proud to belong to. Many boys felt that some teachers seemed more like friends. Any mutual 'retribution' happened on the games field in the end of term staff-versus-boys match – a close run game when the boys let off all the steam that they wanted, as players or spectators, and no one was ever (seriously) injured.

Many ex-service teachers had trained after demobilisation. Others had left better paid jobs in industry for a secure job teaching newly introduced technology subjects. Many found it hard to raise a family on their salary and consequently 'moonlighted' with an evening, weekend, or holiday job, to supplement their income.

The Lanfranc Boys

Money was tight for many young families in Croydon and extra cash was needed for necessities, let alone luxuries. Accordingly many couples limited themselves to one child – a decision that some Lanfranc parents were to rue bitterly. Those with large families clothed offspring in hand-me-downs or second hand clothes from jumble sales and 'Bring and Buy'. Unless well-heeled, school uniform was 'Sunday best' and some felt stigmatised by having to wear it to church. In 1960 every Croydon school was easily identified by its uniform.

Striped blazers and summer boaters were unheard of at Lanfranc, yet despite being lower down the educational strata, a uniform of school cap; smart dark blazer with the school badge, a white shirt, school tie, and grey flannel trousers was worn. Prefects distinguished their blazer with a golden-yellow trim. Although his boys ragged around, sometimes entering school dusty and dishevelled, when given the order to smarten up, Tommy Fowle knew they scrubbed up well and could look as smart as any of Croydon's elite. Lanfranc's school badge was a circular heraldic shield, divided into quadrants, emblazoned in blue and yellow. When it was designed no one could ever have anticipated that one day its intricate pattern would be perfectly replicated in blue and yellow flowers, or that it would be seen all over the world.

Lanfranc's 'rough, tough' reputation was channelled under Tommy Fowle's headship. Fist fights occasionally happened in the playground at Lanfranc, attracting a crowd, but as soon as the teacher on duty arrived the fight terminated. In fights outside school, if one boy said he'd had enough the fight ended – usually amicably and invariably forging better relationships between the protagonists. Croydon was famous for the boxing champions that it had produced over the years, and the sport of boxing was encouraged at Lanfranc, under the supervision of Norman Cook. Consistently producing Croydon School boxing champions, there wasn't a school in Croydon that matched the raw energy of Lanfranc's boxers. Every boy, whether he liked it or not, was encouraged to 'have a go' and many unlikely fighters found themselves representing their House, praying that friends had done a good job hyping their fighting potential, hoping to be spared by getting a bye. Boxing increased a boy's self-confidence, enabling him to stand up for himself. It was character forming, but bullying was not. To avoid bullying there were separate playgrounds for the lower and upper school, nevertheless gangs of bigger boys picked on the vulnerable outside school.

Most boys played football in the streets near their homes, so 'good' and 'bad' gangs of boys existed, and these social groupings were also a part of school life. Dick Turpin had reputedly once terrorised the area, and many a highwayman had swung from the gibbet at Thornton Heath Pond. Pursuing this tradition Lanfranc's bullies 'held up' lone youngsters as they arrived at the school's back entrance, menacingly demanding their dinner money with the old refrain *'Stand and deliver, your money or your life!'* Consequently youngsters stuck together and found it paid to have a bike, preferably a racing bike with speed and manoeuvrability. Lucky boys with older brothers at Lanfranc relied on them for 'protection', enabling these youngsters to be cocksure! Those without guardians developed their own survival strategy, became streetwise, eventually taking Lanfranc's subculture in their stride. Many a Lanfranc Boy today, vows that it helped them develop resilience, especially those who joined the armed services.

The minimum school leaving age in 1960 was 15, so despite there being a small fifth year, most boys left with some technical qualifications after their fourth year. Of those boys who stayed on to obtain further certificates, some became school prefects, led by the Head Boy and the Vice Captain. Senior boys assisted the headmaster and staff in various ways including maintaining discipline. The Fifth year for 1960-61 consisted of boys aged 15-16, working for G.C.E. (General Certificate of Education) and R.S.A. (Royal Society of Arts) examinations. Fourteen boys already knew that they were to be made up to prefects. Clive Grumett was elected Head Boy and Roger Taylor Vice-Captain, ably assisted by other hand-picked boys. Their parents were proud that their sons were staying on and were considered mature enough to be prefects. In one year's time they would leave school and their adult lives begin. They had so much to live for – yet half of the fourteen prefects would never see their 17th birthday.

Staying until the end of the Fourth or Fifth form was not the only option. Croydon Education Committee provided the 13+ Examination as a way out from Secondary Moderns for 'late developers'. Lanfranc boys passing this exam transferred to Croydon Secondary Technical School considered an echelon higher. Some candidates rued the day they passed the 13+, preferring their old school, its sporting prowess, and happy ambience. No other Croydon school could compare with Lanfranc for sporting (but not athletic) success. Nevertheless Lanfranc's boys took part in cross-country running around Mitcham Common, every competitor jumping the muddy ditch christened 'Beacham's Brook' after the teacher whose station it was. Individuals and teams showed incredible determination and were encouraged to victory by their enthusiastic masters. Whether kicking a soccer ball, running with a rugby ball, bowling a leg-break, chasing over the Common, or punching in the ring – a 'Lanfranc grit' developed and many boys represented Croydon Schools and even played for Surrey. Two outstanding Lanfranc cricketers, John Wells and Trevor Condell looked set for a promising future with Surrey Cricket Club. Who could have foreseen that instead of leather and willow, *floral* balls, bats, and stumps, would commemorate their last innings? Or that Croydon boxing champion Reggie Chapple's ultimate date with destiny was not to resounding cheers, but tears – at the sight of boxing gloves made from sweet scented flowers commemorating his fame?

Progressive Tommy Fowle was proud of 'his' boys. He eschewed an examination system which at eleven categorised a boy for life. The new bias curriculum included English, Maths, Science, History, Geography, Music, Art, and Religious Knowledge, together with practical Woodwork and Metalwork. Although earmarked for technical trades the boys were encouraged to develop *all* their personal skills, and the school's popular annual Eisteddfod, organised by Ron Cox, afforded opportunities for certificates and prizes in numerous categories, including even cake baking. Drama was encouraged, and coached by English teacher Jim Hemmings, Lanfranc's young thespians acting mature roles – to the considerable surprise of their parents. Nothing was too good for his boys and Tommy Fowle approved educational opportunities, whether a day trip to London's Oval to see England's cricketers (a never to be forgotten treat), or experiences further afield. A firm believer in the adage 'travel broadens the mind', he encouraged school trips abroad. He was educating young men to go out into the world and make a success of their lives in whichever way they chose. Their future was paramount to him.

The Lanfranc school year 1960-1961

In July 1960, as John F. Kennedy was nominated for President by America's Democrats, Lanfranc's school calendar for 1960-61 chronicled a cornucopia of events. Turning a blind eye to dates for school and public examinations (never a pleasant prospect), the boy's interest focused on sports fixtures for the autumn, spring, and summer terms, and then on the much speculated upon 'School Journeys'. A number of lucky lads had enjoyed half term in Switzerland, whilst forty boys were due to visit Bruges. The big question was – what had Messrs Beacham and Budd planned for next summer? It elicited whoops of excitement.

John Beacham and George Budd organised the school trips, recruiting other staff as co-leaders. John had taken seven trips from Lanfranc, all successful, the previous being to Bolzano in the Northern Italian Alps where the boys unanimously voted to do the whole trip again. The recent Switzerland trip had been very popular too but he'd deliberated on the destination for 1961. Bruges was to have excursions into France, Germany, and Holland, but in largely urban areas where the landscape was uninterestingly *flat*. Italy and Switzerland with alpine pastures and lakes were breaths of fresh air, so to keep older boys interested the choice necessitated a *new* country, undoubtedly one with mountains. A geographer, John reasoned that rugged landscapes offered memorable geographical examples useful in answering exam questions. Experienced in handling large groups of 'live wires' he also reasoned that strenuous 'adventure' activities such as climbing and canoeing had the added bonus of tiring the boys out, reducing the chance of any silly behaviour. He knew boys only got up to mischief when they were bored and badly supervised. Accordingly next summer's half-term trip was planned to visit Austria, whilst the summer holidays trip was to Norway. Beacham and Budd were besieged by boys itching to learn about the planned holidays – and their answers had them cock-a-hoop. All previous school trips were by train but word spread like wildfire, the revelation was that the Norway trip was going by PLANE! The Norway holiday was going to be a brilliant FIRST! Lucky boys who could get on this trip would FLY from London to a place called 'Stir-Van-Gore' somewhere in Norway. Next year was going to be Lanfranc's BEST YEAR YET!

In common with the majority of British at this time, the Lanfranc boys were almost entirely ignorant about Norway, except perhaps that it was a Scandinavian country across the North Sea, famous for beautiful blondes, incredible mountains, and fjords. No one could have foreseen that in a year everyone in Britain would know exactly where **Stavanger** was, and that its name, powerfully evocative and synonymous with tragedy, would become linked with Lanfranc – and indelibly etched on their hearts.

The trip organised for Whitsun was a ten day rail trip to Radfeld in Austria. The summer holiday proposal was to fly to Stavanger's Sola Airport in Norway in August for eight days. Austria would cost £20 and accommodate 70 boys plus four staff. Norway was more expensive at £27. 10/- and could only take 34 boys and two staff because of the 36 passenger seats on the plane. Beacham and Budd were to lead the Austrian, whilst John Beacham and his head of department, Ron Cox, were to take the Norwegian trip. Ron Cox 'moonlighted' to support his wife and son, but not during school holidays. Delighted with the prospect of visiting Norway with its rich Viking history and mind-blowing landscape, Ron provisionally accepted.

Excitement for both holidays gripped the boys from the start – but the buzz generated for the Norway trip was enormous. The problem was the major difference in price, some boys knowing they daren't ask for either option as family finances were tight. Some rued having only one parent to finance a holiday, others that their fathers drank any excess funds, knowing they'd only get a clip round the ear if they had the audacity to ask. Nevertheless many crossed their fingers when they informed their parents. Almost all desperately pleaded for Norway because this trip was going by AIR – and the lucky boys would FLY. Persuaded and cajoled, so many boys received permission for Norway that it had to be restricted to the upper school only. Canny boys hedged their bets, realising that if they asked for the most expensive trip and were turned down, then they might be lucky with the other! Advertising school trips well in advance meant that parents and boys had plenty of time to save up and pay for the holiday.

'Beacham's and Budd's Tours' had achieved legendary popularity, and boys from previous trips were desperate to go again – with their pals if possible. Some parents were inveigled into agreeing, with the provision of paying by weekly instalments of ten shillings. Hopeful lads offered to provide their pocket money for the trip from their own earnings. Some even agreed to fund it entirely themselves, through their out of school jobs delivering milk or by newspaper rounds. The greater cost for Norway meant that many lads had their hopes of flying dashed and the long list of hopefuls diminished. Clive Grumett, Patrick Wilson, Dave King, Alan Spicer, Raymond Le Riche, Geoff Wood, Paul Sexton,

Tim Willis, Colin Dawes, and Bruce Guest all wanted to go with their friends but their parents couldn't afford another trip. Alan Oliver and Charles Ella were both from families of seven, so their hopes fell by the wayside. Two felt they simply couldn't ask. John Hunt's sick father wasn't working, whilst Derek Wade knew his father had terminal cancer. Some, like John Martin *begged* to go. His mother hated dashing his hopes, but as lone bread-winner she needed a new oven – they had to eat! Others, like Leslie Bentley and David Randall, were given the agonising choice between flying to Norway or of having a new bike. They both chose a bike. Ian Bell and Alan Foster (who dreamed of a career as a pilot) had just passed the 13+ examination but yearned to go with their old friends. Others like Barry Lee and Zed Buckley were bitterly disappointed to be moving from Croydon and starting at new schools. Still, they had left their mark at Lanfranc. Their names were carved on their form's wooden Totem Pole that Syd Gubby had erected in the grounds.

Preliminary lists were drawn up and the boys left for the summer holidays knowing they needed to save their pocket money (if they had any), or that they had to start earning. (As many were Boy Scouts used to 'Bob a Job' week they were already entrepreneurs.) But the glorious summer holiday lay ahead; and next year was 365 days away!

The Summer Holidays of 1960

Nothing was more blissful to any schoolchild in the Sixties than the start of the summer holidays. Glorious weeks of freedom stretched ahead, infinite time when they were at liberty to do what they pleased without having to stick to a timetable, or sit up straight in class, hand in homework on time, or face whatever demons school had for them. Lanfranc's pupils relished summer so much that sensitive pupils even had 'school holiday' nightmares about returning to school partway through, and were intensely relieved to find they'd been dreaming! Cricket matches, fishing expeditions, cycling and camping trips with friends, seaside family holidays or staying with relatives in the country – all or some of these lay before the majority of the Lanfranc boys. Some may even have longed to be like Francis Chichester who had just sailed single-handed across The Atlantic in his yacht Gypsy Moth II.

Despite their urge for freedom, forty Lanfranc boys (including 13+ school leaver Ian Bell), commenced their summer holiday on an educational trip to Belgium. John Beacham, George Budd, and Ken Naish the Art master, cleverly timetabled a mix of culture and fun visiting Bruges, hiring pedal cars for a 'Grand Prix' at Blankenburg, swimming in the North Sea, visiting Dunkirk, and haggling in a Dutch market at Middelburg. Pocket money was administered by 'Buddy' and handed out on a daily basis so that no one spent all their money at once, but boys knew the itinerary and saved up their money to haggle for souvenirs at a market. A canal trip from Bruges culminated in a guided tour of a windmill where 'Buddy' translated information from French into English – to the boy's utter amazement. They thought it was the most enjoyable holiday they'd ever spent. They discovered that their masters were like older mates. Derek Meacher even took a photo of them. Ian Bell was sad to leave Lanfranc and his parents who met him made sure they thanked Messrs Budd, Beacham, and Naish for taking him.

Some boys carried the best of school seamlessly into the summer holidays. Thirteen year old wicket keeper Trevor Condell was such an exceptional player that he played cricket for Lanfranc, Croydon, and Surrey under 15's. He enjoyed every day of his holidays – if playing cricket. His mother was proud of him – despite his cricket whites always returning filthy! Blonde, slight bodied Trevor was a very capable wicket keeper and batsman, but flinging himself about the pitch he was quickly dishevelled, covered in dust from head to foot, cricket pads flopping over his knees, and his shirt un-tucked! Always cheerful and supportive, he could bowl a devastating leg-spin but was happiest wearing his wicket keepers gloves. Cricketers from other schools liked Trevor and thought him a 'lovely chap'. 'How's That!' magazine featured him in classic wicket keepers stance behind the stumps, on their front page. He dreamt of playing for Surrey County C.C.

Fellow cricketer John Wells did too. John was another 'lovely chap', reminiscent of Tommy Steele with fair swept-back hair and a chirpy personality. But John was deadly serious as a fast bowler who had captained Croydon's victorious Primary Schools Cricket Team. At Lanfranc he'd been awarded cricket colours two years running. When not playing seriously John played for fun with his married sister Shirley. Their Waddon home was close to playing fields and although Shirley had a young baby, every free moment was spent batting, bowling, or playing football. He adored his baby nephew and couldn't wait for him to grow up so that he could teach him to bat. John's elder brother Ken joined him in rowdy games of street football, where stray balls bashed against neighbours front windows. John was such a popular, pleasant character, who entertained their children, that few neighbours were cross, and errant footballs were returned.

Camping was a pursuit that many boys enjoyed, especially those from families who couldn't afford a week at the seaside. Quentin Green ('Greenfly') and his pals Michael O'Rourke (affectionately nicknamed 'Ear-Oles'), and Charlie Armour, camped at Sheepcoate Valley in Brighton. Quentin's father lent them his brand new 'Igloo' inflatable tent, transported them all, inflated the tent, and left them to it. The thirteen year olds had a great week fending for themselves, going to bed late, and rising even later. Quentin enjoyed lying in as normally he delivered papers at seven o'clock. Money he'd saved up from his 'round' he now spent on chips and 'Knickerbocker Glories' at a local café. They cooked some meals themselves on a Primus, the resulting gloop eaten with relish. One wet morning a Billy-can of bubbling hot baked beans upset over the tent's plastic groundsheet and left tell-tale blisters. Scooped up with dust, grass, and feathers, eating destroyed the evidence of the crime. The tent was very neatly packed when Mr Green arrived to drive them home!

Brighton was a favourite seaside venue that some boys knew from train or car visits with parents. Edward Prosper and school friend Peter Moore decided to cycle to Brighton, but kept it secret from Eddie's parents. On the day, Eddie cycled from Thornton Heath and met Peter at Merstham, where they commenced the 80 mile round-trip. Cycling to school was easy, but to Brighton a different matter. Muscles burned and throats dried, peddling the steep slope of the South Downs, but free-wheeling down the other side, feet free of whirring pedals, was literally a breeze! Triumphantly speeding through Brighton's famous gates – rain started. Brighton Pier in drizzle wasn't much fun, or the narrow gauge coastal railway. Their legs ached and Peter decided not to cycle but to take the train back to Redhill. Eddie insisted on cycling. Agreeing to rendezvous at Redhill station, Eddie departed early to coincide with Peter's train so they could cycle back to Merstham together. It was raining hard when tired Eddie liaised with Peter. The two rode off, yellow cycle capes billowing. After a long, wet, and windy ride to Merstham, Eddie rode his solo stretch home, heart in mouth. He was far too late to explain his absence as just 'spending a day with Peter'. His worried parents demanded to know exactly where he'd been and read him the Riot Act when he owned up to his 'secret day out'!

Good looking Richard Lawrence, about to enter the fourth year, accompanied his parents and younger brother and sister, on holiday at Bembridge on the Isle of Wight. The Lawrence's made friends with the Storey family from Caversham, with children the same age. Spending glorious days playing on the beach together, Richard was attracted to Carol Storey, a pretty girl his age. When the adults gathered in the evening at the hotel bar, bringing out crisps and fizzy drinks for the younger kids, these two walked off hand in hand to watch moonlight sparkle on the sea. It was an innocent teenage holiday romance. When it was time to leave Bembridge, Richard sorrowfully kissed Carol goodbye. They both vowed to keep in touch.

Geoff Brown was popular in and out of school. His numerous friends included his best mates Derek Goddard and Dave Heyden, his younger brother Ian, and girlfriend Maureen Kay – who shared Geoff's sense of adventure. Outings organised by Geoff's Youth Leader parents invariably involved healthy country walks, and he and Maureen enjoyed cycling to his grandparent's farm at Gomshall where he and Ian helped out. The brothers drove the farm tractor, towing their younger sister Janet, in a trailer over the bumpy fields. Dave Heyden's parents owned a bungalow at Shoreham-on-Sea and the friends often stayed. One day Geoff and Dave were at sea in a two man canoe when it turned turtle and they struggled to escape. Mr Heyden rescued them, relieved they hadn't drowned.

Robert Martin, always known as 'Bobby', was an only child the same age as his cousin Patricia. They spent happy days together with non-identical twins Peter and Geoffrey Crouch at Wandle and Beddington Parks catching sticklebacks. Patricia knew Bobby would do anything to please her, so she asked him to partner her ballroom dancing. Following suit the Crouch twins took up dancing too, realising it was a good way to find a girlfriend! The cousins always holidayed together at the seaside. Playing in the sea on a Li-Lo, they propelled their 'raft' off from shore enjoying the sun and salt water. Deep in conversation about the white sports car they dreamt of buying together, they didn't notice the shore recede far behind. The tide had turned and they were drifting out to sea. Their parents shouted and waved from the shore and others joined them – but it was too late. They drifted further holding on tightly to the now sagging Li-lo. The local Lifeboat came to their rescue in time, adding to their adventure. But their distraught parents had feared they would never see them alive again.

Only child Robert Roffey, his friends Jim Knight, and John and Philip Russell, also had a close call with water. Intending to fish the River Mole near its confluence with the Thames, they took an early train from Waddon Marsh Halt, via Wimbledon, to Hampton Court. Pairing to fish on separate stretches with promising pools, Robert and Philip, John and Jim were happy to hook pike, perch, carp, or tench. All went well until a splash, followed by urgent shouting, alerted Jim and John that someone had fallen in. They discovered Philip in a deep pool, gasping and submerging. Then Robert, valiantly trying to grab him, fell in himself. Horrified, because neither could swim, Jim and John's shouts alerted two young boys who ran from their bungalow on the opposite bank and launched their dinghy. They pulled the floundering lads out and took them home, where they dried and were lent clothes. Asked for their telephone number to arrange for the clothes to be returned, Philip gave his home number. The four returned home unaware that Philip and John's parents had been informed and were anxiously waiting at Waddon Marsh Halt. They could have drowned.

Brian Mitchell was a very keen member of the 67th Croydon Scout Group whose H.Q. was 'The Endeavour' in Melfort Road. Second in command of Seagull patrol, every summer he went off to camp where he learned camp skills including map reading, first-aid, tracking, and camp cooking. Field games and midnight hikes were exciting and he acted like an older brother to young scouts who had never been away from home before. His Patrol Leader was his friend Paul Fairweather with whom he learned resourcefulness and responsibility during shared Scouting adventures. Family holidays for Brian were spent caravanning at Hastings. Brian and his niece Shirley explored Hastings' winding old streets, and fishing fleet, hauled up on the shingle.

Not every boy was lucky, and some found holiday times worse than school because they were *expected* to work at home. Peter Huggin's parents ran a sweet shop, and friends felt that timid Peter didn't have much freedom to enjoy life. Others had to look after younger brothers or sisters whilst their parents worked, or help in family butcher's or grocer's shops, delivering orders and running errands. Some had morning *and* evening paper rounds. One hard-pressed Lanfranc boy from a broken home had *all* these responsibilities and his life wasn't fun at all. A clip round the ear was what he could expect if he asked for time off. Life was tough for these boys and they looked forward to the start of term to be back with their mates and to be able to 'relax' a bit in the relative tranquillity of their classroom.

Just a few boys *had* returned willingly to Lanfranc during the summer holidays. Boys like Quentin Green and his friend Geoffrey Parr were on a long rota of helpers who took their turns at looking after George Budd's laboratory animals, housed in hutches next to the school vegetable patch and gardens. Quentin whizzed in to school on his bike. Geoffrey took two buses from South Croydon. They didn't want any stray dog or urban fox 'liberating' or worse still, *eating* Buddy's rats and rabbits before school started!

Most homes had a black and white television and sports mad boys indulged in news reports of the Rome Olympics – where Cassius Clay won the gold medal for heavy weight boxing. On the news too was U.S.A.F. pilot, Gary Powers, who was sentenced to 10 years in a Russian prison for espionage. The Cold War was polarising international politics.

Autumn Term 1960

New boys starting at Lanfranc came from Primary Schools scattered throughout Croydon. Leonard Dee, from South Norwood Primary, met up with two older friends who had 'survived' their first year at Lanfranc. Gregory Allen, alias 'Eggy' and his friend Clive (nicknamed 'Carthorse') offered to look after Len, and invited him to cycle to school with them. From Norwood they coasted downhill towards Crystal Palace football ground, passing under the railway to White

Horse Lane. Now on the flat they had to pedal. Len had a racing bike with drop handle bars but 'Eggy' had an uncomfortable, heavy, 'sit up and beg' bike, with antiquated rod brakes. Keeping together they rode via side streets to the Bus Garage at Thornton Heath, then the shortest route to Aurelia Road, and via the cemetery footpath that emerged near Lanfranc's back entrance. It was a long, six mile, bike ride.

Walking the short distance to school was new boy, Graham Reygate, who lived in Mitcham Road and played street cricket with Alan Lee and Michael Benson. They offered to look after him until he established himself. No self-appointed guardian could ensure a new boy's first day run totally smoothly. Fresh from Primary schools and full of excitement, Graham and his class left their first lesson and ran noisily to their next, unwittingly passing Angus Tarn's Maths classroom. 'MacTarn' shot out like a trap door spider, enraged at their raucous audacity. The new comers stood in fear and trembling as he ticked them off, before walking, silently and sedately, to their next lesson – where, naturally, they were reprimanded for being late! New boys had to learn the ropes quickly at Lanfranc.

Tommy Fowle kept an eye on his new arrivals *and* all his older lads. He knew all their names (and some of their nicknames too). Every day on his school tours he left his office, his observations enabling him to keep his finger on Lanfranc's throbbing pulse. Touring his domain at different times and by different routes he glanced through the wire reinforced window of each classroom door, slipping into classes that looked troublesome to sit amongst the boys. The transformation in behaviour was amazing. More often he simply looked in – and learnt a lot. There was a happy, expectant atmosphere at the start of this new school year and he was quietly confident. The school was doing extremely well in all sporting activities, whilst improving academically. New boys would soon learn that Lanfranc was a school to be proud of.

Leaving his office near the main entrance he looked in at the Technical Drawing room next door, where boys were sharpening pencils, with set squares and protractors at the ready. He popped into his secretary's office from whence the school's loud speaker system operated, and then walked across the foyer into the

TWO POPULAR MASTERS

John Beacham (32)

George Budd (47)

THE LANFRANC BOYS

There are no photos for Edwin Murray (15) or for Gregory Allen (13).

John Bradbery (16)

Peter Boyes (16)

Geoffrey Brown (16)

Edward Gilder (16)

Derek Goddard (16)

David Hendley (16)

Brian Mitchell (16)

Roger Taylor (16)

Reggie Chapple (15)  *Trevor Condell (14)*

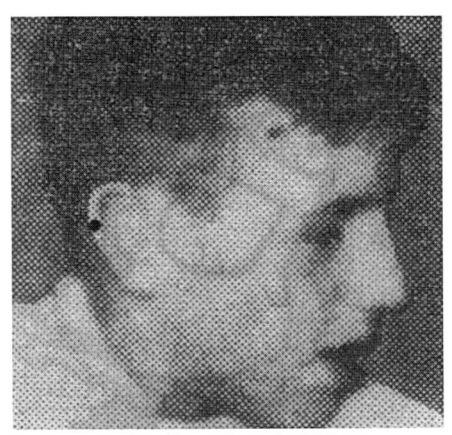

Geoffrey Crouch (15)  *Clifford Gaskin (15)*

David Hatchard (15)  *Richard Lawrence (15)*

Robert Martin (15)   *Edward Prosper (15)*

Robert Roffey (15)   *John Adams (14)*

Michael Benson (14)   *David Gore (14)*

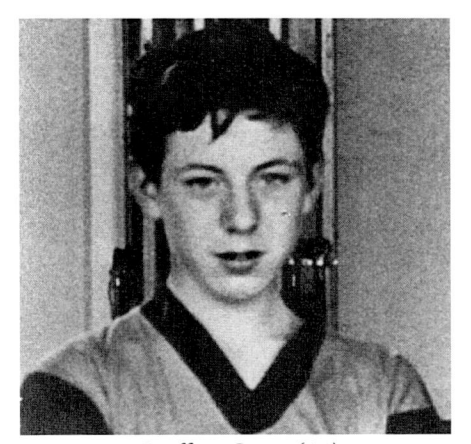

Geoffrey Green (14)

Anthony Harrison (14)

Quentin Green (13)

Peter Huggins (14)

John Phelps (14)

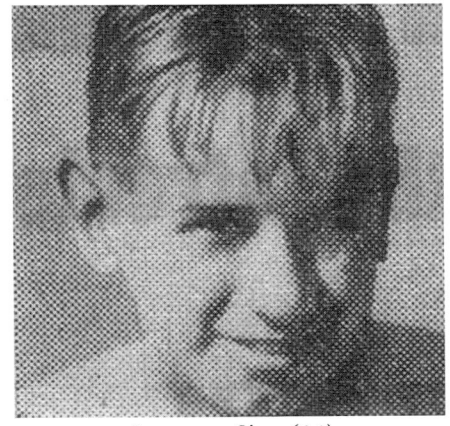

Lawrence Sims (14)

Colin Smith (14)

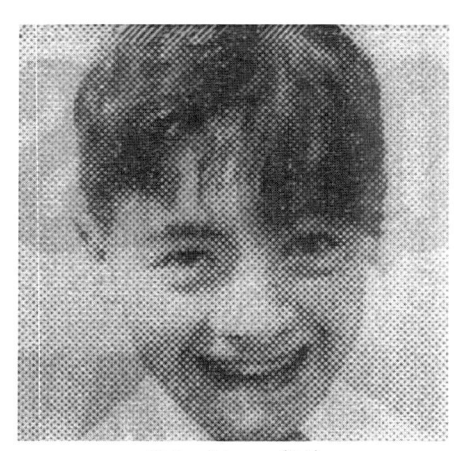

Peter Stacey (14)

John Wells (14)

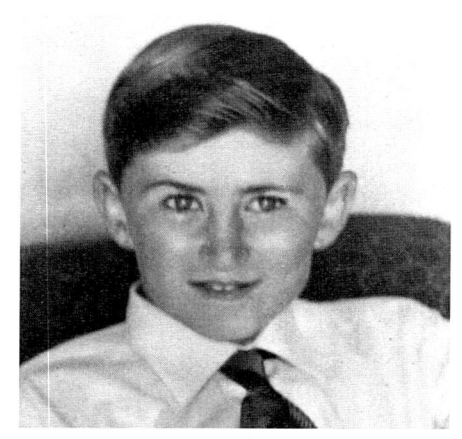

Martin White (14)

Roger White (14)

Alan Lee (13)

light, bright school hall. Nothing presaged it would become a sepulchral Chapel of Rest. It connected with the school canteen and could hold a lot of people – ideal for school plays, or inter-house boxing matches. He strode on to the prefects Common Room where 'studying' fifth formers, were recounting holiday exploits. They immediately jumped to their feet with 'Good morning Sir!' He was particularly pleased with his prefects this year. Clive Grumett was School Captain and Roger Taylor Vice-Captain, with a group of carefully selected prefects which included John Bradbery, Peter Boyes, Geoffrey Brown, Derek Goddard, Robert Edmeads, and David Hendley. He would rely on them to support the teaching staff in numerous ways – and to dish out detentions to any deserving miscreant.

He continued on towards the two storey classroom block where Maths, English, Geography, Religious Instruction, and History were taught. All was well except one lost new boy, who was shepherded into Jim Hemmings classroom, its walls decorated with slogans from Milton and Shakespeare. Taking the corridor to the metalwork and woodwork labs he passed an old car being rebuilt. Syd Gubby had his glue pot on the boil with a couple of bottles of school milk warming for coffee break. Upstairs in the science labs George Budd was speaking to his new charges in his quiet, firm manner, whilst senior boys in Mr Taylor's class were discovering, the 'metre rule' way, just how much about Physics they had forgotten since last term. Downstairs again he strode to the gym where Norman Cook was overseeing pairs of boys engaged in his 'speed and reflex' game, winners being the first to slap the other's back. From the gym he visited the Music room and then took the stairs to the Art room where Miss Jones already had new boys enthralled. Savouring lunch smells, he returned via the canteen and popped into the kitchen to see the cooks. He knew that these good-hearted ladies fed them all well, everyone's favourite being chocolate sponge and custard. Completing his circuit Tommy Fowle felt confident it would be a good year – culminating magnificently with the first school trip from Lanfranc to fly abroad. In due course he would ask Messrs Beacham and Budd how the Norway trip was progressing.

By the end of the summer term flying to Norway had become the most popular choice but now deposits for one or other holiday had to be paid. Dithering seniors wondered whether to choose Austria which was cheaper, two days longer, but by train, or Norway which was more expensive, shorter, and by air. Lists changed constantly. Eventually the majority were pleased to visit the Tyrol, the high-light being a planned visit to Hitler's hideaway at Berchtesgarten. Norway was financially beyond the majority. Norway-listed boys were the 'elite' but places weren't taken up quickly. Weekly payments commenced and those enrolled handed over a ten shilling note (50p) or a sweaty handful of half-crowns, florins, shillings, sixpences, three penny bits, pennies, half pennies, and even scraped together farthings! They watched like hawks as 'Buddy' credited their instalments on their payment card, knowing they'd have to watch their behaviour if more hard-earned parental largesse was to be forthcoming.

Few parents found they could afford Norway and this list was fluid as boys pulled out or changed places to Austria. John Beacham had a nucleus of fifth years, but a disappointingly small number of fourth years. The Norway option proved divisive and the cause of envy. Both holidays offered mountain adventures, but the cheaper Austria trip, although two days longer, was going by *train* and they all wanted to *fly*!

Aviation was a passion most Lanfranc boys shared, having grown up watching aircraft at Croydon airport. Some fathers had served in WWII with the R.A.F., giving their sons wooden models that became the foundation of their model aircraft collection. At school many a red herring (and paper plane or dart), was 'launched' in boring lessons to seduce ex RAF masters into recounting wartime exploits; and some boys, like David Henley and Alan Foster intended a career in aviation. Most boys from an early age had *pretended* to fly – zooming around, arms outspread, playing 'Spitfire versus Messchersmitt'! They knew something of their father's fearless wartime exploits. Now their fathers looked glum as Nikita Khrushchev banged his shoe on the table at The United Nations.

Ignoring the rapidly chilling Cold War, Messrs. Beacham and Cox were pleased to have trusted fifth year helpers on the Norway list. Strict prefect Derek Goddard was universally liked for his infectious smile and irrepressible sense of humour. His best friend Geoffrey Brown was popular too. An excellent sprinter, Geoff was a fast Rugby Wing three-quarter, Peter Boyes, school cine-projectionist, ran Lanfranc's film-shows at the end of term whilst teachers finished reports. No one cat-called if the film broke as they all knew Peter's father, a member of Croydon Fire Brigade, had recently died. No one dreamt of cheeking John Bradbery either because he was prefect in charge of the school Tuck Shop, a fast-selling snack outlet run in 10 minutes break time with help from fourth former Edward Prosper and pals. Gentle giant David Hendley, a respected member of the Air Training Corps, ensured no queue barging! Crystal Palace fan Edward Gilder had kudos with the other boys. Lanfranc's pupils were soccer mad and Edward's father took him to home games at Selhurst Park – enabling 'Ted' to recount the matches first hand. The 'star of the school' as far as some Lanfranc *Girls* were concerned was Roger Taylor the Vice Captain. Good looking, well spoken, he had played the role of Benvolio in 'Romeo and Juliet' and his 'gentlemanliness' made the young actresses hearts flutter. Roger was scientific and artistic, making both transistor radios and also scenery for his model railway. Another hit with girls was Brian Mitchell who was training as a silversmith whilst attending evening school at Lanfranc to take GCE and RSA exams. These soon-to-be school leavers were such good friends that they didn't want the fun of school trips to end. 'Ted' Gilder even had a cherished walking stick covered in silver tourist badges, proving where he'd been on school holidays. So too did fourth year boxing champion 'Reggie' Chapple. Reggie's stick survived. Sadly, Ted's stick didn't.

It was decided that George Budd and John Beacham with accompanying colleagues, would lead the 70 strong Austria trip, but Ron Cox had second thoughts about whether he should spare his precious holiday time for Norway, as his second job had meant his wife Audrey and son David saw little of him. Norman Cook stepped in and said he would accompany the Norway trip. John was concerned because A.I.R. Tours of Lancashire, organising the package, chartered Vickers Viking planes which carried 36 passengers. Only a full complement of 34 boys would keep the price affordable. Emphasising adventure aspects of Norway to his fourth year geographers, he hoped more would sign up after the autumn half-term break.

On Wednesday November 2nd the boys returned willingly to school after half term because it was a half-day holiday! That day Croydon awaited the official visit from Queen Elizabeth II to mark the town's Millennium. Many townsfolk hoped the Queen would confer 'City' status upon Croydon. Given the afternoon off for this momentous event, Lanfranc boys lined the Royal route together with hundreds of flag-waving, cheering school children and adults. Many boys eagerly anticipated standing there again on Saturday 5th for the annual 'London to Brighton Veteran Car Run', to be followed that evening, Guy Fawkes Night, by bonfires and exploding fireworks. Used only to cheering 'old crocks' with be-goggled drivers, this day euphoric crowds greeted a shiny Rolls Royce and police motor-cycle escort. It was the first time a reigning monarch had visited the town for centuries and Queen Elizabeth and Prince Philip won the hearts of the crowds by smiling and waving graciously, especially towards the children. A fanfare of trumpets and cheering crowds greeted them at the Town Hall. Everyone wanted a glimpse of their beautiful young Queen – mother of young Charles and Anne, and baby Andrew. Streamers and bunting decorated the buildings and the town buzzed with a hopeful excitement for Croydon's future.

The Royal couple opened Croydon's Technical and Art Colleges, took tea at the Archbishop's 'Old Palace' (founded by Archbishop Lanfranc), and attended a service at Croydon Parish Church together with the Archbishop, Dr. Geoffrey Fisher, an official guest. The Royal Visit was an unqualified success. Some Lanfranc seniors, evening students at the new colleges, saw the Royal visitors close up. It was a proud day for the Borough and although 'City' status was *not* conferred, the County Borough of Croydon basked in civic glory. Everybody felt the town was on the 'up', and despite political concerns about Europe's Iron Curtain and the intensifying Cold War, a bright light of optimism prevailed. Croydon's 'New Millennium' had begun and everyone felt that one day soon it would be on the World map. The first scent of the 'Swinging Sixties' was in the air. Changes were happening in Britain, including that same day, the publishers of Penguin Books finally won their court case to publish D.H Lawrence's previously banned, 'Lady Chatterley's Lover'.

Mid-morning and lunch breaks were free time for the boys and staff. 'Lady C' became subversive lunch-time reading but usage of 'four letter words' were still regarded as 'obscenities' by moral John Beacham. His colleagues renamed their lunch time card game 'Chase the Lady' instead of 'Black Bitch', when John played. Some masters took the trolleybus into Croydon to shop during the lunch hour, but science teachers rarely had this free time. George Budd always had experiments to set up and money for the Austria and Norway trips to collect and bank.

By the end of the autumn term George had important matters to discuss with John. Jim Towers had been asked to go to Norway instead of Norman Cook who had pulled out of the trip because he had charge of Norbury's huge playing field as well as coordinating Croydon's school football matches during the summer holidays. Quite a number of Lanfranc teachers, being ex-Servicemen, had entered the profession after two-year or even one-year Emergency courses as non-graduates, because they had young families or wanted to get married. They had been welcomed, but governing bodies had a hidden agenda. For promotion to Departmental Headships and beyond; they favoured graduates because they were seen as enhancing the status of Secondary Modern Schools. Even for graduates, the pay was poor, as compared with other professions, and annual increments derisory. Hence there was a lot of disillusionment and the need for 'moonlighting'. Unappreciated by Croydon Education Committee, many joined the National Union of Teachers (NUT). George Budd was Assistant Secretary of Croydon's branch and helped establish the Teachers Club in Croydon – where he proudly pulled the first pint in what became a thriving social and training organisation.

Having survived the war, Lanfranc's ex-servicemen teachers had high hopes. Despite frustrations for promotion and the necessity of second jobs to pay their mortgages, they were determined to instil optimism and endeavour into their pupils – a sentiment endorsed by headmaster Tommy Fowle. Living standards had gradually improved since 'Super Mac' – Prime Minister MacMillan had famously said 'Britons have never had it so good'! Optimism was the only positive way forward. Britain's fragile post-war economy was improving and aside from threats emanating from table-thumping Nikita Khrushchev, if one could ignore the threat of nuclear war, in 1960 the preferred future looked rosy, (even if the alternative was unimaginably bleak). For Lanfranc's youngsters the U.S.S.R. seemed a long way off and from their Croydon-based viewpoint the dawn of the 60's seemed especially bright.

The Swinging Sixties were evident in modern music and new fashions from Carnaby Street, and Lanfranc's pupils lived in a great location to enjoy its benefits. Bermondsey boy Tommy Steele and Marty Wilde from Blackheath had catapulted to fame and fortune. London's velvet collared Teddy Boys with 'duck-arsed' hairstyles, were on their way *out*, and scooter riding Mods and motor-biking Rockers on their way *in*. Many Lanfranc boys were fans of G.I. Elvis Presley in Germany, whilst others favoured Cliff Richard who resembled their English teacher Harry Barlow. Some boys cultivated their particular idol's hairstyle. At Youth Clubs they jived with girlfriends to Rock and Roll music reverberating from 45 rpm records. Pop Music was all the rage yet some boys loved Folk and Country music, especially records by Ewan MacColl and Peggy Seeger, who lived in Croydon. With such youthful optimism, no one could have believed that thirteen months later, Ewan and Peggy would release a song about Lanfranc's unlucky boys who had chosen the Norway trip.

Music was leisure pleasure, but leather on willow, boots, or skin, excited other passions. Sport was a very serious pursuit at Lanfranc. At a national level it was followed with patriotism, at school level cricket, football, rugby, and boxing, were pursued with fervour. Lanfranc boys had local champions to emulate, such as Peter May, England's brilliant cricket captain; Johnny Byrne, star Crystal Palace footballer, and Dave Charnley the 'Deptford Destroyer' Commonwealth and European Lightweight boxing champion. It was a great time to be young, male, and living within the social and cultural influences of South London.

Speech Day that November was eagerly anticipated. Prizes were only awarded to the most deserving, but all looked forward to cheering friends when they received their prize. Many 'Old Boys' aged 17 returned to receive G.C.E. and R.S.A. certificates, assured of rousing applause because they were men now, earning MONEY! The packed school hall hushed as Tommy Fowle gave his headmaster's report. His charisma gave parents confidence that under his benevolent charge their sons received every opportunity to do well. He gave a résumé of the school's achievements, and commended the great variety of clubs available for pupils. Congratulating all involved in the school's highly acclaimed 'Romeo and Juliet', he thanked producer Jim Hemmings and his team of helpers, including John Beacham who made the sets and arranged the music. He also thanked Ron Cox for organising the school's 9th Annual Eisteddfod, which had over 4,000 entries, with almost all of the school's pupils taking part. Underscoring the all-round competitive nature of Lanfranc, parents learnt that golden opportunities lay ahead for their sons in the 60's, and that the recipe for success was hard work coupled with good behaviour. The staff, sitting with him on the platform nodded assent.

Many of the prefects were prize winners. Head boy Clive Grumett, along with David Hendley and Brian Mitchell received the mechanical Trades Course National Certificate. Vice-Captain Roger Taylor together with John Bradbury, Peter Boyes, Geoffrey Brown, Edward Gilder, Derek Goddard, received City and Guilds awards. Peter Boyes, Roger Taylor, John Bradbery and David Hendley also won Fourth year prizes for Maths and Metalwork, History, Geography, and Technical Drawing and Maths respectively. All were going to Norway except head boy Clive. Seated amongst the current Fourth years were prize winners, and others, also on the list for Norway. Croydon Boxing Champion Reggie Chapple won boxing colours; 'legendary' wicket-keeper Trevor Condell already having cricket colours was awarded football colours; and studious twin Geoffrey Crouch won the Third year Maths prize. With them sat R.A.F. mad Clifford Gaskin, tropical fish keeper David Hatchard, 'chip off the old block' Richard Lawrence, magician and Trokart enthusiast Robert Martin, hard-working 'grafter' Edward Prosper, and ballroom dancing medal winner Robert Roffey.

Amongst Third Years awarded prizes were David Gore who won the Maths prize, Quentin Green who won the Music prize, and 'sporting legend' John Wells awarded school cricket colours. Second Year pupils Gregory Allen won the Science prize, and Alan Lee the Technical Drawing prize for their First year work. Finally Head boy Clive Grumett, who had prepared a tongue in cheek speech with help from Mr Hemmings, rose to his feet to politely request a day's holiday – as tradition demanded. Could it have been due to Speech Day that some proud parents decided to 'reward' their prizewinning sons by allowing them to go to Norway? Parents earn a living by the sweat of their brow, and preferred to go without themselves so that their children could have the best opportunities in life. Rewarding good work would be an incentive for a bright future.

December brought dreaded smog besides dreaded school exams. Despite the 1956 Clean Air Act, Croydon was still afflicted by London's killer fogs. In 1947 two trains had collided in smog at South Croydon and 32 people had died, so everyone hated the choking orange-tinted miasma. Buses, when they came, appeared in long retinues preceded by a walking conductor; cyclists pedalled slowly following the kerb (sometimes bumping into parked cars); whilst boys on foot purposefully counted the number of trolley bus poles (13 exactly) down the Mitcham Road to the school gates. But December wasn't all gloom because after exams, boxing and badminton matches between the four rival Houses of Livingstone, Edison, Caxton, and Pasteur took place. In the House Drama Festival of one-act plays, fourth year Clifford Gaskin's first ever production of 'Shivering Shocks' won the competition for Caxton. December 21st was marked by the Carol Service followed by a film put on by Peter Boyes as staff signed reports. Classes were dismissed and boys raced home, some painstakingly unsealing their reports, furtively reading them, and resealing or disposing of them, fearing a bad report would mean their school holiday would be forfeit. Whatever their report comments, good or bad, the best thing was that Christmas laid ahead! Carefree themselves, their parents were uneasy at the way the United States was racheting up the Cold War stakes, building five atomic submarines armed with 80 Polaris missiles.

Christmas Holidays 1960

Croydon's shops were patronised by boys with a few shillings to spend, keen to find bargains. Mothers might have been made a jewellery box in Syd Gubby's woodwork class, but fathers were harder to please. Sisters were lucky to get a sixpenny bag of bath salts or bath cubes from Woolworths, whilst brothers might get a jar of BrylCream or a comb. Teachers and boys had two days to complete Christmas shopping and buses into town were busy, offloading passengers to join jostling crowds at Croydon's North End in Allders, Grants, or Kennards. Full of last minute shoppers, Allders was popular because it had an escalator; Grants was 'posh'; but Kennards with its Arcade of small shops was best because it had a pet shop, a stamp shop, sixpenny Donkey rides at the far end, and upstairs – a small zoo! The down-sloping Arcade with its pleasant whiff of donkeys was a magic place for children. Ted Gilder and his sister

Christine often visited, pressing their noses wistfully against the pet shop window watching tumbling mongrel puppies, kittens chasing their tails, and baby rabbits twitching whiskers and pink noses. Too old to believe in Santa most Lanfranc boys hoped their parents had heeded their broad hints. Martin White hoped his parents would visit the craft model shop for the new plane kit he wanted. No one, except Lawrence Sims ('Lol' to his friends), who was a dedicated follower of fashion, wanted clothes for Christmas. Leaving their offspring happily entertained in Kennards Arcade most adult shoppers migrated down Crown Hill to Surrey Street – Croydon's historic market.

Selling their wares under decorated stalls the Surrey Street traders were a thriving relic of medieval times, with long established trader families – many of whose members were Old Lanfrancians. The prettiest barrow was the flower stall where bunches and pots of flowers from Holland, mistletoe, holly, and spruce trees, stood with locally made Christmas wreaths 'stubbed up' with red berries, and 'mossed up' with evergreens to last the festive season. The winter atmosphere was jolly and no one could have envisaged an eighteen foot long floral wreath of letters spelling 'Lanfranc Boys' being 'mossed up' in abject summer gloom. The frosty air held no hint of future tragedy. Shoppers bought chestnuts, Brussels sprouts, mandarins and nuts, at cheaper than High Street prices. Butcher's stalls dangled plucked turkeys, but most people could only afford a capon or chicken, or a joint of ham or pork, and last minute buying at Surrey Street was essential because few homes had a refrigerator. Geoffrey Green ('Beanie'), and his younger sister Susan shopped together with their father who always went just before Christmas to buy nuts, fruit, and sweets for their stockings. Geoff and Susan loved the bustle and excitement generated by last minute buying as twilight loomed and everyone wished each other 'Happy Christmas'. A glow of anticipation made the dark market, lit with stall lights, a magical place where everyone was full of good cheer. They loved returning home because they knew their mother had decorated their Christmas tree and transformed their home.

At the other Green household, in Norbury, Quentin and his sister encouraged their five year old brother Nigel to lick and link long paper chains, whilst they inflated giant balloons, and amused him by letting them zoom erratically around their lounge, making rude noises. Nigel asked Quentin to sing 'that funny song about your teacher' and Quentin obligingly piped *'Mr Beacham's got a bunion, and a face like a pickled onion, a nose like a squashed tomato, and cauliflower ears!'* to Nigel's delighted laughter. Then Quentin sang Carols to them both, practising for the Christmas service at St Philip's church where he was head chorister. He was looking forward to Christmas Day knowing it might be his last Christmas in the choir if his voice broke. He didn't know it would be his last Christmas.

Carol singers gathered outside Croydon's homes to sing a few verses before knocking on doors in hope of a donation. Anthony Harrison loved singing, and he wryly recalled a previous Christmas Eve when he'd gone missing from home. He'd heard Carol singers, and slipped out of the house to join them. Anthony was the Harrison's youngest child, a 'joyful surprise' for his parents who had two grown up children. His brother was in the Navy so it was his parents and sister, who set out in the dark to search for him. Sister Judy found him having a whale of a time singing his heart out, unwilling to return.

Many Lanfranc boys had parents who didn't attend church but sent them to Sunday school, whilst they enjoyed an hour of peace. Prizes were awarded for good attendance but the best reward was the Sunday school Christmas party! Children gorged on a feast of meat paste sandwiches, jam sandwiches, cakes, jelly and ice cream, washed down with orange juice or tea. They each had a cracker (pulled with a deafening bang) containing a paper hat, riddle, and toy, and they enjoyed playing *'Blind Man's Buff', 'Pin the Tail on the Donkey', 'Musical Chairs',* and *'Pass the Parcel'.* Mayhem was allowed in the church hall, but Michael Benson together with his young brother Derek had to cover their embarrassment when the adults organising their Christmas party were surprised to find that the tea had turned purple. Unknown to them the crepe paper of Micky's Christmas cracker had found its way into the kettle!

For older boys their Church Youth Club parties involved dancing, intellectual games such as a treasure hunt, and the chance to hold a piece of mistletoe over a chosen girl's unsuspecting head and steal a kiss. Geoffrey Brown enjoyed their party at St Stephen's with his adoring girlfriend Maureen Kay. His best friend

Derek Goddard, grinning broadly, took his chances with some mistletoe! Few girls would have refused happy Derek.

On Christmas Day Tommy Fowle was with his wife and daughter, glad to relax and forget school. George Budd was at home in Coulsdon with his wife Margery, sons Geoff 18, and Tim 9, watching the Queen's broadcast on their old 9 inch brown Bakelite, Bush Television. Johnny Beacham was at home with his recently widowed mother and other family members, the highlight for them all being the Christmas Day service at church. Lanfranc's pupils had variously awoken before the crack of dawn to open presents left by their bedsides, *or* to wait in agonising suspense until permitted to open anything. Most scoffed the contents of their chocolate 'Selection Boxes' immediately, read their Eagle, Beano, or Dandy comic Annuals, played with new sports equipment, investigated model plane or Meccano kits, and tried on 'useful' new clothes (ugh!) before tucking in to Christmas dinner. At 3.00pm they watched The Queen's speech, followed by Billy Smart's Christmas Circus, or played cards, *Monopoly*, or charades, and basked in the heat of flames roaring up the chimneys of rarely lit fires in their front rooms. Some boys, like Brian Mitchell and his cousin Shirley, put on after dinner entertainment in the form of a performing music show for the adults in their family, ensconced in comfortable chairs. With TV programmes featuring Harry Belafonte, Tommy Steele, and Cyril Stapleton and his Orchestra, for all these Lanfranc families, Christmas 1960 would be remembered as the last 'happy' Christmas.

Spring Term 1961

Times were changing. Farthings minted since the 13th century ceased to be legal tender; Dwight Eisenhower severed relations with Cuba; a Soviet spy ring was uncovered in London, John F. Kennedy became the 35th President of the U.S.; and a pop group called 'The Beatles' performed at the Cavern Club in Liverpool. Now into the Spring Term bachelor John Beacham (when not on duty outside where inter-playground snowball fights were currently the highlight of the school day), was often to be found in the science and crafts building fraternising with George Budd and the craft teachers. Whilst woodwork master Syd Gubby boiled the kettle for tea, and Neville Mearns debated the fortunes of the M.C.C.,

George and John grappled with travel, accommodation, itineraries, and insurance. Everything had to be done by the book for Croydon Education Committee. They were interrupted from time to time by boys with instalments of money (no farthings anymore), or boys stifling tears of disappointment, explaining why they had to relinquish their place. 'Buddy' was always sympathetic. He knew the difficulties of earning enough money, himself spending three evenings a week teaching evening classes to make ends meet. It was a gargantuan task to organise two foreign holidays simultaneously, especially with boys constantly dropping out and more needed to take their places. Luckily Messrs Beacham and Budd had become well experienced. Norway was originally only open to the upper school as it was to be much more of an 'adventure holiday', staying at a mountain youth hostel and setting out from there to trek, climb mountains, and canoe in lakes and fjords. It wasn't considered suitable for anyone under the age of 15 (although younger boys had applied and been given places), but whilst the Austria trip was almost fully subscribed, filling the Norway trip was proving problematic, especially as the price had just been put up by the travel company. Some boys had asked to be transferred to the Austria trip because they wanted to be with their friends, whilst others who signed up had been forced by circumstances to drop out. Doug Kerr was such a boy who had rushed home, heart in mouth and fingers crossed, hoping that all would be well and that he could still go. But his hopes were dashed. Neither his parents nor his elder brother could afford the extra money. Another, Colin Francis, had a dilemma. A member of The Salvation Army, he'd been offered a free place at a Scout Jamboree if he came as a helper. The Jamboree was scheduled for the same time as the Norway trip. His parents decided he'd go to the free Scout Jamboree instead. With diminishing numbers, Beacham and Budd decided to open the trip to the lower school or it wouldn't be viable.

An article advertising the trip, written for 'The Lanfrancian', was published in February, the month when inter-house cross-country races took place and many white clad boys slipped at 'Beacham's brook' – ending up wet and brown, whilst some muddy exhibitionists, egged on by Michael Jones, elected to *swim* through Mitcham Pond rather than run the long way round it! Proud of having 'survived' the course, especially the watery parts, Mr. Beacham's **'School Journey to Norway, August 1961'** was read with interest. *'This year a school party is flying for the first time, to Stavanger in Norway. The first and second nights are spent at Mosvangen Youth Hostel, Stavanger, and on the morning of the third day, the journey is made by steamer and coach to the Preikestolen Mountain Lodge. The last part of the journey is on foot (one hour) but baggage is transported by cable. The party will be staying in a Youth Hostel featured in the film 'Passport to Norway' made by Richard Dimbleby and shown on B.B.C. Television. The Hostel has two, three, and four bedded rooms, hot and cold water and shower baths, and is very comfortable. Visitors are not expected to do any work in the hostel, as this is taken care of by a resident staff. The party stays here until the morning of the seventh day, and will find facilities for bathing, trout fishing, and badminton, as well as being able to make fjord excursions by boat and to take walks through the surrounding countryside (notably to the Pulpit Rock – 3 ½ hours). The party returns to Stavanger after lunch on the seventh day. On the last day of their stay, lunch will be taken at the famous Mortepumpen in the Hotel Atlantic.'*

Third year boys learnt that there were fifteen places up for grabs! The excitement was intense. Quentin Green asked his parents, but his racing bike had been stolen and the metallic green frame found sawn into several pieces. Choosing between a bike or Norway, the bike won because he lived far from Lanfranc. John Adams lived near school, taking the short cut through Croydon Cemetery. He asked his mother Eileen who, wanting the best for her son, decided to sell her Premium Bonds to help pay. Michael Benson and his best friend Geoffrey Green both wanted to go. As they were doing well at school both sets of parents consented. The boys told their old junior school friends Diana Murphy and Brenda Ireland, now pupils at Lanfranc Girls School. The girls always waited for 'Beanie' and 'Micky' after school because they loved to chase them home! David Gore didn't have the same freedom to be chased by girls. He had filled the position as 'man in the house' for his widowed mother, although he managed to find time to plane spot at London Airport and was also a member of the school Quiz Team. His mother wanted to reward David for being such a help to her, particularly for growing everything in the garden. Keen footballer Anthony Harrison, indulged because he was the youngest, was given permission to go. Peter Huggins helped out in his parent's sweet shop and the trip was to be a reward for his unpaid after-school help. Edwin Murray pleaded with his parents to let him go, even though his mother didn't like the thought of him flying to Norway. There had just been a plane crash near Brussels, Belgium that had killed 73 people. She gave in to his entreaties with misgivings. John Phelps, another school Quiz Team member, and Lawrence Sims an artistic boy full of 'go' both managed to obtain their parent's permission. Colin Smith, a boy renowned for always having a smile on his face had been a consolation prize winner in the Eisteddfod, which was a high achievement, so his parents said he could go. Peter Stacey was another aircraft-mad boy who was an expert on all makes and types of planes and even knew from whence they operated, persuaded his parents that he *had* to go. John Wells was tipped to be the school's new cricket captain. Enormously proud of his achievements, his parents felt he'd earned a place. Martin White and Roger White, friends not brothers, sat next to each other at school and lived near each other in Norwood. Martin wanted to go and Roger persuaded his parents to let him go too. Denis Field's widowed mother worked on the domestic staff at the school, knew all about the school trips, and was determined to scrape together the payments. These additions filled all but two places and without these two essential party members John Beacham knew the price would have to go up, undermining the ability of existing parents to meet the increases. Serious discussions between him and George ensued, but there was another problem in store – Jim Towers announced his wife was pregnant. He too had to drop out because 'the patter of little feet' by the end of the year necessitated a holiday job to earn more money. Dependable, good hearted George Budd said he would go to help instead.

The Norway party was made up of eight fifth form school leavers, all reliable boys… men almost. They also had nine fourth formers including top sportsmen with school colours, some prize winners, and other decent lads who would soon become school prefects. The fifteen third formers were also good eggs, several with school sports colours, and others with school prizes. But who would take the last two places? Two second years asked if they could go. Gregory Allen cycled each day from Upper Norwood, in all weathers, on his ancient bike and his mother was a respected art teacher at another Croydon school. Alan

Lee lived close to the school, was form captain, but outside school was always into mischief. John and George needed to fill the places so agreed these two could go too. On reviewing the final list they decided that they were a good bunch of boys with not a bad lad amongst them. In fact they were many of Lanfranc's best. At last everything augured well. John Beacham got down to constructing scenery for Jim Hemming's end of term production of 'She Stoops to Conquer' (which made a change from Shakespeare), with a light heart.

The Easter Holidays gave many 'school trip' boys the chance to earn pocket money for their holiday. Many paper-boys amongst them read headlines that on April 8th the second worst peacetime maritime disaster since *The Titanic* had happened when the British passenger ship *M.V. Dara* was targeted by Omani rebels, and had been blown up off Dubai. The death toll of 238 would have been much higher but for the swift action of Norwegian merchant seamen who risked their own lives, sailing their oil and gas-filled Tanker in dangerously close, in order to launch lifeboats. On April 12th the Russians triumphed in the start of the 'Space Race' when Yuri Gargarin became the first man in space. Adolf Eichmann's trial began in Jerusalem, and Cuba's Bay of Pigs was invaded by United States – backed Cuban exiles. Still recovering from WWII, Communism and the Eastern Block's desire for supremacy was a sinister cloud.

As Lanfranc's Summer Term commenced the first Russian nuclear-powered submarine was commissioned, and not to be outdone, on May 5th the United State's Alan Shepherd became the first American in space. School life, however, was too busy for the boys to be concerned about the escalating arms and space races, summer was the term for cricket, swimming, and sports events, and they intended Lanfranc to win!

A boy with an eye for a pretty girl was Brian Mitchell. He'd spoken to Lady Edridge school girl Denise Schröder when she'd got off her bus after school. Introducing himself as 'Brian', he'd asked if they could meet again, and she'd agreed. It wasn't easy 'chatting up' Denise, who was wary of Brian's direct approach, but he was determined to persevere as she was special. He didn't tell her he was going to Norway. It would be something to talk about when he returned. Eddie Prosper was a Boys Brigade drummer who felt very grown up in his smart uniform and he also had a girl friend from Lady Edridge, named Barbara Whiffen. She lived near him and was a nice girl who his mother liked. It made him feel very mature to boast he was going to Norway!

Fourteen year old Colin Smith felt macho every Saturday when he went ice skating at Streatham Ice Rink. He loved speed skating and jumping barrels placed on the ice, but best of all he loved all the friends he'd made amongst both skaters and staff at the rink. At home in Norwood he recounted his brilliant skating sessions – but not his dare-devil tricks! A little 'dare-devil' living nearby was Angela White, three year old sister of Martin White. She was fascinated by the model planes Martin made from balsa wood and doped paper. Secretly picking up his latest model under construction, she marvelled at its lightness and transparency – until her chubby finger went straight through. She was filled with horrified, guilty delight, because the taut tissue paper had made a lovely 'pop' sound. This was so satisfying that she 'popped' all the little 'windows' before carefully replacing the plane. When Martin discovered his wrecked model he confronted her with the evidence, and unable to be dishonest to a brother she adored, said truthfully 'I wanted to poke it, so I did poke it!' Martin was helpless with laughter.

Now that everything for Norway seemed set in stone, John Beacham contacted Croydon Education Committee with full details of the school holiday. Did someone there say *they* would see to insurance for the trip for him? For some reason John Beacham must have thought so. What Croydon Education did do was to contact the Phoenix Insurance Company, who on May 17th filled out an insurance policy for John and George covering them both for *'Personal liability in respect of school journey from London to Stavanger, Norway, covering liability of teachers in charge. Limit of liability, any one accident, £5000.'* The Norway trip was going with Cunard Eagle Airways Ltd, and both John and George knew that Croydon Education Committee had covered them and the 70 boys going to Austria.

On May 19th these lucky boys going to Austria met at East Croydon for their train to Folkestone. A Croydon Advertiser reporter took a group photo and interviewed John Beacham, who said it was his ninth school trip abroad, and that Lanfranc's pupils were *always* well supervised and behaved themselves –

unlike some schools abroad he'd seen. Three second year boys, John Cooke, Doug Kerr, and Mick Cantwell, bagged seats together. John and Doug had hoped to go to Norway, but John had changed because all of his friends were going to Austria, and Doug changed because neither his parents nor elder brother could afford it. Now they were on a 'high', thrilled to be off with 'Beacham and Buddy' to Austria! On the ferry they chatted up some girls from a northern school who sounded just like characters in the new T.V. series 'Coronation Street'. Hailing from Scotland, chubby good-natured Doug Kerr got on so famously with them that one girl nicknamed him 'Cuddles' – a name that stuck throughout the holiday. Aboard the train to Basle some had paid for couchettes whilst others just had seats. Doug had a couchette and slept well. John and Mick had such hard seats that they slept on the luggage racks. Arriving in Basle at dawn, they sleepily breakfasted in the station buffet before a brisk, mandatory, guided tour to wake them up and educationally utilise two free hours before travelling to Rattenburg. Nine long hours of travelling and a long walk from the station later they arrived to find that their hotel, 'Pension Kaiserblick', was overbooked. Boys were selected to walk to another 'hotel'. Picking up their bags John, Mick, and Doug accompanied Mr Barlow on another long walk. The Austrian valley had arable fields, orchards, and pastures where cows with bells grazed melodically. The boys were amazed to see snow-covered mountains. Eventually arriving at a large, ancient, log-built chalet with a wide sloping roof and balconies along the front, they found cows inside! Given a Spartan dormitory with metal bedsteads and nothing else they were assured that this was only temporary. Eating with the others, they discovered Austrian food was rather highly flavoured, but when hunger got the better of them they decided it was good stuff! Exhausted after their long day they slept well despite the 'cowshed' smell. Austria was a revelation. Not at all like Croydon.

The three liked their accommodation and when offered beds at 'Pension Kaiserblick' they opted to stay where they were. The 'cow-shedders' enjoyed an unprecedented amount of freedom. They also enjoyed Innsbruck, Salzburg, cable-car journeys at Myrahoffen, and fun days at Achensee and Zellann Zee lakes, where they swam. Doug Kerr was dared to jump in from the jetty, only comprehending as he hit the water, exactly what a lake 'fed from a glacier' meant! It was an amazing school trip despite cancellation of the holiday highlight. They'd sung about Hitler and his henchmen, to the tune *'Colonel Bogey'* on their way to his mountain hideaway at Berchtesgarten – only to find it was closed!

From their daily 'pocket money' many saved up to buy special souvenirs. Doug bought a carved wooden plate but as souvenir shops sold incredible affordable knives most boys wanted one. They were *forbidden* to buy knives, but many secretly did! Ten days passed quickly and they returned to Basle. The homeward journey felt longer and the seats harder, yet they were unanimous that the 'Austria Trip' was a fabulous holiday. The three friends had much to tell their parents. Peter Crouch had adventures to tell his twin brother Geoffrey – who was going on the Norway trip. The non-identical brothers were in different classes and Peter had opted to join his friends going to Austria instead. Norway had a lot to beat after what he'd experienced in Austria. Except, of course, that Geoff would be flying… and that was impossible to beat.

With the Austria holiday completed, John Beacham concentrated upon the Norway trip. On June 26th he wrote to A.I.R. Tours, sending them the passenger list and other forms, adding that *'with regard to insurance, that is already in hand through the insurance company of the local Education Authority'*.

The second half of Summer Term was dedicated to swimming galas, public and school examinations, cricket, and sports, in ideal, dry sunny weather. The political climate wasn't so favourable, with the Berlin Crisis just beginning; Rudolf Nureyev requesting asylum in Paris; and submarine USS Theodore Roosevelt commencing its first patrol loaded with Polaris missiles. But for the Lanfranc boys going to Norway nothing mattered, except getting there, and enjoying it! One boy was feeling very miserable however. Dennis Field's mother couldn't afford the last instalments, and told him so. George Budd and John Beacham were very sorry for Dennis, but had to find yet another boy to fill this last place. They told their third year forms, and two boys were keen to take up the place. Quentin Green earnestly asked his parents if he could go – if he paid back for his new bike himself from his paper-round earnings. He was excited to think he might go with his friends – who hadn't stopped talking about flying.

Ronald Green agreed, pleased to give Quentin his first holiday abroad. At school the next day George Budd tossed a coin between the two hopefuls, and asked Quentin to call. 'Heads!' shouted Quentin. 'Heads' it was. Quentin was jubilant!

Another boy who was on top of the world at this time was Dave King. He had achieved the 'impossible'. In a house cricket match he had to face formidable bowler John Wells. Dave stood at the wicket in flimsy shorts and ill fitting cricket pads in fear and trembling as John walked so far back to take his run that Dave could hardly see him in the distance. John set off to bowl and Dave was panic stricken. John's pace was amazingly fast, and as he reached the wicket he zinged a 'Yorker' intended to go under the bat and hit the stumps. Very few were clever enough to achieve this but John Wells was one. Dave was so terrified that he didn't move, but, backside bent in an un-fetching posture, he stood his ground with his bat firmly rooted in the ground. 'Well played!' shouted Neville Mearns the teacher umpiring. Dave looked up to see him looking at him admiringly. Then he realised. He had blocked a ball from John Wells. He wasn't out! He couldn't believe it because John Wells bowled like an athlete, with every muscle in his body working in harmony. Dave was never to forget that he was 'one of the few' that 'legendary' John Wells never got out. John thereafter, went on to bowl out the opposition in the Croydon schools final for humiliating totals, yet he was such a 'lovely chirpy guy' that everyone liked him.

Derek Meacher ('Del' to his friends) was best mates with Edwin Murray and Ed had a wonderful idea to make money. He'd seen racing pigeons circling in the sky near his home and he wanted to capture some pigeons, breed them, and train the chicks to race. Envisaging future prize money he inveigled Del, who thought the scheme was hare-brained, to help him build a pigeon coop. Having no money they had to scavenge useable wood and they gleaned discarded crates at Surrey Street market after school. They spent evenings building the coop in Ed's back garden (watched with misgivings by Ed's nurse elder sister, Patricia) – but had no pigeons to put in it. Ed made umpteen unsuccessful attempts to catch pigeons in the street when eventually Del suggested they wait until the pigeons roosted and were dozy, the perfect place to grab sleeping birds being under the nearby railway bridge where there was some convenient scaffolding. Going out one evening after dark Ed climbed the scaffolding whilst Del held their bikes. Sleeping with an eye open the pigeons were quickly alerted and mayhem ensued – the flock flapping wildly under the girders trying to escape and liberally dropping dried and fresh guano. Disturbed by the racket a local householder accosted the lads and told them, in the vernacular, to clear off or he would call the police! They didn't fare any better at Ed's home either. Patricia didn't want 'racing' or any other kind of pigeons leaving 'calling cards' on her nurse uniform drying on the washing line.

Mrs Roffey and Mrs Martin, Robert Roffey's and John Martin's mothers were very close friends. They were also both quite superstitious, and sometimes went together to visit a Medium. On one occasion John Martin went with them and waited with his mother in the waiting room together with other clients, whilst Joan Roffey went in for her consultation. During her 'reading' the Medium asked if her son ever did any parachuting. 'No' said Joan. She thought nothing of it, and left. Shortly afterwards the Medium came into the waiting room and was very upset by what she had 'seen' for Mrs Roffey.

Lanfranc School Sport's Day marked the end of the scholastic year. Most boys going to Norway represented their houses for an event. Tommy Fowle looked on approvingly at his lads. He was proud of them all. They had such vitality! He bid farewell to his leavers knowing he'd see them again in November for Speech Day, when they would collect their awards. His physics teacher Mr Taylor was leaving to live in Australia and he wished him all the best for his new life. He knew 'Mighty Mouse' and his cane and metre rule would be sorely missed! He wished George and John a carefree trip to Norway. As he packed up his brief case at the end of term he heaved a sigh of satisfied relief. All was right with Lanfranc – his world.

BLACK AUGUST

Six weeks of freedom commenced. Lanfranc's cycle-mad boys had the chance to whizz off together and visit other towns. Keith Scotcher was with Bobby Martin and others on a ride to Epsom and back when Bobby mentioned his forthcoming holiday to Norway and said he was 'off' on August 9th. This stuck in Keith's mind because the 9th was his 15th birthday. Some boys felt envious of friends going to Norway. Ian Greest had paid the deposit but his father lost his job and had been close to tears when telling Ian he couldn't go. Oddly, his mother had felt differently. To compensate they all went camping in Cornwall. His parents were listening to their radio when they heard awful news. Ian's mother rushed into Ian's tent gasping, 'There's been a terrible plane crash! I hope it's not the boys! Thirty people have been killed on a holiday flight somewhere in Europe!' Ian's heart missed a beat but investigation proved that it wasn't Lanfranc's plane at all. They weren't going until August 9th and this was August 6th. Also the plane had crashed in *Budapest* which was in *Hungary* and Ian's friends were going to *Stavanger* which was in *Norway*. Foreign place names, although quite distinct, seemed confusingly similar to many adults who had never been abroad. Ian's mother was so relieved. For some time she had felt strangely glad that her only child wasn't going.

Circling the Earth and able to pick out every country without consulting an Atlas, Gherman Titov became the second Russian in space.

Stamp collectors knew their geography better than most. One Lanfranc boy who was a keen stamp collector visited the little stamp shop in Kennards Arcade, where he had seen an old first day cover of Scouting Jamboree stamps that he wanted. He hadn't enough money, so he asked the stamp shop owner if he would put them by for him until he returned from Norway and had saved some more money. The shop man knew him well and kindly agreed.

8th August

By August 8th, the day before their great adventure, the Lanfranc boys were busy gathering their essentials for the Norway trip. Many had been bought 'Norway-proof' anoraks and shoes. New clothes often stretched family budgets to the limit, so Quentin Green had been bought a large anorak, in the hope that he'd grow into it. Geoffrey Green had new 'casual' shoes, which had caused a heated argument, because his Dad thought them 'too modern'. Michael Benson had a new suit. He tried it on that day and sat glumly playing records in his front room, with his young brother Derek. 'You look very grown up Micky', said Derek. Michael didn't answer. 'You must be getting really excited about the trip…' Derek pursued. Michael looked up with a puzzled expression on his face. 'For some reason I'm not really looking forward to going', he replied. 'Why on earth not Mick? You're so lucky! I wish I was going! Michael just shrugged his shoulders and played another record.

Some boys had pets to arrange care for. Derek Goddard's beloved 'wobbly-legged' stick insects weren't a problem. His parents were to supply fresh privet leaves and water, every two days. David Hatchard trusted his teacher father to care for his tropical fish, whilst his mother would walk Sally his beloved terrier. He stroked Sally and wished he could take her with him as he knew she'd love the mountains... Originally he hadn't wanted to go to Norway but his devoted parents insisted it would be 'good for him'. Now he was getting excited, especially as he had been bought new sandals for the trip.

Another boy smelt freedom. Peter Huggins, an only child, had friends who dreamt of owning a sweet shop – but not he! The occasional cigarette sneaked from his parent's shop helped him find friends, when shared behind the bike sheds, but it was a survival tactic. He felt a bit of a loner and hoped going to Norway would create new friendships and give him some kudos. It wasn't many boys who could boast they had flown!

One boy who may have felt a little nervous about flying was Alan Lee. He had saved up his paper round money to help pay for the trip and now persuaded his postman father to take him to London Airport so that he could see planes take off. How could something so big and heavy 'float' in the air?

School leaver David Hendley had celebrated his 16th birthday on July 29th, the first day of the school holidays. Fascinated by aircraft, his bedroom ceiling was full of swooping model planes, the walls covered in aircraft designs, whilst books on design and construction filled his shelves. He was about to be an apprentice aircraft draftsman. He couldn't wait to fly.

Peter Stacey had a similarly decorated bedroom, and interest in planes. Although desperately keen to fly, however, his main concern was to ensure that his 'adopted' hedgehog didn't do a moonlight flit whilst he was away. His parents were detailed to provide saucers of bread and milk to induce it to stay in their garden. David Gore was also concerned about his garden. He asked his mother Lily to water his flowers and vegetables, and to pick whatever needed picking. He was so excited at the thought of flying. Avid plane spotting visits to London Airport and a bedroom full of model aircraft had convinced his widowed mother that if she could possibly afford it, David should go.

Helping at home was expected, and many a Lanfranc boy found himself running errands for his parents that day. Quentin Green was asked to deliver a message to their next door neighbour. Hearing hammering, Quentin went round to the back door, but being small and light on his feet William Barr didn't see or hear him coming. Suddenly finding Quentin beside him, he jumped in surprise and whacked the hammer down on his thumb. The air turned blue with the invective of an ex-Naval rating. Quentin swiftly delivered his message and ran home, leaving Mr. Barr hopping around holding his throbbing thumb.

In Croydon, Valerie Gore felt depressed. She had an unaccountable, overwhelming feeling that she was going to die, and that somehow this was linked to her young brother-in-law David going to Norway. She couldn't wait for him to go and come back again. Feeling silly to have such weird feelings she went with her husband Jim to say goodbye. She was anxious to tell David that she and Jim would meet him at East Croydon Station on his return – as though making this a statement would ensure his safe homecoming.

One girl with no strange feelings was Maureen Kay, Geoffrey Brown's girlfriend. She, Geoff and his brother Ian, plus best friend Derek Goddard spent a happy-go-lucky evening together fooling around, cracking jokes. Geoff and Derek had left school and were soon to start jobs. Maureen couldn't wait for them to come back again, tell her all about their adventures in Norway, and continue their own happy adventures with St Stephen's Youth Club. She adored Geoff.

Another boy who had left Lanfranc and was looking forward to becoming a commercial artist was Lawrence Sims. He was busy that evening drawing in his bedroom, listening to the latest 'Pop' music, when his friend Bill Tarbuck called round and helped him pack. On Lol's bed was a pair of long, green, 'beetle' boots with red toe caps and two and a half inch high-heels. Liberally interpreting the trip's clothing list for 'stout' shoes, he envisaged these fashion boots suitable for walking in the mountains!

Meanwhile, looking out of her bedroom window in Aurelia Road, young Janis Wilding secretly watched Michael Benson emerge from the newsagents shop laden with sweets and comics. She knew he was packing for his trip to Norway, and yet she'd never ever been away on holiday. She felt so envious!

Whilst all the Lanfranc boys packed their last minute belongings, across the other side of the world, a 22 year old member of the Woman's Royal Army Corps, NCO Corporal Brenda Morris, was preparing to fly home. She had just completed two years duty in Singapore with the Royal Corps of Signals, and was due to be demobbed. She'd hoped to cruise home, stopping at exotic places, but she'd drawn the short straw. A Regimental Sergeant Major (RSM), had broken her leg and was to be medically evacuated home, and Brenda was ordered to escort her. They were checked aboard the first scheduled flight, the RSM with her broken leg protruding into the aisle, Brenda next to her and the window. Sad to leave her friends and 'lovely' Singapore Brenda was returning home the 'unexciting' way. Little did she know what excitement lay in store for her, or that her journey would culminate with meeting ill-fated school boys from Croydon.

As the Norway trip boys retired to bed everything went according to plan with Brenda's flight. Whilst they slept her plane flew westwards, landing in the dark to refuel in Calcutta, and again in Bombay. As a beautiful sunrise greeted her near Istanbul, sparks ignited drops of fuel leaking from the wing Brenda was sitting by. Flames licked over it and they started to lose height dropping to

10,000 feet. She was convinced the plane was going to crash and the RSM said 'I think we should say a prayer…' Cool action by the pilot averted calamity, and the flames were largely extinguished. With spasmodic fire bursts still threatening, however, the Captain announced that Rome Airport was on standby for an emergency landing… Brenda looked intently at the shape of the Greek coastline below, believing it might be one of the last things she would ever see if they crashed landed at Rome, or before…

The Lanfranc boys by this time were up and leaving home when, to Brenda's surprise, the plane turned deliberately northwest by the Adriatic and flew between Yugoslavia and Italy towards the Alps. They were going to limp home to London.

The Eagle Family – London 8th August

Founder Chairman of Cunard Eagle Airways Ltd. 38 year old Harold R. Bamberg divided his time between his offices in Central London and London Airport. His company was held in high esteem having been praised in The House of Commons as one of the most enterprising air firms in Europe. He'd recently amalgamated his 'Eagle' company with the Cunard Steamship Company and his airline's business future looked very bright. His maxim was 'There's no substitute for getting into business and learning the hard way' and now he was about to show the 'big boys' in British aviation how successful an independent airline like his could be. Government sponsored B.E.A. and B.O.A.C., jealous of Eagle, were irritated by its new partnership with the Cunard shipping line. Jaunty Harold Bamberg was about to make them even more so, because he'd ordered two Boeing 707 jets for trans-Atlantic work at a cost of £6,000,000. They would add to his fleet of 18 aircraft very nicely. Constantly upgrading, his fleet comprised mainly Viscounts and Britannias plus five elderly Vikings.

Eagle employees felt they were part of one big happy family, with Harold Bamberg at the head. He had every reason to feel proud of 'his family' as he had come a long way since setting up Eagle Aviation Ltd in 1948. Leaving school at 17, he'd joined the wartime R.A.F. where he had risen to the position of sergeant pilot. Demobbed from the R.A.F. aged 25 he'd set up his company, with only

£100 capital. Investing in two old Handley Page Halifax bombers, he'd converted them to transport fruit and vegetables from Spain and Italy, to his base at Aldermaston, for Covent Garden's market. Having achieved credibility, he'd been contracted to help with the Berlin airlift, and in 1950 his company had moved to Luton, where the following year he'd won a War Office contract to transport troops between the U.K. and Rhodesia. This continued when he moved to Blackbushe Airport a year later. With expansion he'd gathered a prestigious team of Directors and some notable wartime pilots. During 1953 he'd set up 'Eagle Airways' to expand further into passenger charter flights, and scheduled services run from Blackbushe to British and European destinations. They were a young dynamic company that the government contracted for ambulance flights in the Korean War, aid in the Suez crisis, and evacuation during the Hungarian uprising. Later, as London Airport became congested they pioneered flights from Birmingham, Manchester, Newcastle, and other provincial airports.

Post-war austerity had almost gone, and by 1957 Harold Bamberg collaborated with Henry Lunn, and expanded Eagle into package tourism, operating 22 Vickers Vikings purchased from B.E.A. as well as setting up Eagle Airways-Bermuda, for trans-Atlantic flights. Eagle was growing steadily, whilst still maintaining their War Office troop contract, when disaster struck. Harold Bamberg didn't like to think about it. It was awful. During the war he'd accepted that friends in the R.A.F. died, and he might have died himself, but in peacetime? It was bad luck. One of his Vikings had taken off on a troop flight from Blackbushe, when it immediately developed engine failure. Returning hastily, it crashed, killing all five crew and 29 out of 30 passengers. It haunted him, especially as the date was May 1st. May Day! *M'aide!* He knew he had to get this accident into perspective. It was Eagle's only accident with fatalities, and that particular year it was the 21st out of 57 aviation accidents world-wide, in which a total of 1,004 people had died. Air crashes happened. It was a fact of aviation. But it still weighed heavily on him. He'd lost five fine crew members, whilst the lives of so many had been ruined. Just one person survived, – injured. It was hard being at the top and having to accept ultimate responsibility for his airline. He'd decided to sell off several of his Vikings after that, buying newer and larger aircraft.

Harold Bamberg was pleased he'd been able to move his entire fleet to London Airport the previous year, and expand in partnership with Cunard. He had two new Britannias, so he sold three of his remaining eight Viking 'work horses' used on their medium and short haul flights. They'd clocked up several thousand flying hours, and had been flown with two pilots and a radio engineer. Now the Viking's radio engineers worked on his new prestigious aircraft as it had been agreed that Vikings only needed two pilots, plus a stewardess. The First Officer would double as radio engineer and keep the Captain of the plane informed about weather conditions and radio messages.

Five Vickers Vikings left out of 22. Affectionately nicknamed 'Pigs' because of their stocky fuselage, they were good little planes, a variant of the Vickers Wellington. After the war the Ministry of Aircraft Production had ordered three prototypes Wellington Transport Aircraft from Vickers-Armstrong Limited, to be medium-short haul passenger aircraft. The wing and undercarriage design from the wartime Vickers Wellington had been combined with a new design of fuselage. The 1945 prototype had crashed in 1946, due to double engine failure (miraculously with no fatalities), after which two more prototypes were produced. After successful trials, 163 Vikings of several different variants were produced until 1948, when production stopped. B.E.A. had bought a large fleet but had sold many on. Harold Bamberg had bought his from them during 1954 and 1955.

This summer Eagle's remaining five Vikings had been working hard on scheduled domestic and chartered holiday flights. A.I.R. Tours arranged package holidays for school children and had chartered Eagle for school trips to Stavanger in Norway. As these holidays were back-to-back flights, into and out of Stavanger's Sola Airport, they dovetailed nicely. Two such flights were booked for tomorrow, a flight out from London at 9.30 British Summer Time (BST) and a return flight from Sola in the afternoon. He looked over the roster. Yes, Captain Philip Watts was taking Papa Mike together with First Officer R.L.M. Smalley, and stewardess Susan Endicott. They were a good team to assign to their first trip to Sola Airport which his experts had graded as an 'A' – an 'easy' airport at which to land. No problems there then, especially as pilot Philip Watts was extremely experienced and had such an excellent war record. Harold liked employing decorated war veterans and Philip Watts had been on active service aged18 from 1939, and despite the odds, had survived the war. Philip Watts's real surname was Karginoff, his paternal grandfather being Russian, but he'd changed his name to his maternal grandfather's in order to join the R.A.F. where he'd flown Spitfires, Mosquitos, and Gloster Meteors. Philip Watts had served with great distinction and had been decorated with the United Kingdom Air Crew Europe Star. Harold Bamberg noted that his usual co-pilot was off sick, and that R.L.M. Smalley, a good young recruit, also ex-R.A.F. although not nearly so experienced, had been deputed to stand in. This trip would teach him about a new airport – Philip Watts too of course. They'd both enjoy having bubbly, dependable, Susan Endicott as their flight stewardess. Susan was outstanding. It was a pity she had handed in her notice – but someone else had obviously spotted her vivacity, charm, and good looks!

Viking Papa Mike would soon have to be sold. It had first flown for B.E.A. in May 1947 and had averaged 120 hours per calendar month, clocking 11,132 hours and 45 minutes with them before joining Eagle in July 1953. During its eight years with Eagle, Papa Mike, (officially named 'Lord Rodney'), had averaged 101 hours per calendar month, and flown 9,752 hours. Its total flying time now was 20,884 hours and 46 minutes, and it was 14 years old. Decisions would be made soon, in the meantime he was doing his best to create a profitable, dependable, independent airline – and to keep the acquisitive hands of government sponsored airlines off his contracts. They were jealous he knew it and what would happen to his 'Eagle Family' if they got their way?

Soon to leave the 'Eagle family' was graduate ex-teacher Susan Endicott, who hailed from Paignton in Devon. Susan was relaxing in the garden of her flat in Kensington Gardens, which she shared with her sister and two girl friends. The 22 year old was happily day-dreaming. She loved working for Cunard Eagle Airways, having visited wonderful places, but her job was only a stop-gap between teaching (which she hadn't enjoyed), and marriage, followed by her intended career in cancer research. She had just one more flight to do before quitting. Although missing her sister Ann, currently holidaying home in Devon, life was good. Susan was deeply in love with a wonderful man, Army Officer Chris Moysey, and they were about to announce their engagement. In a few days time, on August 22nd she would be 23, a perfect age to marry and be Mrs Christopher Moysey. Chris was currently on leave from Germany and she was able to spend free time with him – so her life really couldn't get any better!

They had been together for four years whilst he'd been at The Royal Military Academy, Sandhurst and she'd been at London University studying Zoology. Graduating well she'd then taken a Masters degree at London University's School of Tropical Medicine, intending to research into the causes of cancer which had ended the life of a young Devonshire friend. When Chris was posted to Germany, she'd taught biology in a badly disciplined London East End school. The girls weren't interested in learning and played up, so knowing Sue's ability with foreign languages, a friend suggested she become a stewardess instead. She passed Eagle's exams with flying colours, and a temporary career took off – literally. Inseparable from her sister, Ann Endicott had joined her in London, but was currently home in Paignton, knowing how much their mother missed them. Sue expected a telephone call from them both at 6.00pm precisely.

In Paignton, Ann and Jean Endicott dialled from their local telephone box on the dot of six o'clock. Jean Endicott spoke first, delighted to chat with her sparkling daughter. Ann spoke next, telling Susan their news, and asking Susan to write to tell her everything that she was doing. 'I will Annie, I promise! As soon as I can…' Susan said as their money dropped into the box and the connection terminated. Ann adored her petite elder sister who looked after her in London, making sure Ann was incorporated into her own happy, busy, social life. Now at home in Devon, Ann was perturbed because her mother had acted very oddly. They had both been relaxing in the garden when, without a word, her mother had abruptly disappeared through their French doors. Concerned, Ann discovered her mother rummaging for Sue's baby photos. On finding the special album, she looked longingly at them all. 'Why are you looking at them now?' Ann asked. 'I don't know… I just had to…' Jean had replied. Normally so level-headed, Ann thought her mother's behaviour very odd.

In the evening of August 8th, First Officer Reginald L. M. Smalley, known as Murray to his friends, was on his way home to Lightwater in Surrey. He had drawn the short straw to accompany Captain Philip Watts on a trip to Stavanger the next day. He'd worked ten and a half hours but the scheduled co-pilot was ill – so bang went his rest day! He was looking forward to seeing his wife Nina in their new house 'Pippins' as he'd spent all of June working every hour permitted flying between Cyprus, a chain of airports in North Africa, and finally Malta, then back again. He had plenty of sunshine, but off duty he desperately missed Nina and their small daughter Karen. This evening he'd only have time for dinner with Nina, as afterwards he had to prepare flight plans for the next day. Before going to bed at 2230 hours Greenwich Mean Time (GMT which is one hour behind British Summer Time) he kissed his sleeping daughter goodnight. He had to be up early to arrive at London Airport by 0700 hours GMT.

Living not far away in Camberley, Captain Philip Watts enjoyed an evening at home. He'd read a 'good night' story to his son Simon, an adventure of 'Black Bob' the 'Dandy Wonder Dog' a resourceful Border Collie sheep dog featured in 'The Dandy' comic. Philip kissed Simon goodnight and went to join his wife. He had to rise early to fly school boys to Norway. He'd not flown to Sola Airport, Stavanger before. It was new to him, and could be interesting, otherwise tomorrow was just a bus trip transporting a school party from Croydon – a place he knew from living in nearby Addiscombe. He thought they'd all be getting excited at the prospect of flying. And who could blame them? Not him. Being an airline pilot, flying for a living, was the best job in the world!

England Wednesday 9th August

All the Lanfranc boys going to Norway were up early to rendezvous outside Croydon Town Hall by 7.30am (BST), for a flight leaving London Airport at 9.30am (BST). Leaving his home in Coulsdon, George Budd stuck his head around his son's bedroom doors to say 'goodbye', before his wife Margery saw him off, with some trepidation. She had a fear of flying, whilst being ex RAF George was looking forward to the flight. This was the first school trip where she hadn't come as a helper because numbers were smaller. George had tried quoting statistics to prove that flying was the safest way to travel, but Margery wasn't convinced. She had not been keen on the trip at all and was very apprehensive. 'There's more chance I could get killed crossing the road' George reassured her, as he waved goodbye.

Papa Mike, pre 1961

Viking G-AHPM, wearing its final Cunard Eagle Airways livery at Heathrow in late 1960 (David Cotterell)

The cockpit of a Viking.

The passenger cabin of a Viking.

Captain Philip Watts.

Pilot Philip Watts during WWII.

Pilot R.L. Murray Smalley.

First Officer R.L.M. Smalley.

Susan Endicott, graduation photo.

Stewardess Susan Endicott, Eagle application photo

Susan Endicott and friend at Torquay, Devon.

John Beacham lived with his brother Dennis and his family at 31, Birdhurst Road, South Croydon. Normally, before departing on a school trip, he said goodbye to his eleven year old nephew Ian, but this morning he left very early. Ian heard him leaving as his bedroom was next to the front door, and a strange sensation came over him. He felt he wouldn't see his Uncle John again, so he jumped out of bed in order to wave him goodbye. As he watched John walking up the road with his rucksack on his back the youngster couldn't understand the odd feeling that possessed him. He'd seen his favourite uncle set out on many foreign trips before, so why did he feel so peculiar this time?

In Thornton Heath, Violet Murray, mother of Edwin Murray, was in a state of anguish, wishing she'd never agreed to let her son go. She felt quite ill at the thought of him flying. Violet Murray wasn't alone because John Well's mother also wished he wasn't going. John was her youngest and all his life she'd feared he'd be taken from her prematurely. It was a feeling she'd struggled with and hadn't wanted John to know about. How could she have stopped her son, one of the most popular boys in the school, from going on this exciting trip?

In Norbury Quentin Green's sister sat in bed wondering what on earth she'd 'heard' inside her head. Something had told her to say 'I'll never see you again' to her brother, but she couldn't say it! Where had that authoritative 'voice' come from? She'd wanted a kiss from Quentin and had received a peck on her cheek… In Mitcham, her namesake Susan Green faced a similar situation. Her brother Geoffrey was standing in their hall and Susan was feeling sad because she was going to miss him, when her mother said 'Aren't you going to kiss Susan goodbye?' He pulled a face and said 'No!' Then he laughed, gave her a big hug instead, and disappeared out of the front door.

Leaving his home nearby was Geoffrey's friend Michael Benson, accompanied by his father and younger brother Derek – who couldn't figure out why his unaccountably glum brother wasn't looking forward to the trip. Another brother who, by contrast, couldn't wait to go was David Hendley. Tall and smart in his new clothes he came into his sister Julia's bedroom to say goodbye, excited to be fulfilling his passion to fly. Panic ensued when his father couldn't start the car and he thought he'd miss the bus to London Airport. Finally it started. In

Upper Norwood, wearing his brother's old shoes and his own favourite jumper, Martin White waved cheerfully as he left home. Martin had wanted Bernard to come too, but being three years older, Bernard didn't want to cramp his young brother's style. His three year old sister Angela wanted to know why Martin was going away. She didn't understand the existence of other countries but was fascinated by the moon and always demanded to know, when it was half or crescent, where the 'other piece of the moon' had gone. Martin announced that he was going away to find it for her. Edward Gilder's parents took a photo of him as he left. He had his special stick covered in silver badges with him. Before he left home Edwin Murray roughly made a sand castle from a pile of builder's sand by his back door and stuck a Union Jack flag on the top. It was a triumphant gesture of a youngster with no misgivings. His mother Violet Murray recalled this, her last memory of him, when all the flags in Croydon flew at half mast…

Outside Croydon's Town Hall, George Budd and John Beacham checked each boy off on their list as they arrived. Then, at 7.45 am the coach set off for London Airport. All 34 boys were aboard. No press photographer had been there to take a group photograph.

(All times are now given in Greenwich Mean Time – GMT.)

Captain Philip Watts and First Officer Murray Smalley were already at the Airport. An hour earlier 40 year old Philip Watts had kissed his wife goodbye saying 'It's just a bus trip – I'll see you soon.' Murray Smalley had bid his wife Nina and daughter Karen farewell, expecting to be back home for dinner. On his Mediterranean travels he had bought a special ring for Nina and looked forward to giving it to her. Both men reported for duty at 0705 hours, and went together to the Operator's Movement Control Office, where maps and Navigational data for the route to Stavanger, prepared for them, were filed in a Navigation Bag. Murray Smalley took charge of this bag and checked its contents. It all seemed perfectly correct to the First Officer, but the type of route chart provided was one concerned with route facilities and not landing aids. As far as both pilots were concerned, however, this was a routine flight, albeit their first to Stavanger Sola Airport. They'd be home by early evening.

First Officer Smalley then attended a Meteorological Office briefing where he also obtained a Flight Forecast Folder. Captain Watts didn't attend this weather briefing but remained in the Movement Control Office, where he checked the aircraft documents for Viking G-AHPM – code named Papa Mike. The documents he checked included the load and trim sheets, invaluable data for the Captain to assess how the engines of his plane would have to react to the load being carried. In this case it was a passenger load of 34 schoolboys and two masters, plus their luggage, plus him, First Officer Smalley, and their stewardess, pretty 22 year old Susan Endicott. Not a heavy load.

Around 0745 hours, First Officer Smalley filed his Air Traffic Control Flight Plan. His navigational route was to fly via Watford and Clacton, and then off airways to Stavanger. He estimated that the flight time would be 2 hours and 30 minutes, well within their fuel endurance of five and one quarter hours. Cunard Eagle Airways had graded all the airports they used, world-wide, into A, B, or C categories according to the technical difficulty of touch-down and take-off. Stavanger's Sola Airport was graded 'A', not necessitating any special instruction, nor the need for a pilot who had landed there previously. Captain Watts was a very experienced pilot with approximately 8,000 flying hours of which 3,730 hours were in Vikings, whilst First Officer Smalley had 1,744 flying hours of which 262 were in Vikings. Sola Airport on its level coastal land might have been graded an 'easy' airport by Eagle Airways, but high land lay not far to the east. Rogaland, the region in which Stavanger lay, was famous for its high peaks and deep fjords. That was what made it a popular tourist destination.

Pretty Susan Endicott, band-box smart in her Cunard Eagle Airways uniform of maroon suit, black high-heeled court shoes, and white gloves, was happily looking forward to the day. It was to be her last job as a stewardess, because on her return, she and Chris Moysey were to announce their engagement. Her last return trip, to Norway a country she'd never flown to before, and one last postcard to send Ann – who had quite a collection of foreign cards she'd sent, usually detailing some funny or exciting experience. Susan left the flat in Kensington Gardens very happy that morning, looking forward to seeing her beloved Chris again that evening, and of telling everyone their wonderful news.

En route to London Airport, Messrs Beacham and Budd, as they always did when taking a school holiday, laid down their rules and regulations for the trip. The boys were going to have the time of their lives in Norway, indeed they *all* were – but as young envoys of their school they were expected to have *exemplary* behaviour. There was no argument about that, as the boys knew they'd have plenty of fun with 'Buddy' and 'Billy Beacham'.

At the airport the group ticket issued by A.I.R. Tours was checked and the party's special collective passport duly stamped. Luggage was taken, but with duffle bags and pockets stuffed with comics, magazines, chocolate, and sweets, the boys filed out to the plane. It wasn't the biggest plane they could see at the airport, and it certainly wasn't the *newest*, but in Cunard Eagle Airways livery it was smart and best of all – it was *all* theirs. Nobody else was flying with them. This Vickers Viking G-AHPM was Lanfranc's plane.

At 0835 hours Papa Mike taxied from the embarkation point to a holding area near the runway. Everyone was ordered to strap themselves into their seats, and stewardess Susan took round sweets to suck, to help equalise air pressure in their ears with the rapid change in altitude after take-off. She also gave each boy an Eagle courtesy pack which contained a brochure with a brief history of the airline and a map of their route; souvenirs to add to their small enamelled A.I.R. Tours School Travel Group badges. The plane taxied to the end of the runway and the boys were variously thrilled, or nervous, whilst their Pilot, Captain Watts, spent ten minutes performing the obligatory pre-take-off engine and instrument checks. Papa Mike's engines were fired up singly and run to maximum revs, the aircraft juddering and shaking alarmingly. The boys knew that in a moment, when the other engine was fired up, they'd be flying! The second engine was fired up on its own, and revved, but failed to seemingly shake the plane apart with its vibrations. Far from hurtling down the vast grey runway at top speed and rising skywards, to their surprise and disappointment 'their plane' taxied back to the airport's Central Area, and they were told to disembark. There was a fault and although to turn back was an enormous disappointment, they all knew it was better to be safe than sorry.

During a magneto drop test of the port engine Captain Watts had gradually opened up the throttle as required, and had spotted a drop of 100 revs per minute on the right hand magneto. This was serious, and there was nothing else to be done but to taxi back again, and request ground support to get to work immediately. With the safety of his passengers at heart, not to mention himself and his crew, Captain Watts was not going to fly Viking Papa Mike until the fault was located and fixed. He knew that with a faulty magneto there was a danger that the affected engine would quit in flight. Memories of what had happened when a port engine had failed on a similar Viking at Blackbushe Airport four years previously, came ominously to mind. This one had to go back for the mechanics to sort out. Papa Mike wasn't going to fly until it passed muster.

The air crew retired to the Operations Room to wait, whilst mechanics from Eagle Aircraft Services Ltd, based at the ex-BOAC hangars close to runway 05/23, were called out to find the fault. They were used to dealing with the company's dwindling fleet of Vickers Vikings. Once the pride of Eagle's fleet, now the aircraft were ageing, and their numbers dropped each year as aircraft were withdrawn from service. Like the song 'ten green bottles' mishaps sometimes occurred, or they were deemed un-flyable, so that whilst in 1957 there had been 22, in 1958 there were 15, then in 1959 – ten, in 1960 eight, and by 1961 there were just five left in service. The 'Pigs' were on their way out. Nevertheless, two Vikings operated on lightly loaded routes from London to Manchester, whilst three operated on a government troop contract to Malta. In between these scheduled flights Eagle's Vikings were utilised for ad-hoc charters – such as this one to Stavanger on behalf of A.I.R. Tours. With decommissioned Vikings used for spares, the fault on Papa Mike now had to be found.

Papa Mike was a Vickers Viking 1A type 610 aircraft. Built by Vickers-Armstrong Ltd. at Weybridge in 1946, it was registered and acquired that year by British European Airways. With 5 hours and 15 minutes total flying time it first flew for BEA in March 1947, who put it into service in mid-May. BEA owned the plane, which they named 'Verdera' until 1953, when they sold it to Eagle Airways Ltd, who renamed it 'Lord Rodney' after a British Admiral. Under military contract and disguised in RAF colours, with the military code XF632, 'Lord Rodney' carried troops and their families from Blackbushe airport to Cyprus, Gibraltar, Malta, Tripoli, and Fayid in the Canal Zone. In February 1955, with 11,132 hours and 45 minutes flying time accumulated, it was transferred to Eagle Aircraft Services Ltd. In 1957 it was converted to a 610/3B type, with the addition of a freight door, and transferred back to Eagle Airways Ltd the same year. In January 1961, coming up to 14 years old, it was transferred to Cunard Eagle Airways Ltd. No longer 'Lord Rodney' the Viking was painted in the Cunard Eagle Airways livery of silver, red, and white with a huge stylised white 'Eagle' E on a black painted tail fin. Its code was G-AHPM, the last two letters its call sign – Papa Mike.

Two technicians got to work straight away, to discover what was wrong with the port engine magneto – an electrical generator that provided the electrical current to the engine's spark plugs, which was vital for the continuous running of the Viking's port internal-combustion engine. Problems with magnetos happened from time to time with piston aircraft. Potentially serious, the problem wasn't major and eventually the fault was traced to a plug lead that needed to be replaced. This spare part had to found. The job should normally have taken an hour.

Meanwhile, as the boys read their comics, or watched aircraft taking off and landing, at 0945 hours First Officer Murray Smalley revisited the Meteorological Office. He obtained an additional briefing about actual weather conditions in Stavanger from data which had come in at 0850 hours, and also 0920 hours. The Aero reports of surface south easterly winds, varying between 30 and 32 knots, and gusting between 46 and 49 knots, indicated it wasn't a perfect August summer's day in Norway, but there was nothing at that stage in the Aero report to worry about. Someone who was very worried, however, was Edwin Murray's mother. Violet Murray couldn't concentrate on her work in the dental laboratory factory at Broad Green at all. She confided in her friend Irene Raff that she was terrified of her son flying, but that she'd been persuaded against her better judgement to let him go.

Over the Alps (where by contrast, visibility and weather conditions were good), Brenda Morris was worried too, and she wasn't alone. The Captain of Brenda's aircraft had decided that he could limp safely back to England, preferring an emergency landing at London Airport. He was still several hours out and knew that his passengers were feeling shaken, so to lighten their apprehension, over the loud speaker system he pointed out important features below. Mt Blanc and The Eiger were singled out, and he jokingly asked them to 'breathe in' so that they could get over the snow-covered range. The weather was brilliant sunshine and the view below was spectacularly beautiful – but for some reason they were still losing height.

At London Airport Captain Philip Watts and his team, drinking coffee and feeling frustrated, knew they simply had to sit it out. Philip Watts, a highly decorated wartime RAF Spitfire pilot was used to enforced inactivity followed by sudden orders to 'scramble!' He had no desire to take off with a dodgy engine, especially as he'd been a First Officer at Blackbushe when Viking G-ABJO had developed a fault in its port engine two minutes after take-off, lost height when turning back, struck a hill and caught fire. Five colleagues and all but one of the 30 passengers died so he wasn't going to take any chances. Frustration or not, they would wait until the fault was repaired.

First Officer Murray Smalley hadn't been a pilot for as many years nor had the exacting WWII experiences of his Captain. He loved flying but he was also an artistic man who enjoyed working backstage in his spare time at the Priory Theatre in his old home town of Kenilworth. He'd met his adorable wife Nina through amateur dramatics.

Susan Endicott was in the crew room day-dreaming when another stewardess Olga Nodiroli, known as Nodi, came in from her flight. 'Where are you off to? Olga asked. 'Stavanger – with a load of school boys' Susan replied. 'I expect they'll all be wanting cigarettes after take-off!' she quipped. They chuckled at the thought of this, and Olga left Susan, half sitting on a table, swinging one of her legs and thinking of Chris, her soon to be fiancé – officially.

Work on the faulty engine continued and the Lanfranc party, hungry after an abnormally early breakfast, (or none at all), were given a meal. Interesting though London Airport undoubtedly was, they were missing out on seeing Norway, and they were raring to go. George Budd and John Beacham had the unexpected job of having to 'entertain' the impatient lads. Probably George explained how aircraft wings acted as aerofoils, describing how the difference in air pressure above and below the wing surface enabled 'lift', whilst John talked about London's importance as a hub of international communications. Some boys played cards or pocket chess (Ed Murray had borrowed his friend Derek Meacher's set) but most had their noses glued to the windows of the observation lounge, watching jets take off and land – wishing that 'their' plane was a jet.

Brenda Morris meanwhile was flying across France. When they reached Paris their pilot pointed out the Eiffel Tower – and promised to try and miss it! As they crossed the Channel and saw the white cliffs of Dover approaching there was jubilation on board. They hadn't far to go! At London Airport preparations were underway for the stricken aircraft to make an emergency landing.

Knowing his mother always worried about him, John Wells phoned home to say that their flight was delayed. On the other end of the phone in Waddon, Mrs Wells wanted to tell him to come home, and not to go. But she didn't. At 1410 hours Quentin Green also decided to telephone home, to let his mother know that they hadn't left yet. His sister answered the phone, and he told her and then his mother of the delay – but said they would be leaving very soon. They both said 'God Bless you Quentin' simultaneously as his money ran out and the line went dead. Kathleen had wanted to say 'Don't go!' But she didn't. Rosalind had felt exactly the same. They had the same uneasy feeling that these were the last words that they would speak to Quentin – but somehow they couldn't believe it. Feeling concerned, Kathleen Green called her husband at his office. He'd served in the RAF at Blackbushe Airport during the war. Did Ronald Green recall Eagle's May Day crash of 1957? With his Blackbushe association he might have done. Did a crash at Nurnberg, Germany, on an Eagle flight that he'd arranged, flying pregnant sows to Belgrade in 1953, ring a distant bell? Perhaps it was just the concern he heard in his wife's voice, but whatever it was Ronald Green immediately visited a City of London insurance company. He paid a travel insurance premium taken out for the duration of Quentin's trip, and felt a lot better. He'd been informed that the school trip was covered by insurance anyway, but he felt that by buying additional insurance nothing would ever happen – it was money down the drain, but it gave peace of mind. He never expected them to pay up.

The technicians working on Papa Mike finally replaced the faulty plug lead, and verified it was working properly with a test run of the Viking's engines. The foreman certified in the aircraft's Technical Log, that the plane was now serviceable. All should have been ready for Papa Mike to take off, but Brenda's stricken plane was nearing the end of its limp home, and ambulances and fire engines were lined up on the main runway, ready to deal with a possible crash landing. Brenda and all the passengers on board had their hearts in their mouths…

It was lunchtime at Broad Green's dental factory, and Violet Murray was sick with worry. She couldn't eat her sandwiches and her friend Irene tried to calm her, rationalising by saying that if the boys had left so early, then they'd be in Norway by now and enjoying their holiday – so really she was worrying for nothing. Violet bucked up at this thought, relaxed a little, and ate her lunch.

New Meteorological Office weather information about worsening weather conditions in southern Norway became available, but for some reason wasn't collected by Papa Mike's First Officer.

As the Lanfranc boys waited in the passenger terminal, Brenda's plane touched down safely – to everyone's enormous relief. As these ecstatic passengers entered the Passenger Lounge a big cheer went up from the boys, and others who had been held up. The Lanfranc boys filed past, waving and chatting to the arrivals, glad to be on their way at last. Surprised to be back on terra firma *alive*, with heightened awareness Brenda took in the happy, smiling faces of the boys who seemed so glad to be departing. Handing over the injured RSM to another escort, Brenda Morris departed to Guildford Camp, to obtain her permission to leave the Army.

The Lanfranc party embarked again, George Budd and John Beacham selecting rear seats where they could keep an eye on all the excited boys. The bucket seats were paired either side of a narrow gangway in the utilitarian aircraft. An oft-set narrow door at the front led to the cockpit – a door every boy wanted to investigate and be allowed to enter. At 1329 hours, five hours behind schedule, G-AHPM took off, climbing rapidly to 4000 feet. Susan Endicott had taken off her high heeled court shoes and was wearing flat heeled shoes, best for walking over the steps covering a spar in the middle of the fuselage when carrying a tray in each hand. She distributed more sweets and these were being assiduously sucked (and more requested), to assist ears to 'pop' in the unpressurised aircraft. As the plane levelled off the boys settled down and enjoyed looking out of the square Perspex windows. 'Their' stewardess was a definitely a bit of all right, they'd enjoyed a free meal, they were on their way, and didn't the River Thames look funny? Like a wiggly snake! Radar at London Airport routed Papa Mike out of London via Burnham and Watford, where it climbed further to cruising level 90, shortly before reaching Clacton on the Essex coast at 1354 hours. Two minutes later the aircraft reported it had passed Clacton, and was estimating crossing Advisory Route 522, at 1414 hours. In fact it didn't do this. Instead Papa Mike crossed from the Chatham Altimeter Setting Region (ASR) in the Thames estuary, to the Humber ASR. At 1422 hours the aircraft reported that it was clear of Advisory Route 522. This was its last direct contact with U.K. Air Traffic Control (ATC), although a message at 1455 hours that Papa Mike estimated '57 degrees North at 1536 hours' was relayed to Preston by another aircraft. Prior to this, however, at 1504 hours, Copenhagen Control heard the aircraft call and the Danish controller replied *'Go ahead'* but there was no response from Papa Mike. Five hours behind schedule Papa Mike was not following the original flight plan, but was flying direct across the North Sea to Stavanger. They were late and had another school party to pick up and fly home again. What Captain Watts and First Officer Smalley did not know was that the weather conditions in southern Norway had substantially worsened.

Norway Wednesday 9th August

August 9th 1961 was a bad day to be a pilot. Whilst Papa Mike was buffeted on its way five hours behind schedule over the North Sea, across the Atlantic Ocean a new Pan-American DC-8-jet airliner with 72 passengers and nine crew members from Houston Texas, were in dire straits. Stopping at Mexico City en route to Guatemala City an armed Fidel Castro sympathiser had joined the passengers. A few minutes after take-off, Pilot Carl Ballard found a gun in his back, and ordered to turn east towards Cuba. It was a nightmare situation, but guessing an excuse, Ballard played for time by insisting that Havana's runway wasn't long enough for a jet airliner. Surreptitiously he sent a coded message –

'We have been hi-jacked and diverted to Cuba'. It was the fourth hi-jacking of a U.S. airliner in three months and the second within a week. President Kennedy ordered the U.S. Air Force to be alerted. As fighter planes took off from Key West, Pilot Carl Ballard's biggest concern was – what if Havana's main runway *really* wasn't long enough for a four engine jet airliner. Hard steel pushed between his shoulder blades. Havana it was!

Meanwhile, through thick cloud, and with turbulence giving a bumpy ride, veteran Viking Papa Mike neared Norway's south coast. They were almost there, and geographer John Beacham had hoped to point out Rogaland's mountains and fjords – but the cloud base was too low. All the boys were excited. Soon they would be safely down in Stavanger and they hoped that their evening meal at Mosvangen Youth Hostel would be appetising because (despite all the sweets consumed en route), they *so* hungry they could eat a horse – or reindeer! Meanwhile at Mosvangen, two English boys, Bill Cole and Roger Ives, were asked to move their kit to a smaller room because a large group of English school boys was expected. Bill and Roger envisaged their peace being shattered by an invasion of boisterous teenagers.

High above the grey North Sea the relatively easy part of the flight was over. Stewardess Susan Endicott asked the Lanfranc party to fasten their safety belts as they would soon be coming in to land. Comics, packs of cards, and chess sets were packed away in various duffle bags. Captain Philip Watts was at the controls and First Officer Smalley's job was to make contact with Stavanger's Air Traffic Control in order for them to guide Papa Mike down safely. They knew from radio messages that there were other planes taking off, or coming in to land, and neither pilot knew Sola Airport, however, Eagle had classed it 'Grade A' – so there was nothing to worry about.

At 1603 GMT, speaking on 124.7 Mc/s by radio telephone, First Officer Murray Smalley, in precise aviation jargon, gave Stavanger Control their Eagle G-AHPM identification.

'Stavanger Control, Stavanger Control, this is Eagle Golf Alpha Hotel Papa Mike on one two four decimal seven. Do you read? Over.'

Stavanger Control responded immediately. *'Eagle Papa Mike this is Stavanger – reading you five. Go ahead.'*

Assured by the prompt response, First Officer Smalley answered, *'Roger, roger, Papa Mike. We are a Viking aircraft from London to Stavanger off airways, Victor Mike Charlie, joining at the Zulu Zulu beacon for Sola airfield, estimating Zulu Zulu at zero eight past the hour and Sola at one five. Over.'*

The ATC at Stavanger Control replied, *'Eagle Papa Mike, this is Stavanger. I checked that O.K. You are at flight level niner zero?'*

'Roger, roger. Maintaining niner zero', replied the Viking's First Officer.

Three minutes later Stavanger Control called again.

'Eagle Papa Mike this is Stavanger. You are cleared to cross Lima Echo Charlie or Zulu Zulu – cleared Zulu Zulu four thousand feet. Stavanger setting is one thousand millibars. Report leaving niner zero.' (Lima Echo Charlie (LEC) is a consul station beacon close to Zulu Zulu (ZZ) – a very high frequency omnidirectional radio range beacon at Varhuag, 15 nautical miles south of Sola Airport.)

'That is affirmative', replied First Officer Smalley. *'Report leaving niner zero, yea.'*

Stavanger Control replied, *'Roger, roger. Wilco.'*

Six minutes later First Officer Smalley called again *'Stavanger Control from Golf Alpha Hotel Papa Mike. Leaving flight level niner zero on a QNH of one thousand millibars at this time. Over.'*

Stavanger Control replied immediately and Murray Smalley asked *'Can you give me your latest weather please?'*

'Papa Mike – Stavanger. Affirmative. The actual weather for Sola. The wind is two one zero, twenty five knots – two one zero, twenty five. Visibility is ten kilometers and the cloud four eights at five hundred feet, five eights at two thousand five hundred.'

Smalley interpreted this as a south-south-westerly wind blowing at almost 29 miles per hour; that visibility at ground level was quite good; and that clouds, though low, had gaps between and were not a massive hindrance. *'Golf Papa Mike'* he said as he signed off and informed Captain Watts. There was nothing serious in the weather update to worry about. But outside of the Stavanger area the wind was picking up with capriciously strong gusts.

A minute later Stavanger Control called, *'Papa Mike – Stavanger. Report passing through flight level seven zero.'* First Officer Smalley responded, *'Golf Papa Mike. Will do.'*

Two minutes later Stavanger Control enquired, *'Papa Mike – Stavanger. What altitude are you passing through now?'* Smalley replied, *'Papa Mike, Just passing through seven zero this time.'*

Stavanger Control confirmed, *'Seven zero this time. Roger. Then report through five zero.'* *'Roger, roger. Wilco',* came the reply from the Viking, now rapidly descending through cloud layers.

Five minutes later at 1602 hours Stavanger Control asked, *'Eagle Papa Mike – Stavanger. What altitude are you passing through now?'* There was no reply, so Stavanger Control tried again. *'Papa Mike – Stavanger. What altitude are you passing through now?'*

First Officer Smalley replied, *'Papa Mike. I say again. Passing through five zero this time.'* 'I say again.'? Had a message from the Viking not come through? Stavanger Control hadn't received First Officer Smalley's first reply but this wasn't of consequence now as they were about to hand over to the Tower at Sola Airport, so Stavanger replied *'Roger, Papa Mike. Contact Sola Tower one one eight point one.'*

'One eight decimal one. Roger', replied Murray Smalley, already adjusting his knobs to contact Sola Tower on 118.1 MC/s. A minute later at 1603 hours he did. *'Sola Tower this is Eagle Golf Papa Mike. Do you read?'*

Sola Tower replied, *'Golf Alpha Hotel Papa Mike – Sola.'* Sola airport had an 8,000 foot concrete runway, 28 feet above sea level. Although the weather conditions were worsening in southern Norway on that summer's evening, at Sola, conditions were fair for the flights the Air Traffic Controller was guiding to and from the aerodrome. Sverre Hodne was the Duty ATC Officer at Sola Tower that day. A serious and diligent young man, Sverre Hodne had earned the reputation of being highly competent. This afternoon he was expertly 'juggling' all the aircraft entering and leaving Sola's airspace, listening for their radioed messages, answering them precisely, and metaphorically keeping a watchful eye on each one of his charges. Currently he had one plane awaiting take-off clearance and four aircraft arriving. A few seconds later First Officer Smalley radioed again.

'Sola – Papa Mike. Descending. Passed five zero, now four decimal five. Estimating your field one eight. Over.' Murray informed Captain Watts that he estimated they would land at 1618 hours. They were over five hours late but both knew they ought to be able to do the turn-around within their maximum duty hours allowed.

Sverre Hodne replied *'Roger, Golf Papa Mike. Advise Lima Echo Charlie four thousand feet.'*

'Papa Mike, Roger' was the reply.

Whilst he was speaking, Sverre took a bearing with the automatic VHF – very high frequency direction finder, discovering that the QDM – the magnetic bearing from Papa Mike to Sola, was 010 degrees. A little east of due north.

A minute later Sverre Hodne said *'Golf Papa Mike – Sola. Runway in use at Sola is one eight. The surface wind two zero zero at twenty knots, gusting up to three zero knots.'* The wind had veered a little and gusts of about 35 miles per hour could be expected at Sola. High in the sky over the North Sea, First Officer Smalley had interference on his radio and hadn't heard Sverre's message because a few seconds later he called.

'Sola – Eagle Papa Mike. Were you calling us? Over.'

'Roger. Just gave you runway in use one eight. Surface wind two zero zero, twenty five knots, gusty. And runway one eight and QNH is one thousand millibars', Sverre added, to make sure. (QNH is the subscale setting on the altimeter of an aircraft which indicates the aircraft elevation, when the aircraft is on the ground at the aerodrome.)

For some reason Papa Mike did not respond to this, but a minute later, at 1605 hours, First Officer Smalley called Sola Tower.

'Papa Mike. Sola, did you ask us to call over the Lima Echo Charlie beacon at four thousand feet? Over.'

Sverre Hodne responded immediately, '*Papa Mike. That is affirmative. Over Lima Echo Charlie at four thousand feet.*'

'*Roger, roger. Four thousand feet at this time. Will call over Lima Echo Charlie*'.

'*Roger*' said Sverre Hodne. Six minutes later at 1611 hours he called, '*Do you have any revised ETA for Lima Echo Charlie?*'

'*Papa Mike. We are just coming up to Lima Echo Charlie at this time. Over*', said Murray Smalley.

'*Roger. You are then cleared to descend to two thousand feet Zulu Oscar beacon for an ILS approach.*' (An ILS or Instrument Landing Approach was normal, unless very low cloud or fog covered the airport. Today this wasn't a problem. Zulu Oscar was the beacon north of Sola which guided aircraft on a central beam towards the airport on the return loop of their Instrument Landing Approach.)

'*Zulu Oscar beacon for ILS approach. Papa Mike. Roger*', was the reply.

At 1613 hours ATC Hodne asked, '*Golf Papa Mike. What is your altitude, now?*'

Immediately the reply came back, '*Golf Papa Mike. We have left four, descending. Passed three decimal five. Over.*'

'*Roger*' said Sverre Hodne satisfied all was well. He was intent upon guiding them in safely whilst also attending the needs of other pilots. A plane had taken off from Sola and now was away, but he had a Safir aircraft, two aircraft from Scandinavian airlines, and Cunard Eagle's Viking to safely land. It was all in a day's work – work which he loved. He took a QDM, the magnetic heading for Papa Mike to steer, with no wind, to reach the direction finding station. It was 360 degrees, plus or minus 2 degrees. Everything at Sola Tower was being done correctly – by the book. There were never any margins for error on Sverre Hodne's watch. In contact with the Safir aircraft, he'd asked them to tune in to frequency 1267 and they had just radioed back that there was '*some trouble with the frequency.*' He also had Scandinavian flights 546 and 385 to deal with, and they had to join the queue as he separated, held, and then gradually advanced their descents. Sverre Hodne was a meticulous ATC, choreographing a complex, three dimensional, aerial ballet.

Five minutes later at 1618 hours he called, *'Golf Papa Mike – Sola. Could you give me an estimate for Zulu Oscar please?'* (Zulu Oscar is the identification signal of the locator positioned at the Outer marker of the ILS to runway 18.)

First Officer Smalley promptly replied, *'Papa Mike. We estimate Lima India beacon in approximately two minutes. Over.'*

Lima India? **Lima India??** That was a slip, surely, thought Hodne who responded with a corrective query, *'Understand you estimate <u>Zulu Oscar</u> in about two minutes. Over.'*

Murray Smalley simply said *'Roger'* without stating which of the two beacons he was actually estimating.

At this moment Sverre Hodne and others at Sola, heard Papa Mike fly over the airport. Sola's ATC knew that what the Viking now had to do was to proceed on the normal ILS approach. This involved flying north to the Outer Marker, then making a turn to the left (westwards), followed by a turn to the right (eastwards), to swing the aircraft round to travel back south, along the flight path's central line or glide path, completing with a visual landing on runway 18. In the meantime Sverre Hodne had Scandinavian 385 to deal with. They were holding at the island of Rennesøy, whilst Scandinavian 546, second in the queue, was maintaining four thousand feet. ATC Hodne estimated they would land at 1633 hours – about five minutes after Papa Mike.

A minute and a half later Sverre called, *'Papa Mike. Are you at two thousand?'* He didn't get an answer so he called again seconds later, *'Golf Papa Mike – Sola. Are you at two thousand feet?'*

Moments later First Officer Smalley called, *'Stavanger – Eagle Papa Mike. Passed the Zulu Oscar beacon. Will call on approach.'*

Was Papa Mike at 2000 feet? The question hadn't been answered.

Assuming they were Sverre replied, *'Roger, Papa Mike. Check outer marker on final for landing on runway one eight.'* During this transmission Sverre recorded a QDM reading of 180 degrees on the automatic VHF direction finer.

'Roger, roger', replied the Viking's First Officer, followed ten seconds later by, *'Stavanger – Eagle Papa Mike. Request your QFE. Over.'* (The QFE is the atmospheric pressure reading at official aerodrome elevation.)

'*QFE is triple niner millibars*', said Sverre without delay.

'*Triple niner. Roger*', repeated Murray.

ATC Hodne called Scandinavian 546 and cleared it to descend to three thousand feet. They confirmed they were leaving four thousand feet, and Sverre gave them their latest QNH of one zero zero one. Returning to Papa Mike he noted that atmospheric pressure had changed by one degree and so he called at 1622 hours, '*Golf Papa Mike – Sola. The QFE is now one thousand millibars.*' They needed this revised reading to land safely using instruments.

'*One thousand millibars. Papa Mike. Thank you*', responded the Viking's First Officer Murray Smalley at 1622 (49) hours precisely.

It was his last recorded message.

Sverre Hodne did not expect Viking Papa Mike to return on its ILS approach for a further seven or eight, minutes. On calm days it took half that time but now the wind strength around the Stavanger region had picked up, so their turn-around time would be longer. The young ATC was alert, awaiting their return. Meanwhile on Norway's southern coast conditions had deteriorated badly and inland from Stavanger the mountains were sheathed in low cloud, with gusting gale force winds. Low level Sola Airport was fortunate and conditions remained good enough for an Instrument Landing System (ILS) approach, whilst Ground Control Assistance (GCA) using radar, had not been requested. As the young ATC officer waited for Papa Mike to loop back he turned to his other protégées maintaining Scandinavian 546 at three thousand feet and clearing Scandinavian 385 to descend to four thousand feet. He noticed the wind was picking up slightly, but it was still a routine day.

Sola Airport was also a Military Airport for the Royal Norwegian Air Force, and because military pilots relied on radar assisted talk down, to land safely (their cockpits didn't have enough space to incorporate ILS), this assistance was always on hand for civil aviation pilots in times of need. Lieutenant Nils Abrahamsen was the officer in charge of Sola's radar station, and he worked the Norwegian Royal Air Force regulation hours so by 1500 hours GMT (5.00pm local time) he had finished for the day, and gone home. Permanently on call, if any aircraft requested radar assisted landing then within 45 minutes (15 minutes for him to get back to the field plus 30 minutes to set up the radar again), Nils Abrahamsen was ready to operate and talk down pilots who could not see the runway or, rarely, some who were 'lost'. No such call had come that day, and all civil aviation flights into Sola, whilst he had been on duty, had landed safely by ILS alone. He was about to be called back.

Having passed the Zulu Oscar beacon at 1620 hours, Viking Papa Mike continued northwards along the central line, relaying its last message at 1622 (49) hours. What happened next is based upon eye-witness reports. Instead of keeping to the central line until over the sea and then executing the expected return, Papa Mike inconceivably became lost. The Viking was heard and seen, passing over Tungenes Lighthouse, which lay to the west. Here the weather conditions were low cloud and gusting wind. Young Asbjørn Løland was in a boat just off the lighthouse, crab-fishing with his uncle. It was raining hard, and they wanted to finish hauling in the creels as quickly as possible, to go home. Their attention was suddenly drawn to the sound of revving engines and a plane passed overhead, low enough for Asbjørn to see the windows. He'd never seen a plane over that part of the fjord before, and wondered where on earth it was going. Something wasn't right and he said to his uncle 'That plane's going to crash!' They watched it disappear at a low level, between the Island of Bru and onwards towards the mountains. The clouds were hanging so low, that from their boat they couldn't see the contours of Hodnefjell on Fjøløy. A deep depression was moving in and further east the wind gusted at 70mph. The crew of Papa Mike did not know this.

The Viking was heard, and in some cases seen, passing north-eastward over Askje, then Sel-Dale on Rennesøy, near to Talgje island, and on across Finnfast to Finnøy where it veered east across Finnøyfjorden where witnesses saw 'a big plane flying low over the sea'. Eleven year old Arild Drechsler, spending his summer holiday at Reilstad, heard roaring engines when he was at the village shop, and fascinated by planes he located the sound, glimpsing a propeller aircraft flying over the fjord as swirling low clouds briefly parted. 'That was really low!' he said to himself before he walked back home to his cabin through atrocious wind and rain. He was so excited about seeing the plane, that he told his parents as soon as he got home.

Papa Mike was heard, or seen, passing over the Island of Fogn, from whence it flew over Fognafjorden to the mainland between Alsvik and Kjølevik, and on to Voster. Just further east, at Lekvam, farmer Ola Lekvam heard the sound of roaring engines over his farm. He could see nothing as low cloud covered the rocky summits. At Holta, despite it being foggy, five year old Målfrid Holta was playing outside her parent's barn with her seven year old sister Marit. Her mother Magnhild was inside milking the cows, her head pushed into the side of one, milk swishing into the pail, the barn noisy with the lowing beasts. Målfrid and Marit heard a plane fly low overhead, and directly afterwards, a very loud BANG! Målfrid thought it was a thunder clap and ran into the barn frightened because she hated thunderstorms. She told her mother she was scared by the thunder but her mother scoffed, said she hadn't heard it, and told her not to be silly, the weather wasn't right for there to be thunder! Målfrid didn't believe her, and feeling afraid, she stayed in the barn until her mother had finished the milking.

Back at Sola Tower Sverre Hodne was watching the clock. Eagle Papa Mike had not checked inbound at the Outer Marker – and it should have. At 1629 hours and 38 seconds, just less than seven minutes after Papa Mike's last message, Sverre Hodne called again. *'Golf Papa Mike. Are you far from outer marker?'*

There was no answer. Was there some difficulty with Papa Mike's radio?

Twenty seconds later he called again. *'Golf Papa Mike – Sola. Do you read?'*

No answer.

Immediately he tried again. *'Golf Papa Mike – Sola. Do you read?'*

No answer.

And again, *'Golf Papa Mike – Sola. Do you read?'*

Twenty two nail-biting seconds had passed, and Papa Mike had not replied.

Controlling an adrenalin rush, Sverre Hodne remained calm as his training demanded. He immediately informed Stavanger Control Centre that Papa Mike was three to four minutes late on its ILS approach and that they had lost radio contact.

Seconds later he called the closest aircraft, '*Scandinavian five four six, could you try to call Golf Papa Mike?*'

Scandinavian 546 obliged. '*Golf Papa Mike – Scandinavian five four six. Do you read?*' There was no reply.

Scandinavian 546 called back to Sola, '*Sola, no reply.*'

Sverre Hodne in Sola Tower replied, worried, '*He should have been over outer marker, if normal time, about three minutes – three to four minutes ago.*'

'*He should have*' replied the concerned pilot of Scandinavian 546.

Picking up the telephone Sverre immediately asked the OPS to contact the duty helicopter pilot of Sola's RNoAF Rescue Squadron. Then he informed Braathens SAFE (a large Norwegian Airline company), and the Meteorological Office. At 1640 hours the Senior Air Traffic Control Officer in charge, Mr Bredal, arrived at the Area Control office, whilst the duty pilot on Sola's Safir aircraft was also alerted. Coping with the shock of discovering a plane missing on his watch, a nightmare situation for Sverre had just begun. He had been successfully handling all his aeroplanes and now, one had disappeared! Sverre's surname 'Hodne', with dreadful irony, translated into English meant 'Horn' or 'Peak' – the summit of a mountain. One such, and just as innocent, was to haunt and blight, his life.

At 1650 hours Nils Abrahamsen arrived and started up Sola's GCA radar in record quick time. By 1700 hours it was fully operational but Nils could see no trace of the Viking on his screen.

Four minutes later the Safir aircraft was airborne, followed a minute later by the Sikorsky helicopter. Duty Pilots Lt. Per Tjetland in the Safir, and Lt. Jan Magne Taarland and Flight Engineer Sgt. Cato Olsen in the Sikorsky, had scrambled and were aloft within 20 minutes with orders to search for the missing civilian plane in the approach sector and adjacent areas – the weather however, away from Sola was bad. Everything was being done to locate Papa Mike. It was hoped that perhaps it had lost radio contact, and was now flying blind. Kjevik airport near Kristiansand, according to the flight plan was the Viking's alternative airport, but Flesland (Bergen), Lista (Farsund) and Fornebu (Oslo) airports were also alerted. On tenterhooks at Sola Tower, Sverre Hodne knew that he'd instructed Papa Mike to fly at 2,000 feet – a 'safe' height. He called Møvik radar station near Kristiansand in southern Norway – clouds obscured their sky and they needed 'eyes'. Papa Mike had to be located and brought safely down.

Bjørn N. Skogen was a 22 year old Private serving his National Service with the Royal Norwegian Air Force, at their radar station at Møvik. The weather that afternoon was appalling, with intense rainy squalls. Despite its prime usage as part of Norway's 'Cold War' defence, Møvik's radar equipment was old, and all the installations, except the external rotating antenna, were located inside a mountain. Not being protected by an up-to-date inflated plastic dome, they had had to shut down, the rotary antenna wired, so that it wouldn't blow away in the gale. There was nothing else for the technicians to do except take a break until the storm blew itself out. Consequently the whole crew, officers and men, were relaxing in the mess room drinking coffee, except for Private Skogen, who was left in the Ops-room to watch the switchboard, with its hotlines connecting various stations with the network. Suddenly a call came through that was to galvanise them all to activity.

On the hotline from Sola Approach was their ATC Sverre Hodne. Private Skogen answered the telephone and Sverre urgently gave him the flight number, and asked him if Møvik could see the English plane on their screens. Bjørn had to tell him that they were inoperative due to high winds, and so had no information at all. Very concerned, Sverre asked if Møvik Radar Station could start up again, immediately, as the plane in question was missing. This was an emergency, and Bjørn Skogen dashed to speak to the officer in charge, who immediately issued the command to put the antenna back up again. Despite the stormy conditions, within 30 minutes they were fully operational. They scrutinised their scopes, but they could see no trace of Papa Mike. There was, however, a small green spot on their radar. They had the flight plans of several flights displayed on a vertical board, with routes, heights, speeds, and times written. By checking the flight plans they correctly identified this 'spot' as a second Vickers Viking from London Airport (also with a school party), but not Papa Mike. The officer in charge called Sola Tower, and told the ATC that there was no sign of the plane. Sverre quickly told them that it was a plane full of children. At Møvik the atmosphere in their Ops room was filled with gloom. A plane was missing, and they were horrified by the thought of all the children – and their families... Hoping for a miracle, they dreaded what they feared as inevitable news.

In the arrivals and departure area at Sola, a previous school party from Chesterfield Grammar School, their holiday over, were waiting for Papa Mike to take them home. They waited, and waited, happily unaware because no one told them the grim reason for the delay, and the airport authorities prevented outsiders from contacting them. Meanwhile, ATC Sverre Hodne had the awful responsibility of informing Cunard Eagle Airways that their Viking G-AHPM was missing, presumed down... (The news was received with shock at London Airport. Someone quickly informed Harold Bamberg.)

Flight Engineer Karl Nilsen, of the Royal Norwegian Air Force, was off duty from Sola Airport that day and was shopping in Stavanger during the afternoon. He knew nothing of the drama at the ATC tower. He and his wife had eaten a meal in a restaurant, and had just stepped out into the street, when he heard a roaring noise in the low cloud above them. Karl knew instinctively that something was wrong, as no big plane should have been flying low over the city in bad weather. Shops were closing at the time and they made their way home to Sola. The journey took thirty-five minutes, and when they arrived they found an airman with a car waiting outside their house. Karl was informed that there was an Ops alert, a plane was missing, and he had to report for duty immediately. Karl immediately recalled the roar of engines he'd heard over Stavanger. Was it the same? As his wife unloaded their shopping he was whisked away to the hangar at Sola, where he was needed to assist in an air search.

'Rogaland Avis' freelance photographer and National Service airman, 21 year old Egil Eriksson, was at home in Storhaug in the centre of Stavanger. The early evening was gloomy with low cloud, and he was chatting with his in-laws, when his attention was riveted by reverberations from a low-flying plane. He knew it wasn't on the correct flight path. Egil was surprised – and puzzled.

Within minutes of Sverre Hodne calling the emergency services at 1630 hours seven surface vessels immediately put to sea from Stavanger, including the

Norwegian Naval minesweepers Vossa, Utla, Sira, and Sauda, and tourist ships of the 'White fleet'. A Bell-47 helicopter also joined the search. All were ordered to search Sola's approach sector and areas adjacent, including local fjords, and the coast bordering the North Sea. A police official in Skudeneshavn, north of Karmøy Island reported, 'We are having a real autumn storm here, driving rain and heavy cloud, so it will be difficult to see or hear a plane clearly.' They were later joined by a RAF Avro-Shackleton, a Coastal Command plane from a Scottish air base. The air search proved dangerous and difficult, because thick low cloud meant dusk had arrived early, and bad weather was now buffeting Sola aerodrome, with gusting wind and rain. All off duty pilots, mechanics, and flight engineers from the Rescue Squadron were called in because of the emergency.

They knew that the fate of the survivors depended upon the speed with which they could be found. Whilst they scanned the vast area, the second plane seen by Møvik's radar, landed safely at Sola Airport, using ILS. Meanwhile the weather around Stavanger deteriorated and the air search was hampered by strong winds, rain, and a low cloud base that reduced light conditions.

Cunard Eagle, informed that their Viking Papa Mike was overdue and missing, were told that a full scale search was in progress. Harold Bamberg and his team, with years of aviation experience, knew with sinking hearts what this must inevitably mean. Pilots were called in immediately to fly Eagle officials, including their Director of Operations, Captain John Sauvage, out to Norway. The decision was also taken to inform the wives of the two pilots, and the parents of the stewardess, that Papa Mike was missing, believed down. The media were not informed. Sola Tower kept in touch with Eagle Airways every few minutes.

At 1820 hours, the search and rescue operation well under way, Sola Airport rescue centre contacted the Police, and Police Superintendant Breen was informed at Rogaland Police Department. The Police immediately offered their assistance if needed. Norwegian radio put out a message saying that a plane was missing, asking for anyone in the Stavanger region who had heard a plane near them to contact the police immediately. Gradually telephone calls came in from people saying that they had heard aircraft noise overhead, at Talgøfjord. Later calls came in saying they had heard aircraft engines at Brimnes, and at Tasta.

Listening to the radio Egil Eriksson heard the news reports that a passenger plane with many passengers was missing, and he had an answer to the puzzle of hearing a plane over Stavanger. But he was doubly interested. This was a news story, and sensing its importance, he knew he had to cover it! So too thought Stavanger Aftenblad photographer Harald Sem, and reporter Lars Torleiv Øye. These two knew this was going to be such big news that they decided to get a boat ready to take them to – where ever!

Whilst this frantic search was taking place in Rogaland, in Cuba the Pan-American DC-8 landed safely on Havana airport's runway. Despite being taken prisoner along with passengers, the pilot and crew considered themselves very lucky. They were.

When Cunard Eagle's representatives flew in to Sola later that evening in another Vickers Viking, they were very unlucky. Unaccountably their radio packed up on landing, so that there was no communication between the plane and the control tower. Sola's 'Follow Me' car was sent out across the storm-lashed tarmac to guide them in. The night was now wild and a light aircraft parked near a hangar was picked up and bowled over on to its back by a strong gust. In the darkness, with the wind howling and rain lashing down, everyone's thoughts were on whether they would find the missing plane. And if they did, would there be anyone alive?

Twenty six year Ola Lekvam was at Lekvam, his farm high in the hills of Strand above the finger lakes of Bjørheimsvatn and Vostervatn. It was a dull misty evening, he had milked the cows and afterwards he'd sharpened points on to some new fence posts. These were the last routine jobs he did before his life changed irrevocably. The fence posts finished, he went inside out of the wet farmyard, sat down with his parents, and listened to the radio as normal. Suddenly there was an announcement that a plane from England that should have landed at Sola Airport, was missing. Like so many who heard the news-flash that evening the Lekvam's were dismayed. Where could the missing plane be? They never imagined that they would be caught up in the drama about to unfold.

Below their farm, on the coast at Fiskå, was their telephone exchange, connected manually by a telephonist who plugged calls through to customers. The telephonist on duty that evening was Kristen Grødem who, by virtue of the switch board system, could not help overhearing customer's conversations. Kristen had connected a number of calls from locals to Police headquarters about the missing plane, and from what he'd heard he built up a mental map of the direction of its flight path. His hunch was that it could be near Holta – not far from the Lekvam's family farm. Kristen knew that 26 year old Ola Lekvam was not only very fit, but also experienced, as he'd served his National Service in the army in Northern Norway. Above all he knew those hills very well. Kristen took the correct plug and resolutely connected it. It could be a matter of life or death.

The telephone rang at Lekvam's farm. It was very late at night. Ola answered and Grødem said urgently 'Ola! I've heard from telephone conversations that the missing plane has been heard over Rennesøy, Talgje, Alsvik, and Voster. It hasn't been heard in Holta, or Bjørheimsbygd. I'm sure the plane is in the hills right behind your farm. You *have* to go and look for it!' Ola was immediately galvanised by this news but frustratingly there was nothing that he could do straight away. It was too dark to go looking in the hills – he'd never see anything at all. So he set his alarm clock to wake him at dawn, when he hoped the mist and rain would have cleared, so that he could see clearly.

At 2345 hours GMT the air and sea search was called off due to darkness and bad weather. The buffeting winds, heavy rain, and low cloud, had meant that helicopters and planes had not extended the search into the mountains. Frustrated by this, but realising to prolong the search under these conditions was lunacy, the decision was made to set out at first light.

The airmen spent the night in their barracks next to the helicopter pad adjacent to Sola's vast German wartime hangar. Desperate to locate Papa Mike the order had been given to recommence at 0330 hours GMT (0530 a.m. local time). Lt. Arnt Wangsholm was to fly out in a Safir single engine aircraft to recommence the search, this time over Strand, where reports telephoned in to the Police indicated that the missing plane might have crashed. The crew for the Sikorsky

H-19 were Pilot Lt. Jan Magne Taarland, Co-Pilot Lt. Øystein Herstad, and Sgt. Cato Olsen as Flight Engineer. Together with Lt. Arnt Wangsholm they had orders to scramble at first light. Some men snatched a little sleep whilst others spent what felt like, a very long, short night. In other parts of Norway, experts from the Norwegian Aircraft Accident Investigation Commission had their bags packed, ready to depart for Sola Airport on the earliest flight. The head of the Investigation Commission, Director Colonel Johan K. Christie, was under no illusions as to what to expect. A British plane had undoubtedly crashed somewhere and he had an important job to do.

The Norwegian Broadcasting Company had announced several times that evening that a British plane was missing, asking for anyone who had heard a plane to call Rogaland Police. In Stavanger, teenager Kari Ringe was celebrating her 17th birthday, and the news-flash on the radio about the missing plane was an unhappy interruption on her special day. She and her married brother Rolf were Red Cross members. Kari had no idea that soon her big brother would be intimately involved in this event, or that she was to discover her life's vocation.

At 2300 hours, as Norwegian radio broadcasts came to a close for the night, Sofus Tønnessen a leader in Stavanger's Red Cross heard the announcement that the missing British aircraft with 34 English schoolboys aboard had been localised to the Ryfylke area, but that it had not yet been found. The broadcaster again asked everyone who had seen or heard anything in connection with the plane to get in touch with Rogaland Police. Sofus knew that the Red Cross would be needed. But where? And when? The Red Cross Corps Hjelpekorps Commander was Kaare Hidle who had just returned from military service and he wasn't aware of Red Cross members available at short notice to help. Sofus decided to take charge.

At 2325 hours Sofus telephoned Rogaland police to see if anything new was known about the missing aircraft, and whether they needed Red Cross assistance. He spoke with Police Chief Ravn-Tollefsen, who told him there was no definite news, but messages were still coming in from people who had heard the plane, and these had to be analysed to find the most likely location before anything could be done. Nevertheless, he asked Sofus to get around 20 trained personnel for a possible search the next morning. Sofus suggested that his phone number be used as the emergency telephone until 0700 hours the next morning, and after that, his Red Cross colleague Anna Nordland's telephone number. Putting the phone down from this call he immediately telephoned Anna Nordland, and quickly gave her an overview of the situation, asking her if she would arrange to be the person in charge of telephone communications.

England, Wednesday evening 9th August

Blissfully unaware of the nightmare about to unfold, Ann Endicott and her parents had spent the afternoon at Blackpool Sands, a favourite beach near their Paignton home. The weather in Devon that afternoon was sunny and calm, the opposite to weather conditions in Norway. Back home again, Jean Endicott was making tea, when their doorbell rang, and she went to open it. Following her, Ann saw a policeman silhouetted in the sunshine, and was horrified to see her mother collapse. Ann shouted, and her father ran to help his prostrate wife. Captain Endicott couldn't take in the policeman's unbelievable message, but Jean Endicott had. 'Your daughter's plane is missing.' It was as though her worst fears had been confirmed. Although deeply shocked and scared, Ann tried to be encouraging, saying, 'Don't worry Mummy. Sue will be all right, she'll survive...' But it was terrible news, and they hadn't a phone to be in constant contact with Cunard Eagle Airways, so they went to friends who had a telephone, and waited anxiously for updates. They prayed there would be survivors. They prayed that Sue was alive and would be one of them. For the Endicott family in Devon the horrendous nightmare had started.

Handling the emergency at London Airport was Captain John Sauvage, the company's operational director. He knew that if they didn't get good news soon, he would have to fly out to Norway to help in the operations there.

At their homes in Surrey the wives of the two pilots were informed that their husband's plane was missing. They both had to walk a tight rope of emotions, coping with fear, hope, black terror of what the future might hold, yet with young children – still try to carry on as normal.

Near Blackburn, Lancashire, Albert Roberts, a former teacher who ran A.I.R-Tours waited for news by his telephone. In nine years of organising school trips abroad he'd arranged for over 20,000 youngsters to holiday on the Continent and never a mishap. Till now.

In Croydon the families of the Lanfranc boys were totally ignorant of events. Those who had felt very strange misgivings, now felt reasonably happy because they knew the boys must have arrived in Norway, and be enjoying the first evening of their eight day holiday.

'No news was good news' was what Kathleen and Ronald Green felt, and they went out that evening together with their daughter Rosalind to look at a folding caravan for their family holidays. But this wasn't the way that June Chapple, sister of Reggie, felt. Early in the evening, whilst her father drove June and her partner to a restaurant for a meal out, June felt her body became very cold and she was consumed with a dreadful impending feeling… What would happen if Reggie *didn't come back*? 'Oh please God…' she thought. 'Please don't let that happen.'

During the later part of the evening the B.B.C. made radio and television announcements that a plane from London Airport, with an all male passenger list, en route to Norway, was missing. Relatives and friends of the Lanfranc Boys were in various ways, and at different times, about to hear worrying news.

Susan Green, Geoffrey's sister had spent the day at Brighton with her mother. It had been warm and sunny, and they'd taken the train home at 5 o'clock. Susan had eaten her supper, gone to bed early and was asleep when someone threw a stone at her bedroom window. Her father went downstairs to see what was happening, and moments later she heard him cry out. A neighbour had told him the news of the missing plane, but they all hoped they would be found alive. Susan went back to bed again and lay there not knowing what to think. At 13 years old, this was too enormous for her to grasp.

Someone else who couldn't grasp the significance was Dave King, a second year pupil, who had been envious of his friends who were going. He'd retired to bed early, and his elder sister flew up the stairs to his bedroom, saying that Lanfranc's plane was missing. 'Cor! That's fantastic!' said Dave, thinking that the lucky boys had got yet *another* experience. 'Now they've even got an *adventure*!' he said resentfully. 'Dave! This is *serious*!' his sister said. But Dave naively didn't understand. He believed his 'jammy' friends were having even *more* fun, and he thought they'd be impossibly full of themselves when they got back to school again. He wasn't alone in not comprehending. John Martin who had desperately wanted to go, heard the news flash, but didn't realise that the plane could have *crashed!* Neither did Leslie Bentley, on holiday in Hayling Island. He was fishing in a creek when his father told him the plane was missing. Leslie just thought 'Oh well, it will turn up sooner or later.' It was a common belief of youngsters with little experience of life that tragedies only happened to other people, not ones you knew. John Cooke, who had pulled out of the Norway trip and gone to Austria instead, had been out at the cinema watching Walt Disney's '101 Dalmatians'. When he arrived home he saw the news item, but simply didn't connect the two facts of an 'all male passenger list' and the destination 'Stavanger'. On holiday at Eastbourne with a classmate, David Randall heard the news, and he and his chum both thought 'Lanfranc will be famous, –when it all clears up'. Little did they realise just how famous.

If many Lanfranc boys couldn't grasp the seriousness of the situation, there were two boys who did – Keith Scotcher, and Peter Crouch. It was Keith's birthday and when he heard the news flash that a plane with an all male passenger list was missing en route to Stavanger he remembered Bobby Martin telling him the date of his flight. Keith was worried sick. Peter Crouch was too. His twin brother Geoffrey was on the missing plane along with Bobby Martin who was his best friend. Knowing that Bobby's parents went to bed early, and that they might not have heard the news, Peter rode his bike to their house, 15 minutes away. They were in bed, and he had the agonizing responsibility to tell Mr and Mrs Martin that their only son, whom they idolised, was missing. Somehow coping with seeing grief, shock, and terror, all in one, written on their faces, Peter grew up in those brief seconds. He also had to struggle with the realisation that his twin brother was missing and might not return.

Ken Wells, John's elder brother had been out at Hastings for the day with his girl friend Maureen, but on the way home his car broke down at Tonbridge, and they had to leave it at a garage. The courting couple took the train home instead. They'd had a wonderful day out, and apart from the car breaking down, were very happy. Unknown to them bad news had galvanised the Wells household.

Mrs Wells knew it was the Lanfranc boy's plane before it was confirmed. 'That's John's plane!' she cried, on hearing the news flash. When Ken and Maureen arrived home, it was to find his mother and father distressed – and the news that 'a plane was missing'. Mrs Wells was sure it was John's plane. They got in touch with other members of their family nearby and they all waited anxiously...

Irene Raff, friend of Violet Murray, heard the news about the missing plane and felt terrible. She prayed, and prayed, that Violet's boy would be safe.

Mrs Hendley was ironing David's pyjamas whilst her husband and David's elder sister Julia were listening to the radio, when the programme was interrupted and it was announced that an aircraft belonging to Cunard Eagle Airways was missing on a flight to Norway. They all realised immediately that this was the flight that the boys were on. They didn't have a telephone, so Julia 'phoned London Airport from a public phone box, and their worst fears were confirmed. All sorts of horrors went through their minds. Their nightmare had begun.

Not far away in the Brown household in Norbury Crescent, Geoff's young sister Janet woke up when a policeman knocked on their door to tell them that Lanfranc's plane was overdue. She got up and wanted to know more, but her parents pretended nothing was going on and told her to go back to bed. Then they telephoned her grandparents where her brother Ian was staying, and asked them to keep any newspapers away from Ian (who was very close to his older brother), until they were able to get down to see him and tell him what had happened. But Ian overheard and knew something was going on too. Maureen Kay, Geoff Brown's girl friend was in bed when Ernest Brown called at her house, and told her father that the Lanfranc boys were missing. Ernest was on his way to St Stephen's church to pray for them all. Maureen couldn't believe it. She'd been with Geoff yesterday. He was gorgeous, and she was in love with him. How could he be 'missing'? That night the Vicar of St Stephen's church stayed with the Brown's praying, trying to be encouraging, desperately attempting to keep their hopes up. But Ernest Brown wasn't hopeful. He'd been a wartime pilot and believed that 'When you take two feet off the ground you put one in the grave'. Perhaps it was this belief that had stopped him from letting his younger son, Ian, be a member of the trip to Norway as well. His decision hadn't been a matter of cost.

Lily Gore was watching T.V. when the news came through that the plane was missing. When they said the passengers were 'all male' she knew straight away.

Martin Idale was a friend of Brian Mitchell. They were both Patrol Leaders with the 67th Croydon Scout Group, and Martin's father was the treasurer of the Parents and Supporters Association, whilst Brian's father Frank was the auditor. Frank Mitchell was at their house going through the annual accounts, and the television news had been on, but they hadn't paid any attention to it – when the phone rang. It was Edie Mitchell, Brian's mother. 'Is Frank there?' she gasped. 'That plane that's gone down – my Brian's on it!' she shrieked. Frank dashed home, Scout Group accounts forgotten. His married eldest son was away in Scotland visiting in-laws. A telegram was sent that evening saying 'Come home. Brian's plane is missing.'

On hearing the news that a plane with an all male passenger list was missing in Norway, some parents did their best to protect other members of the family. Putting on brave faces, Mr and Mrs Alan White decided not to tell their elder son Bernard, who had been out at Tooting with friends playing in a band, because they didn't want to worry him. Bernard didn't notice that anything seemed wrong, but did think it odd when someone called at their house at 11.00pm. That visitor was 37 year old Rev Michael Percival Smith, Vicar of All Saints Church Upper Norwood. He had been 'phoned by someone at Croydon Town Hall, with news that there had been a terrible accident, and there were eight families in his parish he must visit. 'What terrible accident?' he'd asked. The situation was explained, and eight addresses were given. The young clergyman was thunderstruck. He got down on his knees, and he prayed as he'd never prayed before. Then he went out to visit each family on his list, including both of the two White families, the Gaskins, and the Lawrence's. Four were families he knew. Four were not. Throughout the long night he listened to them, prayed with them all, and did everything he could to keep their flagging hopes up.

Ron Cox, history master at Lanfranc, heard the newsflash on the television just before nine p.m. The initial announcement merely said that a plane with school children on board was missing. Another flash, shortly afterwards stated that the passengers were all male, and the country was Norway. Ron had his mind elsewhere and didn't take much notice as he hadn't remembered the precise date the party was due to go. This was another example of the trusting expectancy that 'nothing ever happens to anyone that you know'.

Mrs Budd had heard the same news report and was worried, although the details didn't fit with the timings of her husband George's flight that morning. Her 18 year old son Geoff was over in Streatham at his girlfriend Thelma's house, whilst her youngest, nine year old Tim, was upstairs asleep. She desperately wanted to contact Geoff, but Thelma didn't have a phone. She popped next door to her neighbour's house, and asked them to help her discover more information. She knew she'd have to wait until Geoff cycled home by 10.30pm. Cycling back through Mitcham, Wallington, and then on to Coulsdon, Geoff arrived home at 10.45pm. Mrs Budd shot through a gap in the shared garden fence, and Geoff expected to be castigated for being late home. Instead it was much worse. His mother was in a dreadful state as she told him the news. At first Geoff was numbed by the shock. Then he tried to be positive – the plane hadn't been found, and there might be survivors. They talked quietly so as not to awaken young Tim, and finally went to bed having unwillingly taken a sleeping pill given by their neighbour. Both mother and son inwardly knew what would be the outcome. A reporter called their number and was told 'We are waiting and praying for news.'

Far away in the Vicarage at Whittlebury, Northamptonshire, John Beacham's sister Myrtle saw the 10 o'clock news on television. She was horrified and immediately called London Airport. Her widowed mother was staying with her and her vicar husband, and their teenage daughters, whilst John was away. They all felt awful, yet Mrs Beacham remained optimistic saying, 'they will all have landed somewhere in those mountains, but John will take care of those boys and get them to safety. John wouldn't let anything happen to them…'

Quentin Green's parents drove home again, and were looking forward to more comfortable camping holidays as they entered their driveway around 9.30pm. They were surprised to see 20 year old Anthony standing outside the front door. He opened the car door as they pulled up, his eyes huge with concern, his voice staccato. He felt there had been a disaster. Quickly he explained what he'd heard on the radio, and Mr Green immediately telephoned London Airport. Officials there wouldn't disclose anything, but took his number, then phoned him back. Tony was right. It was Lanfranc's plane that was missing. Immediately they went down the road to St Phillip's Church and prayed for Quentin, the boys, the masters, and the crew. In the familiar church with its colourful triptych, close to the choir stalls where Quentin sang, and where the day before he'd received a special blessing, they bent their heads and prayed. Holding tears at bay Rosalind silently entreated, pleaded…. Dear God let them all be found safe and sound!

Back home again and powerless to do anything else writer Kathleen Green, a former secretary at Lanfranc Boys School, felt convinced that people should know that it was the Lanfranc School trip and not simply 'all male passengers' that were missing. Ronald telephoned the Daily Express whose reporters arrived in record time from Fleet Street, took details, and left again with a photograph of Quentin and his school badge from his old blazer. Everything had moved very fast, but now it all moved slowly. Seconds seemed like minutes. Nothing seemed real. Rosalind felt as though someone had scrambled her brain with a fork, whilst behind her eyes it felt as though a dam was about to burst.

Cunard Eagle Airway's telephone – SKY 3611, was jammed with calls that night, and three switchboard girls had to put some through to their public relations personnel. All they could be told was that 'the plane is overdue', and to be advised not to come to London Airport. Everyone at Eagle was on tenterhooks, yet given Norway's terrain and current weather conditions, all but the most hopeful realised the plane wasn't 'overdue' – and that the worst must have happened. Harold Bamberg was in constant touch with his staff all that night.

Headmaster Tommy Fowle drove to his school office. When contacted there by the press later he said 'I am just sitting here, hoping and praying that the plane will be found and that they are all safe.' Throughout Croydon, Lanfranc parents spent a sleepless night waiting by the nearest telephone for news. Blood ran like ice through their veins. They shivered with fear and apprehension. It was the longest night of their lives.

In the early hours of the morning, hope was fading. A spokesman for Cunard Eagle Airways said 'There is no doubt that the aircraft is down. Whether it was in the sea, or in the mountains behind Stavanger, we don't know. One very slim chance is that the radio had packed up, and the pilot made an emergency landing somewhere. But that is a very remote hope now.'

Allen Lee's anxious parents left their house to call at Lanfranc hoping for news – but it was in darkness again. A reporter accosted them, and they said that their 13 year old son was on the missing plane. 'We have been everywhere trying to get news' said Mrs Lee. 'What can we do? Nobody seems to know anything.' Postman Mr Lee said that Allen was so keen to go, that he'd taken him to London Airport a few days before. Now he wished he'd never given his consent.

Meanwhile at London Airport, Army Officer Chris Moysey walked in to Eagle's office and said he was the fiancé of Susan Endicott their stewardess. His eyes brimming with tears, he asked 'Please tell me what the news is. I saw Susan off yesterday.'

One mother unaware of events, and delightedly making plans for a wonderful home-coming, was Rene Allen, 'Eggy' Allen's art teacher mum. A single parent, Rene lived with Gregory in Upper Norwood, in a flat in her parent's house. She had scraped together part of the money for the trip, whilst relatives had helped with the rest. Everyone liked Rene, and relatives had wanted Gregory to be like other boys at Lanfranc, and go on an exciting trip. Rene had also squirreled away enough money to buy Gregory a very special birthday present which was wrapped up in protective corrugated cardboard, and standing upright in the kitchen. She knew Gregory would be so thrilled! She never anticipated a knock on her door at five o'clock the next morning.

 J. Collie was the acting Police Inspector Night Duty Officer at Croydon Police Station that night, when a call came through that boys from Lanfranc School were involved in an air accident, and that all next of kin must be traced and informed. As very few people had private telephones, the whole of his police team on duty were seconded to the task, whilst he acted as coordinator. Their delicate job was made more difficult by inaccuracies in the airline's passenger records. Collie's team, a few in cars, most on push bikes, took different areas of Croydon, knocking on doors and delivering the worrying news. Some parents knew already. Others did not.

Whilst the police patrolled Croydon's streets looking for the right houses the news editor of The Croydon Advertiser had furiously telephoned his staff. He needed every journalist he could lay his hands on, and Betty Brownlie was one of his best young reporters and he couldn't get hold of her. Where was she? The paper was going to press in less than 12 hours and he needed to speak to her right NOW!

Betty Brownlie, a 20 year old newly-fledged reporter, was out with her boyfriend, and returned to her flat in Chichester Road around midnight to find her telephone ringing. The news editor barked the news, and said he wanted her in by 7.00am. The big boys from Fleet Street were already out there and she had to get and file her stories, tomorrow, before they went to press!

Police Inspector J. Collie found that the attentions of the press were an added hindrance in his work. Some homes visited had already received visits from journalists, and to make matters worse they then monopolised vital public telephones, calling editors with their stories. He had a difficult night especially as tracing one parent had proved impossible. His team couldn't find the mother of Gregory Allen. Left until last, Inspector Collie made it his responsibility to find the home. Eventually, around 5.00am he discovered Gregory Allen's home was his grandparent's house in Bramley Hill. He knocked loudly and Rene Allen sleepily came to the door. As gently as he could Inspector Collie imparted the grim news. He was never to forget her reaction. Rene couldn't take it in. Completely distraught, she kept on repeating, 'It's his birthday on Saturday. Look there's his new bicycle waiting for him in the kitchen…' Inspector Collie did his best to encourage her to remain hopeful, but it was heartbreaking to see this pretty young mother both inconsolable, and unbelieving that anything could have happened to her only child. She'd bought Gregory a new bike, she kept telling him. 'Gregory won't have to ride his awful old 'bone shaker' to school any more… Look Inspector – it's waiting for him in the kitchen…'

Inspector Collie went home from his night duty physically and emotionally exhausted. As a policeman he'd often had to notify someone of a fatal accident, – which was never an easy task, but this was different. It was all *local* and it was *so many children* from a Croydon school, one famous for its sporting successes. He felt awful.

Norway Thursday 10th August

Police chief Ravn-Tollefsen hadn't gone to bed. Search teams had given up after midnight and were now home, drying out and snatching sleep, but he and his constables were busy answering calls, many of them from newspapers in Norway and Britain. The stormy weather was easing slightly when at 0220 hours GMT, having deduced that the missing plane must be down near Holta in Strand, Ravn-Tollefsen called Sofus Tønnessen again. He asked for the Red Cross team to be ready for departure to Tau, meeting at the Strand quay at 0500 hours – and requested they bring walkie-talkies. Sofus immediately called Anna Nordland and asked her to alert all of their 1st squad. Whilst 48 year old Anna telephoned Red Cross members – none of whom hesitated to respond positively to her request, Sofus contacted his quartermaster. The quartermaster immediately set out for Stavanger's Red Cross equipment store, with a helper, to prepare all the necessary equipment. Anna also made sure that the 2nd Red Cross team was alerted and on standby. As a member of the Red Cross since 1946 Anna was determined to be included in the rescue.

Red Cross member Kjell Idsøe had heard the radio report of the missing plane whilst eating his dinner that evening, so he wasn't surprised by Anna's night-time summons. Ellinor Sandsmark was sound asleep and awakened by Anna's call yet was ready 15 minutes later, just as transport arrived to pick her up. Others in a team of twenty responded with immediacy. All were told to bring warm clothes and food for 12 hours, and to meet on the Strand quay at 0445 hours. Fate had elected that they were to put all their hard training into practise, searching for a missing English aircraft with 39 on board. Sofus selected three girls to be members of the 1st team, one to act as a secretary and two for catering duties. The men (nearly all aged early 20's or younger), would attend to the casualties. Sofus called the quartermaster again, telling him that they needed five first aid bags repacked to contain just large and small compresses, field dressings, bandages, and pain killers. He also requested rails and carrying straps to construct stretchers, plus plenty of ropes, some compasses and maps, and a complete first-aid bag. He knew he had a life and death search and rescue ahead, and that they would provide emergency first aid before the casualties were taken to hospital. He packed his own bag with great care knowing the problems of a mountain search and rescue, and of caring for injured casualties. Sofus had worked in a military field hospital in Korea.

Whilst Sofus finalised his preparations at his home in Stavanger, meanwhile at Lekvam, 20 miles away in Strand, Ola Lekvam pulled on his everyday farming clothes of checked shirt, breeches, thick knee length socks, and boots, plus a weather-proof coat to keep him dry. Ola wondered which of so many places he should search first. He knew it could be like looking for a needle in a haystack.

At 0300 hours men elsewhere awoke and dressed quickly – with feelings of apprehension. All were searchers, most official, one unofficial. At Sola Airport the Saab Safir and Sikorsky, were being made ready for take-off. Still tired from the search the night before, the pilots stepped into their flying suits wondering how long they would be out before they found anything. Pilot Lt. Arnt Wangsholm was to fly the Saab Safir and endeavour to spot the downed Viking, whilst Sikorsky Pilot Lt. Jan Magne Taarland and his co-pilot Lt. Øystein Herstad and Flight Engineer Sgt. Cato Olsen, would be in the vicinity to make a landing to investigate. They were the professionals – and they were glad that the weather conditions had improved.

The airmen left their colleagues in the barracks where most had remained awake that night, and jogged to the hangar where their aircraft were waiting. The night had been wild and no one had righted the small plane that had been picked up by a gust and tossed onto its back. Thankful that it was quieter now Lt. Arnt Wangsholm started the Safir's engine and taxied on to the empty runway. Pilot Lt. Jan Magne Taarland started the Sikorsky's rotor blades. At Lekvam, Ola had decided on his search strategy.

Sofus had called the Red Cross Corps Commander elected for 1961, Kaare Hidle, at his workplace and put him in the picture. Kaare Hidle agreed with all the decisions Sofus had taken, saying he'd find someone to take over at his duties at work, drive home and get ready, and then contact Sofus to discuss their plans before they met at the quayside. Sofus called the Red Cross at Sandnes, hoping to borrow their two 'Simrad' radio telephone sets as well. But at that early hour his calls weren't answered.

It was still dark in the hills when Ola set off. He wanted to get to the highest vantage point if he was to search the hills between Lekvam, Voster, and Holta. As the sky began to lighten he climbed Varafjellet from where there were panoramic views over Lekvam and Holta. He knew the area like the back of his hand, every rocky knoll, lochan, and lake, but as he scanned the grey horizon he saw something new in the familiar silhouette. It looked like a cairn standing out on the horizon. But he knew that there *wasn't* a cairn on that steep crag that overlooked Holta and Heia! Realising that the telephonist's hunch was right, with a thumping heart Ola knew what 'the cairn' must be …

As the airmen flew over the countryside towards Stavanger, Ola ran down towards Holta, and sped through the sleeping community. He bypassed the homes of Hendrik Østerhus, and his father's old friend Elias Holta. Everyone was asleep. Not even a dog was awake. From Holta the view of the crag was obscured but when he got to the gate at Gardbrekk, between the cultivated fields and the common pasture of the hills, he saw it again – something jagged and black, perched like a cone on the summit. His heart in his mouth he kept going, apprehensive of what he would discover when he got to the spot. The fearful shape hadn't been there yesterday. Used to walking Strand's rocky terrain known as 'Blokkebærknuten', Ola kept running. Questions filled his thoughts as he pushed himself relentlessly onwards and upwards, stumbling through clumps of heather, bilberries, and myrtle, and avoiding juniper that could trip him. He jumped over a small stream cascading down the hillside, and closer now, he could see it was definitely *not* a new cairn – but the hideously shattered wreckage of a plane. Part of it was hanging over the cliff edge. The effort of relentlessly running made him vomit. He felt sick at heart too. Would he find anyone alive? And if he did, what on earth could he, Ola Lekvam, all on his own, do to help? An intact wheel lay at the foot of the cliff but above he could see twisted, blackened metal. His heart was racing as he reached the summit.

The airmen had not had much sleep. Their night had been plagued by speculation. The most nagging question being why hadn't the missing plane requested Sola's GCA radar? Now grey dawn provided the chance for action. Their orders were to search a wide circle around Holta a small hamlet in the hills north of lakes, Bjørheimsvatn and Tyssdalsvatn, and south of Vostervatnet in

Strand. The police had reported that the Viking had been heard near Fiskå, but no further. They knew it wouldn't be easy to find anything until the sun rose above the eastern mountain tops. The hummocky terrain, smoothed and rounded by ancient glaciers and fretted into weathered blocks like giant bricks, could hide an aircraft in its shadowed hollows. But speed was imperative – any survivors had just spent ten hours in terrible weather in the mountains, – so they had to find it quickly! The aircraft sped over Stavanger, where the city's early risers apprehensively recalled the previous night's dramatic land and sea search. One up and engaged was Red Cross anchor-woman Anna Nordland. At 0355 hours Sofus had called her and learnt that his search team now consisted of 18 strong fit boys and three girls. He was relieved. They had a good team.

Flying onwards between the islands of Vassøy and Lindøy, on course for Holta ahead of the Sikorsky, Safir pilot Lt. Wangsholm increased his altitude. He could see the port of Tau, beyond which Strand's bare summits, menacingly dark, plunged steeply downwards into once glaciated finger-lakes, now feebly reflecting dawn's grey light. Hoping that morning mist, shrouding rocky hollows, would part to reveal an *intact* plane, Lt. Wangsholm flew his small aircraft towards the looming mountains. The Sikorsky was searching at a lower level further west.

In Stavanger Sofus Tønnessen had only two walkie-talkies but the police had requested more if possible. Sofus called nineteen year old Conrad Sæbbø and gave him orders to drive to Sandnes as quickly as possible, waken Sandnes Red Cross members, get into their depot, commandeer their 'Simrads', and return immediately. Conrad set off at 0405 hours with orders to be at the pier at 0500 hours. It was a matter of urgency to get to Sandnes and back in time.

Whilst a new (unofficial) speed record was set between Stavanger and Sandnes, Ola Lekvam clambered as fast as he could to the plateau top of the hummock locally called 'Holtaheia'. Unprepared for the total devastation which lay before him, the impact of what he saw hit him like a fist in the guts. Barren rock twelve hours previously, now what covered it defied imagination. He smelt diesel and saw there had been a widespread fire. A ripped open section of fuselage rested on the top. Wreckage was spread far and wide. Aghast he ran around looking everywhere to see if anyone was alive. He saw only bodies, and tried to count them as he went. Some bodies lay below, down a steep rocky slope. Hoping there might be survivors hidden amongst the heather and juniper he ran down and searched – in vain. His head was spinning. How many had he counted? He couldn't be sure! Again he ran around trying to count… but it was an impossible task and he knew he had to get back to inform the Police. He had seen enough… He felt nauseated, and his knees were suddenly weak. Light rain was falling, wetting the smooth rocks and making them slippery and he wondered desperately how he would manage to get back down quickly. Shock was setting in and he couldn't let it take hold – he *had* to get the news through. Then he spotted a wooden walking stick with silvery metal plates nailed on it. He needed something to support himself with if he was going to get to a telephone quickly – and this ornate stick, flung from the aircraft, was it. (It was Reggie Chapple's walking stick.) Ola felt a terrible responsibility, worsened by being all alone.

As he descended into the shadowy, rocky valley Ola saw two aircraft, one was quite close, the other in the distance. He realised they were searching for the crashed plane. He saw one fly over the summit where he'd just been. He thought it must have seen the wreckage because after circling it flew southwest towards Sola. On less steep ground again he progressed faster with one thought driving him. He was a man with a mission and he knew Elias Holta had a telephone.

Whilst Ola ran downhill to Holta, the stick helping him, in Stavanger Kaare Hidle met up with Sofus, his second in command. Together they double-checked the search and rescue plans. They hoped and prayed they would be in time to save lives. At 0435 hours Sofus and Kaare went to the Red Cross store, checked that all equipment was ready, and then took it with them to Strand quay where their team were already waiting. But there was no sign of Conrad Sæbbø and the extra walkie-talkies.

Lt. Jan Taarland aloft in the Sikorsky received a radio call from Lt. Arnt Wangsholm in the Safir whom they could see in the distance. He had located wreckage of the plane. It was 0515 hours. They sped towards the Safir which they could see circling a low summit. As they approached, Lt. Wangsholm, his job done, flew his Safir back to base. On the blackened top of Holtaheia the crew of the Sikorsky saw the crashed plane. Its tail overhung the cliff edge and its fuselage looked as though it had somersaulted over the top. One wing had broken off at impact and had flown onwards 160 yards, landing in a shallow lochan. Wreckage lay scattered everywhere, some of it lodged in cracks in the cliff face. It seemed that the Viking had just missed clearing the peak. If it had been a few metres higher it would have been safely over… but they could see from the direction of the strewn wreckage that it was on course to hit the next, higher summit, just further on… The Viking had been doomed.

Lt. Taarland circled the crash site a couple of times, surveying the devastation from on high, before looking for a landing place downhill from the area. It was imperative that their helicopter's swirling blades shouldn't disturb the distribution of debris, vital to remain in situ for the investigation process. Lt. Taarland informed Sola Tower that he was landing, but the moorland between the crags was boggy and he hovered the Sikorsky in a 'stabilising' manoeuvre over the potentially dangerous ground, in order to provide a quick take-off if any living casualties were found. Sola Tower asked him for the condition of the wreckage and Lt. Taarland replied, on visual analysis of the mangled metal, that he thought it looked a total loss. From below Papa Mike looked bizarrely like a dead monster, with dangling broken tail and shattered body and bones heaped up on top. For the professional aviator the pulverised remains were an anathema. Thirteen hours before it had been a beautiful flying machine. At Sola airbase, helicopter pilot Lt. Per Tjetland and Flight Engineer Karl Nilsen were ordered to fly the Bell-47 to the crash site, and take photographs immediately. Meanwhile at Holtaheia, Lt. Herstad and Sgt. Olsen had climbed up to the summit to investigate. They searched for some time but came back shaking their heads…

At Holta it was still very early, and Elias's door was locked, so Ola picked up a wooden clog left outside and banged hard. Old Elias came sleepily to unlock. 'What's wrong Ola?' he asked. 'Are you trying to knock my house down?' Out of breath Ola gasped about the crashed plane, grabbed the telephone receiver, and via the exchange at Tau contacted the Police in Stavanger. It was 0440 hours. The Police Station had just heard from Sola airport ten minutes before that the missing plane had been found, and that a Sikorsky helicopter was now at the site. Ola was told to stand by until they arrived. The police needed a guide. Ola knew he had to see to his animals. Adrenalin fuelled, he ran back to Lekvam to milk his cows and let them out to graze.

News of the crash spread around Holta, and people from the hamlet were already making their way up as the Sikorsky was preparing to leave. Seeing them Lt. Taarland ordered Lt. Herstad to remain to keep everyone away from the site. More local folk were making their way up. Leaving him as a solitary guard, the Sikorsky gained height but as it drew away the engine 'coughed' repeatedly, shaking the helicopter. This wasn't good news. The two airmen could see wreckage of one crashed aircraft scattered below and they didn't want their Sikorsky to join it! With their engine malfunctioning they made an emergency landing at the coast near Tau, and shut down. Sgt. Olsen checked the engine, finding a fault with the fuel/air mixture. Knowing they had to get back as soon as possible, cautiously they flew back to Sola, where the Sikorsky was grounded. Lt. Taarland immediately gave his report with the tragic news – 'there are no survivors'. It was just on seven o'clock in the morning local time.

Whilst Ola was milking his cows with unaccustomed speed, Conrad Sæbbø roared back to Stavanger, foot on the accelerator, eye constantly on his watch. He'd failed to find anyone at Sandnes to help him get hold of the radio telephones, and now he knew he might miss the boat. Five minutes late he arrived just in time to leap aboard one of the two Norwegian Naval minesweepers at 0505 hours. The search party, divided between the two boats, consisted of Police Chief Ravn-Tollefsen, his second in command Sjøtun, (both from Rogaland police force), 13 military personnel from Sola Air Station, and 21 team members from Stavanger Red Cross. Without further ado the two minesweepers, 'UTLA' and 'VOSSO', headed for Tau. Sofus and Kaare, on board Vosso were disappointed not to have the additional Simrad radio telephones as they knew these would have been invaluable searching Strand's hilly terrain. Despite this they felt otherwise well prepared for the forthcoming search. A short briefing was held by Ravn-Tollefsen at which police officer Sjøtun, Kaare Hidle, Sofus Tønnessen, and four selected Red Cross team leaders were fully briefed. Ellinor Sandsmark was selected to act as secretary to Ravn-Tollefsen, whilst two map readers from the Red Cross would assist military crews from

Sola Air Station. Ravn-Tollefsen told them all that, from information received, it appeared likely that the plane had flown over the large lake called Vostervannet, heading south-eastwards. Telephone messages indicated that the plane stopped just east of this location, as no further sounds of a plane had been heard. It was decided to establish headquarters for the search at Holta farm, which was known to have a telephone. It was agreed that the search would be carried out in groups, who would, as far as possible, keep in contact with each other. The search would start from Holta farm, and continue east over Holtaheia, towards the Tyssdalsvatn. Of the two Simrad sets, they decided to keep one at their headquarters and the other one on top of Holtaheia. The rescue equipment was then distributed, and the group leaders briefed their teams.

At Sola, Colonel Christie, Director of Norway's Air Accident Research, and others including Gullbrand Nyhus, Nils N. Ørstad, and S. Holsten, had started arriving from Oslo and elsewhere. Gathering on arrival in the canteen, they awaited photographs of the accident before preparing their strategy. Pilot Lt. Per Tjetland and Flight Engineer Karl Nilsen were already en route in the air base's Bell-47 helicopter to supply them.

As the Bell-47 flew over the wide fjord, two naval minesweepers (carrying several of their RNoAF colleagues and the Red Cross rescue team), were visible below, creating a frothy wake through the dark water. Karl had orders to take photos of the entire wreckage site, from high above and close to, so that the flight path of the plane could be assessed. He had used the old war time aerial photograph camera, now resting uncomfortably on his lap, before. It was a huge, heavy, but simple contraption, 60cm long, with a 20cm lens, a sight to aim through, and a trigger to shoot with. Under the low cloud base they found the burnt summit of Holtaheia.

Hovering high above, clutching the cumbersome equipment by its large handles and holding the camera from the side window, Karl Nilsen photographed the site from all angles. The landscape below looked grey and grim. Ancient jointed metamorphic rock, weathered by frost action and pocketed with hardy mountain plants, was now incongruously littered by twisted metal that had once been a plane. Pin-men amongst the wide rocky expanse of the plateau, more than fifty local people stood in groups of two's and three's far below. Per Tjetland landed below the cliff whereupon twenty locals came to join him, anxious for further information. Others stared transfixed at the wreckage. Gritting his teeth Karl walked up with the heavy camera. His senses were assaulted as he arrived at the top, but deadening his own feelings he got on with his vital job. Whilst Lt. Herstad and pilot Lt. Per Tjetland cordoned off the site and kept inquisitive locals away Karl stuck it out taking picture after picture from all angles until he had more than 50. Then he staggered down over the wet rocks to the welcoming Perspex 'bubble' of the Bell-47. He was glad to leave. He just wanted to get away.

During this time the Investigation Board assembling at Sola had increased in number as more experts flew in. Important British officials were packing bags to go to Stavanger. Two accident investigators from Britain's Accident Investigation Branch, Mr. N. S. Head and his adviser Mr R.G. Feltham, were preparing to fly out. From his office in Stavanger, Mayor Jan Johnsen had sent a telegram to the British Ambassador in Oslo, Sir John Walker.

Back at Sola again, Karl was sent straight to the photo laboratory where the film was developed immediately. He returned hot-foot, and the investigators immediately examined the prints, selecting images they wanted enlarged. Karl answered questions they fired at him, and was detailed to return to the photo-lab with orders for specific enlargements. At the photo-lab, impulsively he asked for two copies of each print. The enormity of what he'd witnessed had now sunk in and the germ of an idea that Croydon's newspapers might be interested elicited this spontaneous request – but when he collected the two sets of enlargements he changed his mind. Sensational news it certainly was, and it would soon break, but *not* with his photos. It was a sober reassessment. Karl delivered the enlargements to the Investigation Board team, whilst the duplicates he locked away – his job was too important to him.

At Lekvam, Ola finished vigorously milking his cows and turned the bemused beasts out to graze. He looked at other intended jobs awaiting him, but which wouldn't be done. Feeling out of kilter with the day, he climbed into his vehicle and headed back to Holta. He was waiting there when a car roared up the track.

It was the local taxi owned by Harald Hendriksen, and in it Harald Sem and Lars Torleiv Øye from *Stavanger Aftenblad*. Harald Sem was a Norwegian resistance war hero and freelance photographer since 1946. They had heard that the plane might be down near Holta and had left, very early, in their own boat. As minesweepers 'Usso' and 'Vosso' surged across the fjord from Stavanger to Tau. Sem and Øye were guided up to Gardbrekk from whence they could see the wreckage. The 'early birds' of all the reporters who flocked to the scene that day, they weren't deterred by one air force guard! The two men witnessed the awful spectacle, and Harald Sem realised that there were images there that he could *never* use. He photographed the contorted wreck of Papa Mike against the grey sky and they made their way sadly down.

At 0610 hours the minesweepers docked at Tau where the local police sergeant, waiting at the quayside, informed them all that the missing plane had been located by a search plane from Sola. There was, however, no need of a rescue as such because there were no survivors. This was gloomy news for all of them, and threw a whole new perspective on the planned rescue. The teams loaded all their rescue equipment onto a waiting coach, and were driven to Holta farm, where it parked and became the Red Cross preliminary quarters. The Police established their quarters at the farm. The military personnel with them were immediately sent to the scene of the accident, to cordon off the area. As this was two kilometres away as the crow flies, they decided to keep one radio at the farm and one at the site – maintaining contact every half an hour. Strict instructions were announced that no one was to touch anything until the Accident Commission had conducted a full investigation. Physically ready for a rescue operation, the Red Cross members had to remain inactive until further orders. Although he was technically second in command, Sofus had persuaded Kaare to let him take command at the crash site. Sofus thought his work in Korea with war-wounded would have desensitised him to horrific injuries, whilst Kaare, an avalanche search and rescue expert, hadn't the necessary experience.

When reporters Sem and Øye arrived down at Holta, and saw the Red Cross team dressed in anoraks and wellington boots waiting beside the coach, Harald Sem aimed his camera in their direction capturing the scene. The two newsmen departed in their waiting taxi, Lars scribbling his story, Harald with a photographic scoop. His iconic photo of a blackened pyramid of twisted metal, high above a grey landscape of fjords and islands, were to be studied by the select air crash investigation team and by countless millions more – when they were syndicated that day in newspapers throughout the world.

Across The North Sea in England, London Airport was already full of reporters, rushed by their newspapers to get places on the earliest flights to Stavanger. They included Walter Partington of The Daily Express, Brian Groves of The Daily Mail, and the Daily Herald's (anonymous) 'Man-on-the spot'. Dispatched with orders to gather every scrap of information, none of them spoke any Norwegian. But before this invasion of aggressive foreign correspondents (who were to catapult Ola Lekvam to unwanted fame), the young farmer waited disconsolately to guide the Police. It wasn't what he'd envisaged doing this day. He had jobs waiting in his workshop, a place where he enjoyed quietly creating things. He felt out of place. What was he doing there? The day seemed like a bad dream – but he knew it was real. His life had suddenly changed.

At Sola the Investigation Board members, who had gathered at Sola by 11.00am (local time), studied the stark images Karl had taken, and they formalised a work plan for the important job they had to do. Firstly they had to feel assured that the crash site was guarded. Military police were on their way there by naval minesweeper, and Lt. Herstad could be relieved. Lt. Taarland was ordered to fly the Bell-47 back to ensure that the crash site was properly cordoned off, and to bring Lt. Herstad back to base.

Across the fjord in Stavanger, Bill Cole and Roger Ives got up that morning at Mosvangen Youth Hostel, blissfully unaware of the event. They thought the hostel was very quiet and the mood of the staff unaccountably sombre – then the warden broke the news that the expected school boys had not arrived, and that their plane was missing. Bill and Roger ate their breakfast alone, speaking in hushed tones. When the news came through that the plane had been found, and that there were *no* survivors, they simply couldn't take it in. They had pre-booked a trip to the Preikestolen or 'Pulpit Rock', and although after this news their hearts weren't in it, they decided to go on with the trip as planned.

The Osmundsen family, on the shore of Bjørheimsvatn, saw an unusual amount of traffic taking the track up to the hamlet of Holta. As word of the disaster spread they learnt the tragic news, and young Kjell Terje Osmundsen and his father Lars Holta Osmundsen (whose parents were born at Holta), walked up to see if there was anything they could do. Their home was three kilometres away from Holta, and they had a telephone. This telephone and their proximity to the lake were to transform their quiet retreat into an unprecedented hive of activity that long day.

On the wind-swept plateau, Police Chief Ravn-Tollefsen, his second in command Sjøtun, and others, surveyed everything that had once been Papa Mike – and its precious cargo. With sou'westers or hunting caps on their heads, and clad in oilskin coats that flapped open in the gusts, they searched the site with mounting depression. Everyone on the summit wore a long face. They were stunned and glum. Few words were spoken as with hunched shoulders they surveyed the site. It was horrendous. Sofus independently viewed the disaster, solemnly assessing the rightness of his decision. He knew that a division of labour was best. He would take charge at the crash site, whilst Kaare would be in charge of the base tent lower down. His heart was low as he judged that their rescue requirements were completely different. No first aid was needed. Instead they would have to locate, painstakingly extricate, and carefully wrap each body. Many stretcher bearers would be needed, and it would be a long difficult, slippery trek down to the road end. Four men would best be needed to transport each stretcher, and if it was up to his Red Cross team alone, bringing them all down would take too long. Sofus descended to the foot of the cliff and discussed the new plan. On hearing of his need for extra helpers, Ola Lekvam, standing nearby, willingly volunteered, giving the names of Asgaut Warland and Erik Veland, dependable friends of his who were also fit to assist. It was something practical that he knew he could do, otherwise Ola felt useless. Thursday August 10th had turned into the worst day of his life.

It was the worst day of his life for Sofus Tønnessen too. He grimly estimated they needed ropes, stretchers, and protective gloves. Could he rise to this challenge he wondered? It was nothing like he'd experienced in Korea – almost all the casualties here were children. Back at Holta farm he contacted the Jørpeland Home Guard, requesting 40 stretchers and a large tent, and then he contacted his Red Cross base at Stavanger and asked them to provide 20 pairs of rubber gloves. Sofus reported to Kaare the awesome task that awaited them. But they couldn't do anything until the Accident Commission team arrived to commence their investigation. The Red Cross team faced a long wait before they could begin their work.

The Sikorsky helicopter, thoroughly inspected and passed fit to fly again brought in the Norwegian accident investigation team. Officials of the British Ministry of Aviation accident investigations branch led by Mr. Norman Head accompanied them, making seven in all. Immediately they set to work gathering as much information as possible, even down to the direction and location from the wreck of every piece of paper and shred of textile. They had investigated crashes before – although nothing near as bad as this one. Not with so many children involved. They had to shut off emotions and get on with a scientific examination to discover what had happened, so that nothing like this could ever again occur. Lt. Jan Taarland and Lt. Per Tjetland found themselves very busy, making many helicopter flights back and forth to Holtaheia. Crash inspectors and Cunard Eagle Airline representatives all needed the swiftest transport. The British Ambassador, Sir John Walker, fluent in Norwegian, was flown to see the site too. British newspapers were already quoting a London market insurance figure of £17,500 as 'Hull value' for the Viking. It was a worthless carcass now. Except for the media.

Young Egil Eriksson was a very keen newsman. With a nose for a story he'd taken the ferry to Tau where he'd seen rescue personnel. Following them to Holta in his car he noted that many were military police from his own base at Sola, sent to guard the site. Remembering that he had his own military field uniform with him, Egil quickly dressed in it, and set off for the peak where locals were staring at the cliff top in horrified disbelief. One of them was 22 year old Kåre Østerhus from nearby Østerhusbyholta. Another was 50 year old Olav Nervik who, informed by the local telephonist, had driven up from the holiday apartment his family always rented at Tau. Olav saw splintered wreckage littering the rocks and luggage scattered far and wide. One forlorn image struck him – a single high-heeled shoe standing alone. All the locals quietly waited to see if they could help. Amongst them was five year old Målfrid Holta, her sister Marit and three year old brother Karl, together with their parents, and grandparents. The adults were awe-struck. The children were frightened by what they saw. How could anything as cataclysmic have happened here? They spoke in hushed voices. Their hearts were very low. Helicopters noisily flying in and out terrified little Karl, who ran off and hid. It was his parent's turn to fear for *their* son – until they found him cowering amongst some rocks.

Egil took a photo of the locals standing at the foot of the cliff where the tail of the plane over-hung the edge, and debris was wedged fast in crevices in the frost shattered rocks. A twisted cone of contorted metal was silhouetted on the summit. The small helicopter from Sola had settled on the boggy moorland on its floats, and Air Force Military Police were conspicuously guarding the site. Rogaland Police were already on the top viewing the site, and Egil knew he was up against a risky challenge to take photos without being questioned. What he saw on reaching the flat summit hit him between the eyes. With a cameraman's gift to 'see' potential images, what he saw 'in the frame' was horrific. Like photographic plates, his eyes registered and his brain indelibly fixed, terrible enduring images – in split seconds. Paying an instant price for ambition, Egil knew he had important work to do. This was big news, and awful though it was, he had to get pictures for his paper. The crash site was cordoned off but he stepped inside, aware that he shouldn't be there. He snapped candid shots of the investigators and police, but whilst photographing he noticed military policemen watching him suspiciously. Turning around he deftly removed his film, replacing it with a new reel just before they accosted him to confiscate it. Egil obligingly opened his camera, gave them the unexposed roll, and was escorted off as an 'unwanted person'. Relieved that he'd got away with it, he raced back to Stavanger. Egil Eriksson had twelve exposures on the film in his pocket.

Whilst crash investigators continued their grim assessment, back at the 'Rogaland Avis' dark room in Stavanger, Egil set to work developing his film and printing the negatives. Swirling the photographic paper in the chemical trays, the stark images appeared just as he recalled them, 'fixed' in his photographic mind. Nothing could erase them. It was a high price to pay for a keen young photographer, but it had rewards. Interest in the tragedy, in Norway and abroad that day, (and for some time afterwards), increased to such a high demand that Eriksson engaged a photo agency to syndicate his photos. The 'Holtaheia plane crash wasn't just 'Big News' It was WORLD NEWS!

Every newspaper wanted a slice of the cake, and many were prepared to make a meal out of any crumbs of information. August was the 'Silly Season', renowned for being devoid of much interesting news, so the tragedy of the Lanfranc schoolboys spelt increased sales to news editors. Millions of additional newspapers were to roll off the presses all around the world. Everybody waking up to the tragic news that morning wanted to know more. Working on its daily edition, Stavanger Aftenblad included a short column about previous air crashes involving Sola. There had been two military accidents in 1953 and another in 1958. The crash on Holtaheia, however, was the biggest air accident ever to have happened in Norway.

As Military personnel guarded the site, reporters from Oslo, ahead of Britain's newsmen, landed in sea planes on Bjørheimsvatn, in front of the Osmundsen's holiday home. A Pathe News cameraman was among them. Desperate to get to Holtaheia, Harald Hendriksen's taxi made frequent journeys to Holta, from whence the journalists hurried two miles uphill to the base of the cliff – but no further. The journalists, ignorant, or simply hard-nosed, were annoyed not to be allowed closer. One reporter slyly announced that he needed the lavatory and asked when he could go. He was pointed to a location farther inland. It was subterfuge, because he walked uphill above the barriers, dropped his trousers, and aimed his telephoto lens at the site. He was unceremoniously removed by the guards. No member of the press was to take *any* revealing photos.

For Ola Lekvam the day didn't get any better. As it rolled on, he had not only to politely fend off inquisitive locals who had no idea of the horror he wanted to shield them from, but increasingly pushy journalists, who pestered him with questions. Officially helping keep people away, Ola was shocked at the behaviour of the press who didn't take into account the gravity of the situation, and the tragedy that had occurred. Holtaheia had become the unlikely location of a media feeding frenzy, and he was a person these 'sharks' wanted a bite from. Fleshy scraps of information were expertly nibbled from him. When journalists from England arrived (wet, bedraggled, not dressed or shod for mountains, streams, or boggy ground), although he didn't speak any English Ola became a centre of attention. Police Chief Ravn-Tollefsen didn't want the brutal reality of what he had witnessed, publicised. Ola was cautioned to give a minimal interview, before being protected from further unwanted attention. Someone translated, and journalists scribbled every word in shorthand as the besieged farmer hesitantly opened his heart.

"I saw the black remains of the plane perched on the mountain-top" he said.

"In a few minutes I was standing before all that remained of the plane. There was a strong smell of burning.

"I looked at the bodies, at the pieces of plane. It was a terrible sight. I felt hopeless – there was just nothing I could do.

"Rain lightly spattered the scene, but everything was strangely calm and still. I looked at the heavy clouds which still hung in the sky and turned back.

"I had seen enough. I have never felt so useless."

For many others involved, their lives would never be the same again. RNoAF personnel at the crash site realised that they had to take all this in their stride, and get on with their lives, but both Lt Jan Taarland and Flight Engineer Karl Nilsen were concerned for the immediate welfare of the young Red Cross team they saw waiting to help. Lt. Taarland found it particularly disturbing to see the three young girls on the mountain. He knew the Red Cross were mainly college students, not hard core professionals like himself. He felt sorry for them. Karl too was surprised to see Red Cross members far younger than him. 'Do you *really* want them to come up here and see all this?' he asked one young team leader incredulously. 'It isn't a pretty sight!' This was met with a resolute, positive reply. 'Yes…We can do it!' Both airmen were struck by what was expected of the youngsters, whose only qualification was to have passed a proficiency exam in basic first aid. But 'first aid' wasn't even in the description of the job that lay before them! Karl knew he couldn't do what they now had to do. He had acted as a professional, and simply taken photos, but they were volunteers who had now to rescue bodies, so what toll would it take on them?

It wasn't until 1435 hours, when the Red Cross were told that they could move up to the accident site. Carrying the stretchers and tent that had arrived from nearby Jørpeland Home Guard, they climbed to the foot of the rocky summit above Holta. After their prolonged inactivity and frustration, they were keen to get going. Just below the accident site they sat quietly waiting again, mentally psyching themselves for the job they had volunteered to do.

Finally given the order to help they selected a level area 200 metres below the cliff, and erected the large ten loaned by Jørpeland Home Guard, pegging and stoning it firmly to counteract strong winds. Kaare took charge of organising this field station, whilst Sofus joined the investigation team, where he was asked to methodically lay numbers by each body for identification purposes. As he did so he mentally formalised what would have to be done by his team when the order was eventually given for them to commence their rescue. The field station below would be a halfway house from which teams would transport stretchers, each carrying one victim, down to Holta farm. The team members still had no idea of the enormity of the task that lay before them. This wasn't a job for the girls, but then some of the boys were little older than the eldest school boys who were victims of the crash. He knew he would have to choose carefully.

Waiting for further activity, the journalists hung around together, watching updrafts of wind lift and jangle pieces of loose metal on the wreckage above them on the cliff top. Tattered pieces of the plane's interior fluttered in the wind like Buddhist prayer flags. Everything seemed surreal. Under the low cloud base, in grey light, they could see islands studding the fjords far below – the scene resembling a faded water colour painting. Occasionally the sound of church bells tolling drifted up to them. Normally brash (as their job required of them), these men were shocked and affected by what they'd been sent to report. Making the long, wet trek back down again, (many wishing they could have hitched a lift in a helicopter), they knew they had a story that would run and run. The farmer's quotes and their own stories were telephoned back from the Osmundsen's and other 'commandeered' telephones. Editors were holding their front pages, and many of the stories made the late editions that day. Relieved to find that many Norwegians spoke perfect English, Brian Groves of The Daily Mail talked to Colonel Christie, and filed his words. *'This is a tragic day for both our countries. Believe me the whole of Norway is sad. Our sympathies know no bounds.'*

Whilst the crash investigators were systematically and scientifically gathering their information in order to find the reasons for the crash, news reporters demanded instant answers for their readers. Already theories were being bandied around and published as possible causes. John Austin from the Daily Sketch spoke to an investigator who suggested that the crash could have happened if 'the 70 m.p.h. wind caused Capt. Watts to correct his course by 20 degrees' which might have 'whisked the plane through the radio beam before he had the chance to make a further correction; or that the Viking turned right instead of left to face back into the wind for its landing, and was blown violently off course; or the pilot, unable to locate the beam again in the storm, circled for two hours before running out of petrol and losing height.' But it wasn't this third suggestion for they'd found watches that had stopped at 1629 hours.

The Daily Herald's 'man-on-the-spot' had also reached the crash site, got his own story, and was impressed by the Red Cross youngsters who he saw establishing their base camp. He noted the way that they took their hats off and stood, heads bowed in silence, near the top. As soon as he reached a telephone he called the Herald's news desk in Fleet Street, where his story was rushed to the editor – *'I climbed for two hours with rescue teams up the 1,800ft Holtaheia Peak today – as a church bell tolled in the village below. But when we reached the top there was no rescuing to be done. Rain swept across the fjords. We stumbled through a swollen river and over boggy ground to the mountain graveyard of 39 Britons. From below, the wreck of the holiday plane stood out against the skyline like a burnt out Christmas tree. The twisted mass rocked and clanged slightly in the high wind...'* He included the young Norwegian farmer's quotes as well. Reported in almost all British papers, Ola Lekvam's words were to become engraved on hearts in Croydon – where the grieving families waiting for news had also – 'never felt so useless'. The telephone network in Strand was eventually so overloaded that it broke down.

The Red Cross stood by their base camp awaiting orders from the police. Eventually, at 1700 hours, Ravn-Tollefsen informed them that due to identification difficulties, and the ongoing investigation, there was no possibility of them transporting anyone down that day. The bodies of the victims were to remain guarded over night, exactly where they lay. For most of the Red Cross 1st team it was fortunate that they were spared this traumatic job, which others would now have to do. Sofus and Kaare were informed that a team would be needed the following day instead, but they couldn't leave Holta until Civil

Guards arrived to take over from the military guards. When these arrived to guard the crash site for the night, all that day's teams were to be taken back to Tau. The weather had closed in again, and the helicopter that should have taken the four members of the Norwegian investigation team back to Sola, could not take off. Police chief Ravn-Tollefsen was approached by a British journalist from The Daily Worker anxious for a quote. Ravn-Tollefsen had not slept the previous night, had worked hard all day playing a leading role organising the initial identification procedure, and seeing the scattered bodies wished with all his heart that Holtaheia and its neighbouring peak had been a few vital metres lower. Or the plane higher! Politely, but despairingly, he said a few words to inform the British public. *'Those on board must have been killed instantly. The plane was shattered, and pieces of wreckage are spread over a wide area. It is the most frightful thing I have ever seen, or experienced.'*

Kåre Østerhus, who worked with his brother Leif in a lorry transport business called Østerhus Bilruter, received some unexpected business from Rogaland police headquarters, that day. The brothers had been engaged to transport the bodies of the crash victims, from Holta to Tau, the next day. Having visited the crash site Kåre wasn't at all happy. He knew that Leif and he must do their best to help, but what he had witnessed distressed him deeply. This was one job that he wasn't looking forward to.

Bill Cole and Roger Ives had no idea just what a long hard slog it was to the 'Pulpit Rock' and back. It was very late, and to make matters worse, they thought they were lost. With sore feet and aching calf muscles they walked down through the forest, suspecting they'd missed the last ferry, when they came across a woodman. It was getting dark and they *had* missed the boat. The woodman compassionately took them in for the night, pleased to be able to do something to help a couple of boys from a country which had just lost so many.

Meanwhile, across the fjord in Stavanger two English girls, Joan Brown and Maureen Maudlin, who had flown from Coventry on their first holiday abroad, experienced the town's grief throughout the day. Everywhere they went people spoke to them, wanting them to know the sadness they felt at the news. It was clear to the girls that the town's folk felt that the Lanfranc boys were almost like their own sons or brothers.

Stavanger Cathedral was full to overflowing that evening. Almost 2,500 people packed into the 800 year old building with its huge stone columns – it seemed that the whole city wanted to attend. The medieval cathedral, the only one of its kind in Norway, built on its ancient knoll, was unable to take any more and many people stood outside in their raincoats. Bareheaded men held their hats, whilst ladies respectfully wore hats or headscarves. Rain showers threatened and gusts swirled the Union Jack and Norwegian flags flying at half mast to right and left of the entrance on specially erected flagpoles. British residents of Stavanger, and 200 British tourists, including schoolboys from Harlow on a similar school trip, were amongst the congregation who squeezed in to attend the service taken by Stavanger's Bishop Fritjov Birkeli and assisted by Dean Christian Svanholm. Captain John Sauvage of Cunard Eagle Airways, who had flown over the night before, also attended. Everywhere within and around Stavanger flags flew at half mast, in private homes and on all the ships, whilst as the service took place, radio programmes were stopped as Norway mourned. This wasn't a superficial 'official mourning' – the feeling of grief was sincere and went very, very deep.

The Bishop welcomed everyone in Norwegian, saying a few words about why they were all there. Then he spoke in English, and with this surprise the composure of most people broke. It touched the hearts of all the English residents and tourists present and few were without tears in their eyes as he addressed them.

"My dear friends from England gathered at this time here in the cathedral of Stavanger! As you all know a tremendous disaster affecting deeply both Britain and Norway has occurred not very far from here.

*Needless to say that also **our** hearts and minds are stunned with sorrow and horror as we realise that 34 young schoolboys, two of their teachers and a crew of three, all from Britain, lost their lives in the mountains of Rogaland in what appears to be the greatest disaster of its kind in the history of this country. We would of course like to help and comfort. But in a way we feel so utterly helpless all of us in a tragedy like this.*

All these 39 were strangers to us. We didn't know a single one of them. And yet in time of distress and tragedy we all come closer to each other. And as these persons, boys and grown-ups, came to us in the moment of death, we feel that they belong also to us. And so we take part in your sorrow as if they were our own boys. We have these last years witnessed an ever increasing stream of youngsters visiting our shores for holiday. And happy and jubilant as they were excellent ambassadors of Britain, they were always most heartily welcome among us. But we did not expect any of them to find a sudden and violent death here.

What happened yesterday has deeply shocked every one of us.

Quite naturally our thoughts go to the parents and other relatives in Britain of all the boys and the others who passed away so suddenly. Most certainly each father and mother had put all their hopes in their boy. He had been their joy in the past and their more or less proud hope for the future. They had followed him with loving care until this last departure. Now it is brutally over. Their happy dreams about future success have ended here by us in a mountainside. Modern technique gives a lot, but also takes a lot. We have experienced that once more.

We can assure you that our warmest feelings from the city and diocese of Stavanger go to the relatives and to the school in Croydon that lost so much. This terrible sorrow unites us even more than before. Nothing can bring people closer together than suffering and tragedy.

And yet we feel and realise that all our sympathy can produce so little of real value in a situation like this, where human beings become so small and utterly helpless. Together we have to turn to the living God. That is why we are here.'

Having so sensitively delivered the first part of his address with Christian humanity and fellowship, Bishop Birkeli now had the difficult task of linking the horrendous disaster to the concept of a loving God. Everyone clung to his words. Everyone wanted to find the sense in what had happened. The question in so many minds was – why? Why had it happened? Why had it happened in Stavanger?

Bishop Birkeli, still speaking English, led them all in the words of Psalm 121: It was the introduction to the thoughtful, religious part of his address in which he presented a Living God in the atomic age as one who understood the problems of mankind. It was a difficult thing to equate. He ended by saying *'When the living Lord, maker of heaven and earth, has permitted also this to happen we know for certain that His grace will be with all the relatives, and help them and all of us to be prepared for our last journey wherever and whenever it may come, through his salvation and abundant grace. God bless all the dear ones of those who passed away, may their memory be a call to eternity for all their school-mates – and for all of us. Amen.'*

It was a brave, strong address, combining the tragedy of Holtaheia with every Christian's eternal hope. He strengthened some of those present with his own Christian beliefs, understanding, and spiritual acceptance. His sincere words helped those who had faith. For some, inevitably however, the good man's words simply could not explain how a 'loving God' could have let a tragedy like this happen. Many left bewildered at what had befallen the school boys from Croydon – and their own town. But Bishop Birkeli's kind words had helped them all because he had voiced their grief and they had been there to show their love and respect for total strangers.

The Bishop ended the service with the benediction, and everyone filed silently out of the Cathedral, many wiping fresh tears from their eyes. Daily Express journalist Walter Partington had attended the service and telephoned through his report about the occasion saying 'Women wept as they heard him say: *'Our hearts and minds are stunned with horror'*, also quoting his reference to Psalm 121 *'I will lift up mine eyes unto the hills'* and the Bishop's exhortation *'Tonight we must lift them higher again – to God.'* A stock phrase in journalism is 'nothing sells like emotion' and raw emotion was here in abundance. The unusual thing was that hard-boiled newsmen were deeply affected themselves.

Arriving back in Stavanger on *M.S Clipper*, Sofus dismissed his 1st team at Strand pier at 2300 hours. He had no chance to sleep that night because he had to enrol a new crew, and each had to be carefully chosen. They had to be physically strong, and also have the necessary mental strength to cope with what lay before them. With a great deal of thought Sofus hand-picked a new team of 18, and Anna Nordland had asked to be one of them.

That stormy night 30 Norwegian soldiers guarded the crash site. Two of Norway's investigation team had got back to Stavanger on *M.S. Clipper*. Two others spent the night at a nearby farmhouse.

England Thursday 10th August

Across the North Sea in England, as Police Inspector J. Collie went to bed dejected, keen news reporter Betty Brownlie was up and at the news office of The Croydon Advertiser. The editor was already poring over the early editions of the national daily papers which devoted their front pages to the missing plane. They all carried headlines about 'London Boys' in a 'Missing Plane' – with a stock photo of a Vickers Viking. Some had sketch maps of the route from London to Stavanger, whilst others carried photos of the pilot, Captain Philip Watts. All reported that the plane was lost in bad weather, and that a big land and sea search had ensued.

The editor's natural inclination as a news man was to go straight to the heart of the matter. News was news, and this was very big news. Only this was different. Croydon was his town and something awful had happened to a large number of his readers. He couldn't go 'for the jugular' with a news story of this magnitude, when the people concerned were bleeding already. He didn't want a direct approach to inflict more pain. Gathering his eight reporters together he gave them instructions to visit the neighbourhoods of the boys listed on the trip, where they had to circumspectly find out as much as they could, by calling on neighbours and local shops, but *not* any of the families. They were to get their stories – and get back fast!

Betty Brownlie knocked on doors and found everyone very upset, and eager to talk about the lost boys. (1961 was a time when adults referred to other people's boys as 'son' and there was no political correctness that inhibited spontaneous kindly familiarity to a neighbour's or stranger's child.) The owner of a corner shop told Betty that one of the boys had been doing a paper round to earn spending money for the trip. Gathering as much as she could in a short time, Betty dashed back to join the others speedily tapping reports into their typewriters. All were written in time to make the deadline for Croydon's weekly, Friday paper.

Many parents hadn't slept all night. Those who snatched some sleep awoke to find themselves living in a nightmare. There was still no news. The agony of waiting and hoping was stretching them to breaking point. Husbands had to be strong for their wives, when needing every ounce of strength for themselves. Wives, in many cases, had to be strong for husbands and children. The terrible thing was – not knowing anything. For almost all the parents Norway was an unknown country. Many had never seen a mountain in their life, let alone a fjord. The south of England was essentially lowland, with a few low hill ranges, about as different from vertiginous Rogaland as chalk from cheese, yet in ignorance and hope all clung to the impossible dream that the plane had landed somewhere safely. Those parents closest to Lanfranc School gathered at the school gates in the hope that the school would be informed first. Mr Fowle, who had been up all night, knew no more than they, and could tell them nothing. The poor man was struggling to hold the helm of a ship that had lost its compass, and was wallowing in a whirlpool of emotion that threatened to drag it down. Although unrelated to any of them, they were all 'his boys', and he genuinely cared about them. The previous night he had rushed in to school to find the list and addresses of the boys as soon as he'd heard the news. Now there was still no news. What on earth had happened to them? What had become of George Budd and John Beacham? What could he say to all the parents? When would they find them? The 'sails of his ship', like himself, felt shred to pieces. He needed strength. A long standing church warden as well as a headmaster, Tommy Fowle prayed.

He wasn't alone in needing strength. Living close to Lanfranc, and Croydon Cemetery, John Adam's mother, Eileen Adams, heard a voice inside her head say, 'And will you be prepared for bad news?' She answered the rhetorical question in her normal efficient way with, 'Yes'. But she was feeling like nothing on earth. Her wonderful son John was missing, and now she had to be brave for her husband, young daughter, and father.

In Coulsdon Geoff Budd and his mother, despite sleeping pills, had been up before six o'clock creeping about the house and grabbing the telephone handset as soon as it rang, so that it didn't awaken young Tim. Mrs Budd had decided that he must go to stay with her sister in Haslemere as soon as possible, and Geoff was delegated to take him. Thelma had heard the news, phoned from a callbox, and agreed to meet Geoff and Tim on the same train. When he awoke, nine year old Tim was told his father's plane was missing. The last thing the lad wanted was to leave his mother to go to stay with his aunt, but Margery couldn't cope with Tim as well. After boarding the train, as it chugged through the tunnel south of Coulsdon young Tim silently repeated a mantra – 'Crashed, not dead, crashed not dead, crashed not dead'… knowing in his heart that really his father was dead. The blackness of the tunnel matched the blackness in his head.

Helping to lead an Army Cadet Force (ACF) camp, Dennis Beacham, John's brother, on hearing the news left and went home to South Croydon. The awful news was announced at the camp and Lanfranc ACF cadet Alan Oliver was devastated to think his friends and school masters were dead. At a Scout camp elsewhere, Robin Cooper, a good friend of John Phelps and Martin White heard the news. Robin knew both boys from junior school, and they'd journeyed to their different schools on the bus together talking about their school's holiday trips. Robin was due to go to Austria with his school, but all the fun had gone out of it now.

Across the other side of Croydon, Norman Cook and his wife Jean, unaware of the crisis, awoke to their morning newspaper and were aghast to see a photo of Lanfranc's school badge on the front page. Norman broke down and wept. Utterly devastated his first thought was of Tommy Fowle, who he knew had just recovered from a stroke. As quickly as he could, he dressed, downed a cup of tea, and raced to the school to find Tommy Fowle and Syd Gubby at the gate surrounded by scores of parents and crying children, clamouring for more news.

In bed and asleep, John Cooke was enjoying a lie in when his mother burst into his bedroom in tears. John's first thought was that something had happened to his father. Instead she asked if he remembered the news report, and that it was boys from Lanfranc who were missing! John got dressed and went outside to see people in his street huddled in small groups speaking quietly, trying to take in the news. The atmosphere was strangely heavy. Everyone knew a boy on the plane.

Carol Storey was washing in the bathroom at her home in Reading, when her mother rushed upstairs asking 'Was it Stavanger that Richard was going to? There's a plane missing!' Carol knew the trip was a gift to her boyfriend Richard from his grandfather, and that Mr Lawrence was planning to surprise Richard on his return by meeting him in a new gold-coloured Jaguar car. They didn't have long to wait for news. It finally came in a news flash. The B.B.C. interrupted its programme with a brief message to say that the missing plane carrying English school children had been found crashed in the mountains near Stavanger. The last words were chillingly final. 'There are no survivors.' The hearts of parents, siblings, relatives, friends, neighbours, school friends, townsfolk, in fact people all over Britain were pierced by those final words. It was as though a spike of ice had invisibly stabbed right to the centre of hearts, killing hope and replacing it with despair – and real pain. For immediate family members the news was sheer horror. The very name 'Stavanger' struck a chord of terror. The name instilled fear and became synonymous with dread. *Stavanger…* That awful name sounded brutal by its very pronunciation. Even – SAVAGE!

Understandably some emotionally afflicted people reacted viciously to the news. John Adam's grandfather instantly blamed his daughter Eileen, shouting at her 'You shouldn't have let him go on that holiday! Why did you do it?' He was in shock. Eileen was the scapegoat. She had sold her Premium Bonds to help pay. It was her fault!

Lanfranc's staff although numbed by the news immediately dropped everything and rallied to the school. On his way there Ron Cox saw a bill board announcing the crash, and thought he was dreaming.

No one would ever forget where they were, or what they felt, that day when they heard the news.

In Camberley, Surrey, five year old Simon Karginoff, son of Captain Watts, aware that his father wasn't home, was eating the creamy filling from a Custard Cream biscuit which he'd raided from their Huntley and Palmers biscuit tin – when his mother told him. She was inconsolable with grief. Simon couldn't take it in. His Dad was a hero! He'd taken him flying in his plane! So why wasn't he coming home? What did 'dead' mean?

At the office of the Financial Times in London a junior reporter was standing by the telex machine when the news of the air crash came clattering through. As a nineteen year old, Peter Hamilton had met Sue Endicott at a beach party in Torquay and he recalled her kindness to himself as a shy young man. His mind went back to 1960 when he'd met her – a lovely, vivacious young woman, full of high spirits, but generous and gentle as well. He was shocked and devastated.

In Paignton, Devon, Ann Endicott felt as though half of her had been physically torn away. Sue was her other half, she always had been, they were such close sisters. Her world, and her parent's world, collapsed. Chris Moysey was heartbroken. He and Sue were due to announce their engagement and he wished with all his being that she'd never had to do that last flight. She was his 'other half' too.

Derek Benson, Michael's brother awoke that morning and was surprised to find the house full of people. He overheard scraps of conversation, and feared the worst. His father came up to his bedroom, and 10 year old Derek asked 'Has Michael's plane crashed?' 'Yes' his father replied. 'Is Micky dead?' Derek pursued. 'I don't know!' his father replied, breaking down in tears. His mother was sedated and in bed. Derek didn't see her that day, but when the news came through he heard her cry out when his father told her there were no survivors.

Geoff Brown's girl friend, Maureen, awoke early and left her house, wandering 'like a zombie' around the streets, until she ended up at her sister's house – where she was told the news. Her lovely Geoff was dead… At the Brown household everyone was speechless with misery.

Reggie Chapple's family were desolate. His parents idolised their 'champion' son. June's chill premonition had come true.

When Susan Green woke, she washed and put on the clean striped dress that had been placed on the hanger on her bedroom door. A policeman knocked at their house and told them the news. Instantly she knew her life would never be the same again. She was going to have to survive without her dear brother – but how? She depended on Geoff… he was her best friend.

A policeman delivered the bad tidings to Mr and Mrs Hendley and Julia. He told them that wreckage had been sighted on a mountain, and that there was no chance of there being survivors. A terrible, desperate feeling of being totally helpless suddenly descended, and he left them sobbing, their eyes blurred by tears, so heartbroken they couldn't speak.

In the home of Martin White the news of 'no survivors' hit like a bomb shell. The reaction of Mr and Mrs White was shock and disbelief. They imagined that the plane had simply come down and that the boys were out and were in the hills, waiting to be rescued. Martin's brother Bernard now knew, but three year old Angela had no idea. She came into their kitchen to see her father shaving at the sink, a towel round his neck, razor in his hand, and soap lathered over his face, sobbing like he would never stop. Distressed she went to find her mother who was on her knees in front of the hearth, making up the fire as she did every morning. Tears were pouring down her face. Angela didn't know what to do, so she put her arms round her mother's neck, and gave her a kiss, saying " Please don't be sad, Mummy".

Quentin Green's father had thought the same as Mr White, and now wanted to go over and search himself. His mind was tormented by the thought that his young son was wandering, lost in Norway's vast trackless mountains. At first he'd thought his daughter had said there were 'nine survivors' and his hopes had momentarily soared. But she'd bitterly corrected him 'No Daddy. There are NO survivors.' But there *had* to be! Ron irrationally rationalised. How could Quentin be dead when he'd been alive yesterday?

This was a common feeling. How *could* their sons, their brothers be… DEAD? They had been so full of life one day ago! Thursday August 10th was a day unlike any other.

Every household had a newspaper delivered each morning. Some newsagents in Croydon found that one or two of their own 'paper boys' were on the missing plane. Others had Lanfranc boys who worked for them. At the newsagents in Portland Road, South Norwood, the owner was very concerned because Michael O'Rourke was one of his paper boys. The news was splashed across all the front pages. How would the lad react? Everyone was very kind when Mike came to pick up his bag of papers. A friend from another school, who knew Colin Smith, was really sympathetic, but Mike found that delivering all his papers was terribly emotional. His mate Quentin was on the front page of the

Daily Express. He couldn't believe it! So many good mates had died! When he got round to David Hatchard's road he ducked into an alley opposite the Hatchard's house and wept. He felt so sorry for David's mum and dad. He knew they had no other children. Behind their closed door Mr and Mrs Hatchard were so overcome with shock they could hardly speak. All Mrs Hatchard could eat that day was a few tinned peaches supplied by their neighbour. It was the only food that would slip down her constricted throat.

At Cliftonville in Kent, eleven year old Shirley Bradbery was with her parents walking by the sea front. Her father bought a Daily Sketch newspaper and read out the headlines with shock and disbelief. They lived in Livingstone Road, Thornton Heath near to several of the boys. Shirley had a very strange feeling of loss. Although she didn't know any of the boys she felt strongly that she would have met and befriended one of the boys later in her life.

Geoff Budd arrived at his aunt's house in Haslemere later that morning. He had been on tenterhooks the entire journey, and immediately saw from the woeful expression on his Aunt Vi's face, that the worst *had* happened. His girlfriend Thelma took Tim into the garden to gently break the awful news. Tim wondered how he was supposed to react, and not knowing what to say asked rather lamely 'Shall I show you the rest of the garden?'

Anthony Harrison's sister Julia was with her husband visiting his parents in Ayrshire. They saw the news in later additions of the newspapers, which now correctly named Lanfranc as the school concerned, and listed all the names and addresses of the victims. Immediately they packed up to drive home. A long, miserable journey lay ahead, with no joyful homecoming. Far away in northern Iceland, Paul Sowan, a Croydon student, heard the news over his transistor radio in his windswept tent halfway up a mountain.

Leslie Bentley arrived back at West Croydon Station from Hayling Island and found that everyone was staring at his school blazer with its Lanfranc badge. Then his father saw the bill boards. They bought the newspapers, including one that featured the school badge, and Leslie couldn't believe so many from his school were dead. Home again he opened his diary and wrote the heading 'Black August' listing his closest friends.

Chris Taylor and his family, on holiday were just sitting down to dinner and chatting noisily when Chris heard the words 'Air crash' and 'Lanfranc Boys School' emanate from their radio. 'SHUT UP!' he shouted, shocked at his own audacity. They stopped talking and heard the news. Chris was horrified, especially when the awful question occurred to him. *Who* had taken *his* place?

Back home from their camping holiday in Cornwall, Ian Greest's mother, on hearing the catastrophic news, exclaimed emotionally to her only child – 'I thank my lucky stars that your dad lost his job!' Geoffrey Parr was shown a newspaper report by his father and burst into tears. He had been so disappointed not to go, but now his best friend, whom he'd envied, was dead. Clive Grumett, Lanfranc's head boy was on holiday in the Isle of Wight. His father broke the news to him. Half of his closest friends were dead. He was numb with shock. Hundreds of others from Lanfranc felt the same – so many had lost their best mates.

It was a black day for all at Lanfranc. Those boys who had been down to go, but had changed their minds for various reasons, had terrible mixed emotions. Their parents were beside themselves that they hadn't gone on the trip – that their son hadn't died, but any personal feelings of relief these boys felt were swamped by awful feelings that it *could* have been *them*, indeed it *should* have been *them*, followed by the dreadful question – *which boy* took my place? They looked forlornly at the faces of their friends, now grouped together in the later editions of the newspapers – and they *didn't want to know* who had taken their place! Survivor's guilt, a concept completely unknown to them, slipped insidiously into and lodged within the subconscious of those with sensitive minds – never to go away.

At Lanfranc School Tommy Fowle had endured a horrendous day, and so had his staff. Wearing black ties they had all met in the school library joined by officials from the Education Department, and news reporters – who were unusually muted in their questioning of Mr Fowle. The heavy strain of not having slept for 28 hours showed. His voice shook as he spoke of 'his' boys. '*They had plenty of spirit, plenty of character. They were very good types in every way, the sort of boys that helped to set a very satisfactory tone to the school.*' Of his colleagues he said *'They were popular and respected. They had made a big contribution to the life of the school. They were the force behind these overseas trips... without them it is unlikely that we shall be able to continue trips abroad.'* When asked if he would allow another school trip to fly he shook his head. *'I don't think I could ever agree to another party flying – but it is too early to make a decision of that sort.'*

Whilst the meeting was going on, the school caretaker John Hansford came in and tipped off Ron Cox and Norman Cook that two men were wandering around the school. The two teachers slipped away and found the men in George Budd's laboratory. One had a camera, the other was writing scientific formulae on the blackboard. From a tabloid newspaper, they wanted to fudge a photo of 'George Budd's last lesson'. Ron and Norman were so furious at this insensitive intrusion that they would have thrown the men down the stairs – if the reporters hadn't rushed out of the room first! Nevertheless one journalist found school cleaner Mrs Annie Field sitting on a chair crying. She told them how she couldn't raise the £27 that her son Dennis needed to pay for the trip, and that his place was taken by Quentin Green. *'I am so thankful that my son didn't go after all, but my heart goes out to the mother of the boy who took Dennis's place.'* Her son was safe on her married daughter's farm in Kent, aware he was lucky to be alive, unaware that he would soon famously feature in the newspapers. These first journalists left to file their stories. Others arrived asking questions. The tragic news had set off a hive of journalistic activity – and Lanfranc was a honey pot.

Tom Pocock, reporter for the Evening Standard, absorbed the atmosphere. He noticed a small boy in blue jeans, riding his dropped handle-bar bicycle in slow wide figures of eight outside the school, and a group of little boys in bright holiday clothes staring silently at the school buildings. They were there because a scheduled Cycling Proficiency Test in the playground hadn't been cancelled. Tom observed staff gather at the porch, where they shook hands, and talked in whispers. He watched as a shop keeper walked into the hall, shook hands with the school caretaker, saying 'I've just nipped in with the deepest sympathy from us shopkeepers.' One of the masters talked quietly to Tom Pocock about the school. *'We started organising holidays abroad five years ago,'* he said. *'We arranged one or two each year. This was the first time they had gone by air. They were older boys mostly. Three were in the cricket XI.'* The faces of John Wells, Trevor Condell, and Richard Lawrence, seemed to smile at him from a photograph on a notice board. He ducked into the cloakroom thinking that the caretaker would have to change the names above the hooks… Tom Pocock's report captured the sorrowful ambience felt by all the reporters who came and left again, the men in particular touched by photographs of school teams who had lost many of their best sportsmen. Pocock filed his story as *'Silent sadness at Lanfranc'*.

Croydon Council was without its figurehead. Croydon's Mayor, Alderman Mrs Catherine Kettle, was on a coach tour holiday somewhere in Scotland, and telephone calls from the town hall had been too late to catch her at her hotel in the morning, and again when she'd stopped for coffee. But at lunch-time she was found at a hotel in Helmsdale, Sutherland, and told the news. 'I am deeply, deeply grieved' she said. 'This is a terrible tragedy. If need be, I will fly home immediately.'

Flags in Croydon were dropped to half mast, and a palpable gloom had descended on the town. The Chief Education Officer, Mr Rupert Wearing King was finding the situation difficult to cope with. From outside his office his staff heard him pacing round and round, totally unable to do anything rational. Nothing like this had ever happened to him before! But then nothing like this had ever happened to *any* British school before.

In London Harold Bamberg found to his horror that the buck had stopped at his desk. He felt terrible. He had been up all night, in contact with Sola airport and his Director of Operations, Captain John Sauvage. Aside from the bad publicity for his company, he was devastated to have lost two good pilots and one of his best stewardesses. But to have also lost 36 passengers, consisting of 34 schoolboys and their two masters, was almost unbelievable. Almost, but not quite – he'd survived the war whilst so many of his friends and colleagues had died, shot down or in flying accidents, and this wasn't the first fatal accident for his company – but there were *no* survivors this time. Aviation accidents happened from time to time, – but what on earth had caused this one? With a heavy heart he called his secretary and dictated a letter.

'I feel I must write to you today in connection with the tragic loss of life involved in the accident to Viking aircraft G-AHPM near Stavanger.

Words are inadequate at a time like this, but I must extend to you in this bereavement, our heartfelt sympathy. Since the first report that the aircraft was overdue, my staff have been standing by to remit all possible information to those concerned. Our Operations Director and our Flight Captain proceeded to Stavanger forthwith followed by our Chief Inspector. It was however not until early this morning that we were able to provide definitive news as to the whereabouts of the aircraft and the fate of the passengers. As you now know, the crash occurred approximately 21 miles North East of Stavanger, and the cause is not yet known. A full investigation will take place.

I think you would like to know that Captain Watts was able and experienced – and had served with this company for seven years. He and his crew are a great loss and will be mourned here.

Certain arrangements have yet to be made, and we shall be in touch with you again.'

Secretaries in Cunard Eagle's Head Office typed out 36 copies in subdued silence. Harold personally addressed them to the head of each family and signed them *'Yours truly, H.R. Bamberg'* in his own hand.

Elsewhere in London, secretaries not even remotely connected, were also subdued. At Barclays Bank in London's Moorgate, important officials on a fact-finding tour entered the Typing Pool and tried to engage the typists in polite conversation but not one of the dozen girls replied because they were all stunned by the news. The bankers left again, totally mystified.

Complete strangers felt deeply moved by the tragedy. Nothing like it had ever happened before. At the dental factory in Croydon's Broad Green all the workers thought of Violet Murray. Their boss had come in to tell them that Violet wouldn't be in that day – but they already knew that. How could she come in when her son Edwin had died? Irene Raff thought of Violet's 'irrational fears' and couldn't believe how they had come true.

In the households of the bereaved, those who had telephones found that they never stopped ringing. Mainly it was friends and relatives, but often it was the press. Some parents took their handsets off the hook just to get some respite. Every household had visitors, most arriving with flowers. Bill Smith, a good friend of John Bradbery and his parents, drove to see them immediately and found them inconsolable. He had never seen such raw emotion – they were in utter shock. Realising he was out of his depth he asked their neighbour to contact their doctor and vicar. When they arrived Bill walked in a continuous circle in their back garden, choked with salty tears. Another man crying his eyes out was William Barr, the Green's next door neighbour. He wandered round his own garden, castigating himself for unfairly swearing at Quentin. It was too late now to say he was sorry.

The afternoon post brought letters of condolence from relatives and friends, trickles of a future flood of mail already being written by well-wishers who had names and addresses from the papers. Both the National Union of Teachers and the Croydon Head Teacher's Association wrote to Mrs Budd with sincere condolences, saying what an outstanding man her husband George had been and offering their full support to her in every way. Strangers also arrived at her home with offers of help. Realising she was now widowed and her husband's bank account 'locked', a member of the Salvation Army visited offering money to help tide her over. Other strangers were not welcome at all. Press reporters and photographers hung around hoping for new angles on the story, asking Margery questions about her husband's responsibility in taking the trip. She refused to be drawn as she saw elements of the press wanted to apportion blame to her husband and his colleague. Refusing to talk to the press Margery even had to close their windows and curtains as one snooping photographer climbed over their back gate and hid amongst their apple trees hoping for a shot. She was to lodge a formal complaint about media harassment but Mrs Budd was a lady with a high sense of duty and had something more important on her mind. Despite her own loss she wanted to write to all the parents. That day, in her curtained room, she drafted a letter which Geoff had insisted he and Thelma would help handwrite. With three master copies prepared they all sat at her dining room table and wrote 38 letters.

Someone unused to writing letters, least of all a letter of condolence, was Derek Meacher. Del sat down and composed a difficult letter to the family of his good friend Ed Murray. One of the last things that he had done was to lend his pocket chess set to Ed to take with him. To his surprise he had a handwritten reply from Ed's sister Patricia, recalling the happy evenings spent making the pigeon coop and saying that she and her parents agreed his letter had been one of the nicest they had received. Letter writing kept many people busy and Croydon's postmen carried bumper deliveries.

Croydon's clergy were also kept very busy, and it wasn't an easy task. David Gore's mother was visited by Revd Michael Cooper, a young clergyman who was very relieved to find a mutual friend with Mrs Gore, as he didn't know how he would cope. He had to find a way to offer comfort to a recently widowed mother who had now lost her son, as well. Life for some was very unfair and how could he square that with the Christian belief in a Loving God?

This was a particularly vexed question for which there was no immediate answer. Believers needed something offered to them that could help sooth their pain. Atheists needed a logical explanation – and some now railed irrationally with savage recriminations against a God they didn't believe in! Why had God allowed it to happen? Why hadn't God answered their fervent prayers? How could God allow a plane full of boys to smash into a mountain? Very few could comprehend that God wasn't involved in this terrible accident.

Many of Croydon's doctors came when specifically called, but had nothing in their bags to heal broken hearts. Some prescribed aspirins. Most prescribed sedatives. Some mothers unable to cope with their agony were sedated and asleep, and it was thought better to try to keep them that way. Geoffrey Green's mother was one. When Godfrey Winn called at her house she was 'prostrate on her bed'. A surprise interview suggested by Michael Parkinson of The Daily Express, Godfrey Winn was invited in by Geoffrey's married brother. His father was away, having to tend to the animals in his pet shop. They talked about Geoffrey, and then Godfrey Winn departed to see the other Green family. August was traditionally the month when news was usually in short supply, but the sentimentalist writer went away with enough material to write a long article entitled, *'The courage of the family who mourned a son yesterday.'* He too knew that 'nothing sells like emotion' – and there was oceans of it in Croydon.

In Norway preliminary identification of the victims had started, and the police there contacted Croydon Council to request the boy's dental records. Jean Cook was asked to search for them, and to make them ready to be flown out. Jean found it hard to see through her tears. Norman Cook, helping her, found it even harder because he knew all the boys.

Someone who might have wondered whether any of the smiling faces that she had seen, during her visit to Croydon, were any of the Lanfranc boys, was Queen Elizabeth. She was on holiday, cruising off Scotland's Western Isles. The message, sent from the royal yacht Britannia to the Minister of Aviation said*: 'I am shocked to learn of the plane disaster near Stavanger. My husband and I send our sincere sympathy to the families of those who have lost their lives. Elizabeth R.'*

Queen Elizabeth's relative, the King of Norway, sent a message of condolence to her, whilst the Prime Minister of Norway, Mr Gerdhardsen, wrote to Mr Macmillan saying*: 'Allow me to convey to you, sir, and through you, to the bereaved families, the most deep-felt sympathy of the Norwegian Government and the Norwegian people on the occasion of the tragic air disaster in the Norwegian mountains which has caused the untimely loss of so many young lives.'* Mr Macmillan replied thanking him for his kind message and ending *'I am sure that the families of those who so tragically lost their lives will be grateful, as I am, for your sympathy and that of the Norwegian people in this sad disaster.'* Considerate and sympathetic though these messages were, they meant little, at the time, for the grieving families. An all-consuming blackness had engulfed them.

The new (100th) Archbishop of Canterbury, Dr Ramsey, sent a telegram to Croydon Education Committee, saying*: 'I send my deepest sympathy to the town of Croydon in this appalling tragedy. May God comfort those in sorrow.'* Mr Richard Thompson, Parliamentary Secretary, Ministry of Works, and MP for Croydon South, was more practical. He telegraphed Croydon's Chief Education Officer, Mr. R. Wearing King, saying: *'Horrified and distressed by news of air disaster. Am immediately available for help if needed. Deepest sympathy from my wife and self to relatives.'* Practical support, rather than platitudes, was more helpful, and that day the awful responsibility of claiming on insurance for the lives of Lanfranc's victims was already being pursued.

Holding the rudder of Croydon Corporation (as he had done since 1937), was Croydon's Town Clerk, Ernest Taberner. He knew Norway well having married a Norwegian girl who he had met in Norway when he was serving in the Royal Navy during the 1914-1918 war. An efficient man he didn't waste any time before looking through their files, and no doubt with relief, finding a letter dated 25th July to the Phoenix Assurance Co. Ltd. It stated that a party of 34 boys and two masters would be visiting Stavanger, Norway from 9th to the 17th August 1961. Phoenix was swiftly contacted by telephone and notes were made of the conversation for Council members to read. In addition to the indemnity to the Corporation, amongst other things repatriation expenses for death were covered. Phoenix were 'officially' advised of the accident, stating that the Corporation felt that liability rested with the Aircraft Company, and/or the Travel Agency, but that should any liability rest with Croydon Corporation then Phoenix would indemnify the Corporation within the limits stated in the policy. Phoenix also agreed that in the event of the owners of the aircraft not meeting the cost of repatriation, or expense of parents travelling to Stavanger for a funeral, the insurance policy would cover it. Little did the Corporation know what a 'can of worms' they had opened. They thought that the insurance policy was in perfect order. After insurance cover, what principally concerned them were the funeral arrangements. Would a mass funeral take place in Norway? Or would it be in Croydon? Paternalistic plans that would take almost all decision making from the parents were already being visualised. This was leaked to the press and all the parents were horrified to read headlines saying, *'Norway may hold a mass burial'*.

Ex-Army Corporal Brenda Morris hadn't heard the radio news, nor seen the newspaper reports, when on her way home from Guildford Camp via London to North Wales, she visited her uncle and aunt in Walthamstow for the night. They had a television set, and during a special tea of salmon salad, her uncle turned on the 6.00pm news. The news reader spoke sombrely and a picture appeared of the crashed plane – and the boys. Brenda suddenly choked on her food and burst into tears… she knew these were the very boys that she had seen

The wreckage of Papa Mike on the cliff and top of Holtaheia. (E. Eriksson.)

Shattered fuselage of Papa Mike. (The National Archives of Norway.)

Crash investigators and rescuers examine the wreckage. (E. Eriksson.)

Investigators view the wreckage. (E. Eriksson.)

Locals gather near the cliff by the Bell-47 helicopter.

*Investigators Nils K. Jorstad, Colonel Johan Christie,
Police Inspector Gullbrand Nyhus, and police Chief Ravn-Tollefsen. (E. Eriksson.)*

Red Cross Hjelpekorps carry stretchers up the mountain.

Police help carry stretchers up the mountain.

Red Cross Hjelpekorps wait for the command to help.

Red Cross Hjelpekorps carry victim's bodies down the mountain.

Cortege of hearses and Norwegian Army trucks transport the coffins through Stavanger to Sola Airport.

The Red Cross unload the coffins at Sola Airport.

Kaare N. Hidle and Red Cross team place the coffins in the hangar.

The Commander of the Norwegian Air Force supervises before the ceremony at the hangar.

Army trucks and hearses at Sola hangar. Cunard Eagle Airway's Douglas D.C. 6 standing by.

at London Airport! Brenda explained to her bewildered relatives that her own flight had been horrendous and she'd expected to die... but *they* had instead. Those lovely boys... She knew she'd never forget them cheerfully waving goodbye.

As countless people cried themselves to sleep that night, many also knew that they would never forget the last moments they'd shared, either.

Meanwhile the objects of all their affections still lay where they had fallen. The Lanfranc boys, their masters, and the crew of Papa Mike, were all to spend a second night on Holtaheia. This time though they were not alone. They were being guarded.

Harold Bamberg finally went home after one of the worst days of his life. He sat down and vowed to himself that he would make sure that all his aeroplanes were as safe as possible. Aviation accidents happened. But he never wanted another.

Norway Friday 11th August

On Friday 11th August, whilst the 2nd Red Cross team assembled at Strand quay, the woodman who had kindly taken English boys Bill Cole and Roger Ives in for the night, led them back down through the forest, and all the way to the ferry. He had gone out of his way to be kind to them, as it was his way of showing his sorrow for the terrible accident that had befallen their fellow countrymen. He was not alone in expressing such sincere feelings. All over Norway, and especially in Stavanger, British people were receiving heartfelt sympathy.

Whilst Bill and Roger awaited the ferry, savouring their unexpected and unforgettable experience, the 2nd Red Cross team departed Stavanger at 1145 hours, aboard *MS Tau,* for an unexpected experience that they too would never forget. Sofus had selected emotionally strong young men, and had told them the enormity of what lay ahead, but nothing could have prepared them for the task. They began that day as young, carefree, individuals. They were to end it as mature adults.

Their coach, awaiting them at Tau, took them to Holta farm, from whence they immediately trekked up to their base camp. Walking up in single file, their body language showed this wasn't an innocuous training exercise. They didn't have to wait long before they were allowed to move up to the crash site. One volunteer was detailed to guard the tent, as stretcher bearers were to bring victims to this halfway point, whilst another was instructed to guard the barn at Holta, where the bodies would temporarily rest before being brought down to the road. This strategy was devised because the 2nd Red Cross team had been informed that local volunteers would assemble to help later in the day – once all the deceased had been recovered, wrapped, and placed on individual stretchers.

The rescue was carried out with exactitude. Each victim had been identified by a code of letters and numbers, and its position was marked on a map made by the Accident Commission. This was carefully noted before the Red Cross volunteers put each victim into a special paper body bag, and then on to a stretcher. Sofus Tønnessen, Rolf Ringe, and Anna Nordland, had this macabre task. A fourth person made sure each bag was marked with identical letters and numbers, in compliance with the Commission's sketches. Heavy rain had washed the rocks, making their job a little easier. The body bags on their stretchers were then carried by a group of four to the gathering place, where other volunteers wrapped the stretchers in plastic sheeting, ready for transport. The work was done efficiently, and was not interrupted until they had finished. Then they carried all the stretchers down to the base camp tent, to await the arrival of local stretcher bearers who had promised their help. Despite the extra manpower, there still were not enough helpers to carry all the stretchers down to Holta farm simultaneously, so transportation was organised in stages. From the base tent local men formed teams of two or four, and carried the stretchers as gently as possible down to Holta farm, before returning to help again. The Red Cross took it in turns to work in one hour shifts because they rapidly chilled in the strong wind on the mountain.

Kjell Terje Osmundsen and his father knew that the Red Cross would be bringing down the victims that day, and they went up to offer their help. Young Kjell was only allowed to help the rescue team by carrying some of their equipment, whilst his father helped as a fourth man. Walking down with his father and three other stretcher bearers, as they approached the stone-walled fields near Holta, an old man dressed in his Sunday best dark suit and white shirt, opened the gate for them. As they passed through, he turned towards the stretcher and solemnly removed his hat. This act of respect moved young Kjell. He had never seen anyone do this before. Until that moment the excitement of all that had happened at his home the previous day, plus now helping the Red Cross volunteers had seemed an adventure. But an old man sadly doffing his hat, unexpectedly connected him with reality. Lots of people had died. They were mainly boys just a little older than him. The shock of this realisation hit home.

The stretchers were guarded in Holta's barn, and finally, when all 39 victims had been safely brought down, they were placed on board three trucks hired to transport them to the quay at Tau. It had been a long and difficult job as each stretcher had to be brought down gently and with great respect so consequently, each return journey took two hours. It was late by the time that they finished, and all the helpers were thanked and offered a meal of stew, provided by Stavanger Kommune. Although they'd eaten little that day, few could do it justice.

The three trucks, commissioned by Rogaland Police, set off from Holta. One was driven by Adolf Skår, the other two by Leif and Kåre Østerhus. Alone in his cab, with stretchers bearing their tragic loads behind him, Kåre had difficulty blocking out unnerving apprehension. Normally the 12 kilometres to Tau ferry was a 15 minute trip, but that night, driving at a slow pace, the short journey seemed to go on and on. Thoughts about what he was carrying made the hairs on the back of Kåre's neck stand up, whilst his skin crept with goose bumps. He was relieved to arrive at Tau, where British Royal Marines waited to help unload.

Following behind in their coach, the weary Red Cross crews didn't feel like talking. Some were inwardly trying to deal with what they had experienced that day, others simply felt numb – but their job wasn't over. At Tau they helped the Royal Marines to load the stretchers aboard the two waiting boats. At 2300 hours they cast off for Stavanger.

Sitting by her window, watching the activity from their holiday apartment overlooking the dock at Tau, was Kirsti Nervik, a girl the same age as some of the Lanfranc boys. Kirsti's father, Olav Nervik, had returned from being a stretcher bearer late that evening and was disconsolate. Seeing the awful devastation and carrying the bodies of children his daughter's age, had depressed him deeply. Images flashed back before his eyes. One was of that lone high-heeled shoe and he confided this to Kirsti, who was saddened to think of its owner, the young stewardess. Whilst her father had been away at Holtaheia, Kirsti had sat at the window all day long watching the unusual goings on and she had seen the two military boats sail silently in. She watched as stretchers were carried from the trucks, and placed into the boats. Now she witnessed the boats slip from the quayside, and glide on a calm sea into the night. Kirsti kept watching until the glinting specks of their lights, reflected on the rolling black wake, disappeared. Her heart went with the boys, their teachers, and the air crew, as she thought of their families far away. It had been the saddest day she had ever spent at Tau – and one she would never forget.

On his way home to Østerhusbyholta, Kåre Østerhus shivered with relief at having delivered his awesome cargo, but he couldn't erase the spectre of Holtaheia from his mind or the realisation of what he had carried. He had played a small, but essential part in the tragedy, and needed to unburden himself, but no one realised his need to talk. Sleep for Kåre was hard to find that night. Re-occurring nightmares were to haunt him. He wasn't alone in this, for Anna Nordland was to suffer the same fate.

It was after midnight in Stavanger when the boats docked alongside the Harbour Master's Office, and the Red Cross helped place the stretchers on to five waiting trucks. Representatives from Stavanger Kommune, the British Consulate, the church, police authorities, and from the Stavanger Red Cross were waiting at the pier. The Dean of Stavanger, Dr. Christian Svanholm, held a short service of prayers. Anna Nordland had often recited 'Our Father' but never had it left her with such emotion as it did that dark, sinister night. Mayor Jan Johnsen and British Consul Mr. Colin Peck thanked all who had helped. The loaded trucks set off, and the Red Cross team joined cars that drove slowly to Stavanger Hospital, a police car leading the procession. Newsmen waited at the hospital where the Identification Commission, including two pathologists from the R.A.F. Institute of Pathology and Tropical Medicine, were to continue identification. Rogaland Police had thoughtfully detailed English speaking officers to be on duty. The journalists stood back as the stretchers were borne past them and reverently placed in the chapel. It was three thirty in the morning when the Red Cross crew were thanked for their exceptional efforts, and finally dismissed. There was no one to help salve the deep scars inflicted by the horrors they had experienced. They were expected to put it behind them. But no one involved could forget. Weary Rolfe Olaf Ringe sat by his young son's bed watching him whilst he slept; glad his lad was alive. Thoughts of other people's sons and what had happened to them tormented him. Many of the Red Cross rescuers felt unable to say much, or to eat, for days.

Sofus Tønnessen returned home worn out. He had had no sleep for two nights. On his doorstep was a circular wreath of white carnations with a central cross of red carnations. Attached was a card from the Stavanger Red Cross, saying 'Thank you All'. Exhausted physically, and emotionally, Sofus never made it to bed. As he undressed he laid his clothes on to a chair, collapsed into it, and was instantly asleep.

Friday 11th August – Belgium

Croydon Cemetery administrative assistant, 23 year old Chris Mitchell and his wife, were at a bus stop outside the Gare du Nord railway station in Brussels, waiting for a tram, when Chris read the headlines of the newspaper held by the man in front of him. Its banner *'La Mort du Lanfranc'* had caught his eye. A better view of the front page, covered in row after row of photographs of teenage boys, made him freeze. Horrified, Chris asked his wife if she thought there could be *another* Lanfranc somewhere. Fearing the worst, he dashed into the railway station and bought an English paper – and his heart sank. It was the school next door to Croydon Cemetery where he worked. He'd seen many of these boys, as the cemetery shared a boundary with the school, recognising them because many pupils passed the cemetery twice a day, whilst others took short cuts through, saving themselves half a mile walk. The news was unbelievable. One boy was the brother of an old school friend of his…. After a quick discussion they decided to cut short their holiday and return home to Croydon immediately. Chris Mitchell knew he was needed.

England Friday 11th August

In Croydon, all the parents who could bear to, read the newspapers for more information. The crash was still front page news, and associated stories spread into several inside pages as well. *'Norway's bells toll for the Viking children'*, *'MOUNTAIN OF SORROW'*, *'Holiday Britons join in cathedral prayers'*, – Daily Mail journalist Brian Groves' story made the front page headlines, and devastated relatives read the news of what had happened in Norway the previous day. It was as though it was a bad dream from which they would eventually awaken. Numbness, denial, elements of 'doubting Thomas' existed in their minds – how could they believe what had happened? Yet… they knew. They'd been told – *officially*. Only it was still impossible to believe.

Seeing photos of Red Cross volunteers carrying stretchers up a mountainside to bring down the boys bodies, helped provide 'evidence'. Seeing a rocky cliff face littered with smashed metal debris looked unreal. Was all that twisted metal once – their boy's plane? Reading further, there were paragraphs about the possible reasons for the crash, which besides bad weather included 'lost radio contact' and 'no radar'. These theories made no difference to the way they felt, theories were purely academic at this stage. What consumed them was the loss of their loved one. They hadn't the mental energy to grapple with what might have caused it. A 'Roll Call' of small portrait photographs of almost every victim, was spread across double inner pages. The wounds of each family were multiplied by seeing the faces of all the other boys. Their own loved one was simply that – one, amongst so many. This added to the sense of horror, but also offered a strange feeling of belonging. No family was alone. There were many more families suffering the same agony. The tiniest tendrils of a future 'safety net' of mutual understanding, unconnected threads at this early stage, were there.

Photos of each boy were augmented in the Croydon Advertiser with brief comments about them, made by teachers at Lanfranc. It was their 'last report'. All over Croydon, parents and siblings stood in empty bedrooms staring at vacant beds. Minds felt frozen, yet all thought the same thoughts. 'This was his bed. These were his clothes. Those were his books, models, sports equipment, stamp collection, assorted 'treasures'. These were tangibly his. They were here, so why wasn't he? It was impossible that he was 'gone'. Where? Where was he?' Some bedrooms were to become shrines – and remain so.

The citizens of Croydon were all deeply shocked and saddened. The tragedy affected almost everyone, for most people knew of at least one boy who had died. Junior school friends who had parted at eleven for secondary schools discovered old friends who had died. Two teenage sisters, Ann and Frances Samuel were inconsolable for 'little' Quentin with whom they walked to Winterbourne Junior School. Keith Alford was a Croydon boy on holiday in Luxembourg when he saw a picture of his old friend in a newspaper, and was very upset. Keith had sat next to Quentin at Winterbourne and had often listened to him happily singing 'Blue Moon'. Bill Cooper had been good mates with Alan Lee at Elmwood Road School and saw his friend's photo. He was doubly mortified because the photo showed Alan had a scar above his right eye, a scar for which he was innocently responsible. A playtime 'war game', when a stone pretend hand grenade was lobbed by Bill, at Alan hiding behind a dustbin, had gone horribly wrong – and left a permanent scar. They'd been good friends from the start, even sharing gobstoppers, taking it in turns to suck it down to the next colour, or sharing a stick of well chewed liquorice. And when Bill had broken a tooth Alan had tried hard to make him laugh, to forget the pain. Now Bill had a pain that Alan couldn't help alleviate. The pain was the loss of his friend Alan.

Mark Cottington was a Lanfranc boy with two paper rounds. He felt numb and in total disbelief as he delivered his papers in Thornton Heath. Of all the boys who had gone to Norway, there wasn't one bully or horrible boy amongst them – as he judged it. So many nice chaps had died. Why them? Other boys thought the same, and rued the fact that the 'nicest teachers' at Lanfranc had died.

Linda Arwood was on holiday in the country staying with relatives when they heard of the disaster, and she was horrified that it had happened to people from her home town. Then she found that her old school friend Lawrence Sims was a victim. She cried for him, later cutting an article from The Croydon Advertiser listing all the names of the dead, and keeping it as a grim memento. At her home in Buckinghamshire Lesley Corbin opened their daily newspaper and screamed, frightening her mother. Distraught, she'd seen small photos of her old Rockmount Primary School friends – David Hatchard, Richard Lawrence, Clifford Gaskin, and John Phelps. Her parents hid the papers after that and wouldn't let Lesley see the television news.

The Daily Express 'Photo News' published a half page article about Dennis Field. The poignant image of Dennis, trousers half rolled up, jacket slung over his shoulder, fishing rod in hand, was a tear jerker, especially as it was captioned *'He was too hard-up to fly with his friends. So he lived, while they died.'* Other papers picked up the fact that Colin Francis had pulled out to be a helper at a Scout Jamboree. Colin was now so deeply upset that a doctor had prescribed medication.

The fact that everyone's name and address was listed in newspapers meant that the trickle of condolence letters turned into a flood of letters from friends, neighbours, and total strangers. Impossible to reply to them all some parents put up white cards in their front windows thanking everyone living locally for their love and support. Most had to have cards printed with sentiments such as *'Mr and Mrs —— and Family, desire to convey to you their gratitude for your expression of sympathy and condolence in their great sorrow'* – simply in order to cope. Reading letters arriving by morning and afternoon post, and sending off cards in reply, filled in time which now hung heavily. All families felt as though they were in limbo. They had no idea what was happening across the North Sea. When would their loved ones be brought home?

Croydon Council had not been idle. Catching the evening post was an urgent letter to all Council members. A special Council Meeting to take place on Thursday 17th August in order to record the Council's grief at the loss of 34 boys and two masters from Lanfranc School, and the three members of the air crew, and to express their deep sympathy with the bereaved. Places were to be reserved under the public gallery for two members from each bereaved family. The Council had begun to make plans for Thursday 17th of August to be the day of the mass funeral – not in Norway but in Croydon. A letter was to be sent to parents the next day presenting a fait accompli – although personal preferences were, it was stated, to be considered.

A man who considered everyone else first, and placed himself last, was Tommy Fowle. His staff had rallied round and he knew that his ex-head boy Clive Grumett would help when he got home from holiday, but he was desolate, blaming himself as head of the school. That day he visited the parents of every one of his 'lost' boys. The Rotary Club had provided him with a car and driver to help with the heart-rending task. Visits were short and exquisitely painful, yet he pushed on to the end. When he arrived back from his forlorn tour he found that piles of telegrams awaited him. Headmasters, headmistresses, teachers, old boys, friends, strangers, and well-wishers from all over the world had sent messages of support. He was not alone.

Norway Saturday 12th August

At Stavanger's Memorial Hospital, the professional identification experts had worked through the night. Passports and personal effects helped identify some of the 39 bodies, dental records positively identified others. It was a gargantuan, grim task, and it wasn't over by daybreak.

Waking as though from a bad dream were the Red Cross 2nd team. Sofus Tønnessen awoke to find himself undressed, cold, and not in his bed. Others couldn't believe what they had done the previous day. No one wanted to talk about it – unless it was with each other. It hung over them like a dark cloud. Sofus knew that to preserve himself he had to get right away. He called a friend on a small island and said he was coming over. He just wanted to immerse himself in nothing but mindless fishing, until his equilibrium was restored and he could control the haunting images inside his head. He let Kaare Hidle know he had to escape right away. Kaare had been spared the worst aspect of the rescue, but felt the same devastation. Stavanger didn't feel the same to him anymore since the catastrophic death of so many young strangers – but he still had work to do.

Bill Cole and Roger Ives, lads almost the same age as the oldest of the Lanfranc boys, decided to get out of Stavanger where the tragedy has cast a heavy pall over the city. They took a boat and bus sight-seeing trip. Little realising they were heading towards Holtaheia, they were happily seated on the bus and feeling that they had left some of the sadness behind them when the bus driver stopped and pointed out Holtaheia, renamed for the moment as 'Sorgens Fjell' – 'Mountain of Sorrow'. The peak was too far away to make out any details. They had tried to get away to enjoy Rogaland's exceptional beauty but they'd found they couldn't escape the feelings of despair and sadness that afflicted everyone in the region. Had they been able to go to Holtaheia they would have found a cairn of stones at the foot of the cliff covered in bunches of flowers put there by local folk.

Flowers were sent to the Chapel of Rest at Stavanger Memorial Hospital too. Some were from a hospital worker who had lost her two sons during the war. She told a 'News of the World' reporter *'We feel deeply for the bereaved. The boys were so young. Life held out so much for them and now they can never return to* their loved ones. I know of their sorrow. Please tell these English people how grieved we are. We feel for them at this time.' The same reporter nabbed Captain John Sauvage who said, 'The co-operation of the Norwegians has been magnificent. I would like the parents to know that the Norwegians feel deeply for them and will do everything they can in the circumstances.'

The Stavanger Aftenblad received a letter that day. It came from 'A father'. The letter suggested that a memorial fund should be set up, the memorial to take the form of a stone cross. To initiate the fund he sent 50 kroner – £2.10s. a very generous sum of money at a time when few Norwegians were affluent.

Somewhere not far away a coffin maker was sadly finishing an unexpected and very large order.

England Saturday 12th August

In Croydon, notes made by the Town Clerk on the 11th took the form of a bulleted letter, received first post on the morning of Saturday 12th. The Cemeteries Superintendent, Mr Fowle, Police, Registrar of Births and Deaths, Coroner, Recorder, Members of Parliament, the Vicar of Croydon, and the Bishop of Croydon, were all recipients. The Vicar of Croydon was to arrange a Joint Funeral Service, possibly at the Parish Church, to be followed by committal services at the cemetery. The grave was to be 'of the parents' choice, or some kind of communal grave to be provided at the Council's expense. Lanfranc's school hall would be prepared to receive the coffins – with someone to guard them, the suggestion being the local Territorial Unit augmented by Civil Defence volunteers. A meeting, to discuss details of any funeral service, was arranged for that day.

At the time of the meeting there was no definite information as to when the bodies would be returned to Croydon, but it was decided to give the press a statement that the Lanfranc School Hall was being prepared for their reception. The Council were already making preparations for burial (subject to individual parent's wishes), in a joint grave at Mitcham Road cemetery, the committal service to be preceded by a service at the Parish Church.

It was agreed that the leader of the National and Local Government Officers (NALGO) – a British trade union of white collar workers, was to be asked if he could arrange for volunteers to act as administrative officers in charge of Lanfranc School, during the time the bodies were there. Small but important details, such as the fact that a vase of flowers would be placed at the foot of each coffin were minuted, plus the addendum that parent's wreaths could be placed on the top. It was decided that the school would be open from 9.00am until 9.00pm, but admission would be restricted as far as possible to relatives of the deceased and so, for this purpose, some kind of ticket or pass would be issued. The general public was not to be admitted, and police would remain on duty there to preserve order. Special arrangements were to be made for the press to see the coffins, and photographs would be permitted, but this would be at a time when the relatives were not there. The Vicar of Croydon asked that he be notified as soon as it was known that the bodies were on their way to Lanfranc, as he wished to arrange for each of them to be received at the school by a member of the clergy. Croydon Council were planning a ceremonial occasion with as much scrupulous attention to detail as the Queen's visit the previous year, but they had one big problem – they didn't know when Lanfranc's boys and masters would be coming home. They could only set a provisional date for the funeral, but they hoped that it would be at 3.00pm on Thursday 17th August.

In the absence of the Mayor, Alderman Mrs Catherine Kettle, a letter was sent on behalf of her and the Council, to the parents, by Ernest Taberner. As a Solicitor as well as Town Clerk, Ernest Taberner was noted for his capabilities in getting straight to the nub of the matter. In his letter he swiftly expressed their jointly felt deep sympathy; said that the boy's medical records had been sent to Norway; notified them that the Council were planning to make Lanfranc School Hall ready to receive the coffins prior to a funeral service at Croydon Parish Church, followed by a committal at Mitcham Road Cemetery – on a date still to be fixed. Ernest Taberner had held talks with Cemetery Superintendent Len Evans and he hoped that their plans would meet with parent's wishes. Taberner also stated that the Council 'will provide a grave and later will erect and maintain a suitable memorial.' An invitation was given to attend a meeting on the evening of Thursday 17th 'in order to pay tribute to the boys and staff who died in Norway'. With great efficiency these caught the next post and were delivered that day. Peter Stacey's parents, and Gregory Allen's mother, replied the same day, reserving tickets for the scheduled meeting and expressing their gratitude for the difficult work being undertaken by the Council.

Was it because Croydon Council comprehended the devastation of the parents and believed that in such shocking circumstances they should take command? Or was it simply a paternalistic approach and a desire to acquit themselves well as a civic authority? The absence of Mrs Kettle may have made a difference to the decision taking. Had she been immediately at the helm, some feminine sensitivity might have softened masculine logistics. Whatever the reasoning, parents were *not* fully consulted, and many found themselves steamrollered into accepting a mass funeral which, under other circumstances, they wouldn't have considered. Widow, Mrs Boyes, alone amongst the parents, insisted her son Peter would not share in the mass burial but be laid to rest with his recently deceased father. The mother of John Beacham insisted that he would be buried with his father at his elder brother's Parish Church in Somerset. For the majority, however, Croydon's plans met with grateful acceptance, because they were still too shocked by the horror of the tragedy to think practically for themselves.

At Lanfranc School, meanwhile, letters had been sent out to senior boys and recent old boys. Clive Grumett arrived home from holiday to find a message left with a neighbour, asking that he report to school as soon as possible. Lanfranc was an unhappy swarm of activity, with journalists buzzing around hoping to pull something from the honey pot to profitably sell. One, seeing a boy arrive, followed him into George Budd's biology laboratory. George's animals had to be fed, watered, and their cages cleaned. Realising his luck, the reporter composed a picture of one of his volunteer helpers, looking solemnly pensive, by a pet rat's cage. He snapped a touching image which he captioned 'The Lost World of George Budd.'

England Sunday 13th August

Sunday 13th August was like no other Sunday in Croydon. Churches of all denominations were invariably well attended, but this day they were packed. Townsfolk who hadn't been inside a church for years found themselves drawn to fellowship. In all the Parish churches, each Anglican vicar's address should have been a sermon based upon the prescribed Gospel reading. In other churches sermons and addresses would have covered diverse Christian subjects worthy of contemplation. But in all Christian meeting places that day the address centred upon the tragedy, and it was the hardest discourse each minister had ever had to give. Congregations of solemn people, women and girls blotting tears with handkerchiefs, men and boys blowing their noses, listened attentively. They sought reasons, hoped for answers, needed consolation. Many families who had lost sons went to church that day. Some sat ram-rod straight, controlling emotion, others were bent over, weeping. The perplexing question in everyone's mind, not least the minister's was – where did God fit in to all this? There seemed to be no logical answer but the Christian message of Love and Hope was given, and many left comforted. Croydon's population were emotionally fully occupied with what had befallen their town. The fact that East Germany had closed its border with West Germany, and that a barbed-wire boundary was being erected in Berlin, went virtually unnoticed.

Two young boys felt that *they* were virtually unnoticed. Both had lost their fathers. Tim Budd in Haslemere felt in limbo, cut off from his school friends and without his toys and hobbies. He'd not only lost his father but he felt deprived of his mother – and he needed her. He'd asked his Aunt Vi if he could go home and do something to help, but she had said it was better to stay with her so his mother had one less thing to worry about. Five year old Simon Karginoff in Camberley also felt deprived of his mother, except she was with him. Mrs Watts could not cope with the death of her wonderful husband. He had been a decorated hero. He had miraculously survived all the years of the war as a fighter pilot. Why had he been taken from her? It didn't seem to matter that she had a lovely son, she wanted her husband. Simon felt alone.

Writing to Mr Fowle that Sunday was Sir John Walker, H.M. Ambassador, from the British Embassy in Oslo. Since the night of the 9th of August Sir John had been kept very busy.

My dear Headmaster,

On August 10th I sent through the Foreign office a message of condolence to the parents and school friends of those who lost their lives in the tragic crash near Stavanger. I can now write a little more fully to you and, through you, to the bereaved parents and other relatives, about the accident and reactions here to it.

The Norwegians are a very kindly people with a very strong sense of family and a deeply-rooted friendship towards Britain. The feeling of personal loss and sorrow of all the people in and around Stavanger reflects the especially close ties with Britain in that area which mourned as if the boys and masters were beloved members of local families. In Oslo too, and elsewhere in Norway, the same feelings of grievous sorrow and warm sympathy are evident everywhere.

My own distress over the accident was all the more poignant when I saw the wreckage. If it is any comfort to the stricken families, I would ask you to assure them that death was instantaneous and must have taken the boys, the two masters – and the crew – completely unawares.

I hope to enclose with this letter the English translation of the Bishop of Stavanger's Sermon at the Memorial Service in Stavanger Cathedral. He promised to send me a copy as I thought that the bereaved parents might wish to read it and it expresses so well the deep feelings of sympathy and grief of us all over here, British and Norwegians alike.

I have already personally thanked the Mayor of Stavanger and other authorities for all they have done with such willingness and understanding to deal with matters arising here out of the disaster, but I will do so again when I attend the embarkation ceremony.

I enclose a copy of this letter in case you may wish to send one to the Mayor of Croydon.

Yours sincerely,
John Walker. H.M. Ambassador.

Norway Sunday 13th August

In Rogaland on Sunday 13th August all flags still flew at half-mast. Throughout Norway more people than normal attended the state Norwegian Lutheran church, a Protestant Church dating back to the Reformation, which shared much in common with the Anglican Church. The difficult subject of each Minister's address was the plane crash on Holtaheia. Many men of God were hard put to give any comprehensible explanation as to 'Why?' There simply wasn't an answer. Nevertheless heart-felt words were said that permeated, and provided food for sorrowing souls. Mrs Synnove Iversen, a mother from Oslo who felt a particularly empathy for the mothers of the boys, and was at a loss, wrote a letter which she sent to the BBC. It concluded *'Now I want to weep with you. I believe that in some ways it will help, but it is as though something has gone numb inside me. I want to believe there is a God, one who defends the defenceless – so why do such things happen? How I wish I could say some comforting words to you who have been so sorrow-stricken. But what can one say when one refuses to understand what has happened. My message is only to let you know I feel so deeply with you all.'*

Norway Monday 14th August

On Monday 39 empty coffins of varying sizes were brought in to Stavanger's Memorial Hospital. Someone saw to it that flowers were obtained. Plaques bearing each victim's name were engraved, and fixed on the correct casket, as gradually the white wooden boxes received their occupants, and small bunches of delicate flowers affixed by a team of ladies – mothers themselves. As leader of the Red Cross Hjelpekorps, Kaare Hidle had requested that they should be the ones to accompany the coffins to Sola airport, and assist there. The young Red Cross leader was deeply upset by all that he had seen, but was determined that the Red Cross would finish the job. His city of Stavanger didn't feel the same to him now. How could it? He was living through a continuing nightmare.

England Monday 14th August

From all over Britain and the World, letters of condolence were received by Croydon Council. Besides the Queen, Lord Geoffrey Fisher (who had officially opened Lanfranc School) sent a message. Other dignitaries, including the Lord Lieutenant of Surrey, Sir Peter Thorneycroft Minister of Aviation, Sir David Eccles Minister of Education, the Mayor of Stavanger, and the Municipality of Arnhem in Holland. Members of Parliament, Chairmen of Companies, Organisations and Societies, Churches, Synagogues, Town's Women's Guilds, Newspapers, Trade Unions, 72 Mayors or leaders of Urban District Councils the length and breadth of Britain, and 51 private individuals also wrote, many of them sending donations for a memorial fund. The response to the air crash was as heartfelt as it was diverse.

Four Indian journalists on a guest visit to the U.K. sent their deepest sympathy. A Croydon father wrote *'I went to church twice this morning... I am not a church man, but my daughter went to Lanfranc...'* An anonymous message accompanying a money order for £4/10/-d came from Woolwich. From Dreghorn Camp, Edinburgh, a Norwegian Major and his men taking part in the Edinburgh Tattoo sent their condolences. The Daily Mirror Newspapers Publishing Chapel wrote *'In our work as a National Newspaper we have on many occasions been confronted with news of tragic events, but the plane accident which has struck such a blow to you and the people of your borough has been one of the worst tragedies we have had to publish for many years...'* The C.O. of No.66 Croydon Squadron A.T.C. wrote, *'...sympathy and grief in what can only be described as one of the worst aviation accidents ever to have happened to such young passengers...'* The Bishop of Coventry wrote, *'...As a former Bishop of Croydon I feel a particular sense of loss and want to express to you a very deep sympathy.'* The Secretary of the Willesden Free Church who had listened to each news bulletin until hopes of finding survivors had gone wrote, *'It is beyond our powers of understanding to know why such things happen and we feel helpless and unhappy at not being able to do something to help you, but our Prayers and out thoughts are with you....'*. A teacher in Port Talbot, Wales wrote, *'...I have taken groups of pupils on visits to the Continent and have always spent an anxious time until the boys and girls are safely back with their families, so that the shock of this disaster has moved me deeply...'* a contribution to a fund was sent with the letter. Also from Wales, the Ebbwvale Branch of Plaid Cymru prayed that the disaster would not affect other *'goodwill visits made by your authority to other countries.'* A cable from the President of the Indian Youth Congress in New Delhi said, *'...May God Bless the innocent souls.'* Young and old wrote letters, from a teenager in Nottinghamshire, to old folk in a home on the Isle of Wight. From big places, such as the Metropolitan Borough of St Pancras whose Mayor wrote, *'...We were all horrified to hear of this sudden violent and devastating crash which has deprived us of so many of our youngsters on the threshold of their manhood...'* to small places, such as a letter from a villager in Itchen Abbas who wrote, *'The sympathy of everyone in the country is with Croydon and even a small village like this feels involved.'* A letter came from Kenya, another from New Zealand, one from Czechoslovak Airlines, another from a mother and daughter who wanted to relatives to know that they were praying for them. Another from a husband and wife who wrote, '*they must know that the whole nation is mourning with them and the tears of all parents of children mingle with theirs.*' From Paignton in Devon, home of stewardess Susan Endicott, the Chairman of the Council sent their deepest sympathy, whilst Mrs Nina Smalley, widow of First Officer Smalley wrote, '*Please convey to all my grateful thanks on behalf of myself and my small daughter to the townspeople of Croydon for their expression of sympathy at this time. Will you please tell the parents of the boys and masters that they are in our thoughts.*'

Perhaps the most poignant messages came from places that had suffered similar disasters. The Deputy Governor of the Isle of Man wrote sympathetically, remembering their own loss in the 'Winter Hill Disaster' when 35 people from the Isle of Man died (and seven survived) when their plane crashed in bad weather en route to Manchester. Most heartfelt, however, was a message from the Mayor of Heilbronn on the Neckar, in Baden-Wurttemberg, Germany. It said '*With great distress, I have heard of the terrible accident when over 34 scholars and two teachers from one of your schools in Croydon lost their lives. As I understand it, the plane flew into a mountain peak in a storm and was completely destroyed. In this way, an unexpected fate extinguished the lives of these scholars and teachers. We in Heilbronn can appreciate the pain which this catastrophe has called forth, especially in the parents, but most certainly in the whole population. It is a similar fate which many of the parents of our town suffered at Easter 1954, when 10 scholars and three teachers from one of our schools lost their lives in a snow storm, in the Dachstein district of Austria, during a mountain climbing expedition. It is because of this, as we have experienced something similar, that we feel so much for you and I should like to convey to you, on behalf of my Council and the whole population of my town, our deeply felt sympathy. I ask you to convey to the suffering parents and to the school our participation in their sorrow.*' It was 16 years since WWII had ended and many fathers had fought and been wounded for Britain. To receive such a compassionate response from Germany touched many of them deeply. The response to the tragedy was universal and knew no barriers. Enemies once, now these parents felt a mutual sympathy, as Berlin's Brandenburg Gate was locked shut.

Two people who hoped to gain some peace from news of the division of Berlin were Margery and Geoff Budd, who felt that with this worrying world news the media might leave them alone. They had gone to Haslemere to see Tim and Margery's sister, Vi, for two days. Margery found her young son dejected whilst her sister was at a loss to know how to comfort her. Geoff constructed his cousin's train set to amuse his young brother. Young though he was Tim wanted to attend his father's funeral, but Margery was adamant that such a mass funeral was no place for a nine year old. She decided for the best, but she was wrong.

From Monday 14th, as decisions were gradually made both in Norway and Croydon, staff working at the cemetery office were struck by the co-operation that they were getting from all sorts of people. The bodies of the victims were to be flown home. Funeral Directors from all over London offered their hearses to transport the coffins from Gatwick airport. Croydon taxi drivers, at the behest of Mr. F. Goold a taxi driver at East Croydon Station, offered their vehicles and drivers for whatever purpose they were required. Lanfranc school hall was to be used as a Chapel of Rest, and the coffins were to rest on dinner tables. The cemetery office had no idea where dark cloth to cover the tables would come from, but Ernest Taberner turned up trumps. He talked to the managing director of Allders store, and hundreds of yards of cloth appeared within the hour. Everyone wanted to do whatever they could to assist. Reg Searle, the National Union of Public Employees (NUPE) shop steward at the cemetery and crematorium, told Superintendent Len Evans that his men would work all the hours under the sun, and not accept overtime payments. Time was short and offers of help were gratefully received.

The mass grave site selected was a plot near the cemetery's Thornton Road gates, by the Commonwealth War Graves Commission enclosure, and not far from the Civilian War Dead area. Unfortunately this plot was in the middle of a building site because a new mortuary was being built next to where the mass grave would be. Cemetery staff had spent months apologising for this and now, the largest funeral that Croydon had ever seen, was to take place there. This was a big problem but the builders also wanted to help, and they offered to use the mechanical plant they had on site to dig the grave.

A conference took place at the Council offices on Monday 14th at which the Vicar of Croydon, Cemetery Superintendant, Police, and Education department attended. Administrative details had to be arranged so that a mass funeral for Croydon's victims could run smoothly. The school hall had to be prepared for the reception of the coffins on Wednesday 16th, which a London firm of Undertakers, Messrs. Kenyons Ltd., had been instructed by Cunard Eagle Airways to arrange. Visitors to the school hall, to be open from 9.00am until 9.00pm, was to be restricted to relatives and members of Lanfranc staff only, and for this purpose, special cards would be distributed. Clergy were to be in attendance, and any member of the clergy was to be admitted. Special arrangements were to be made for the press to visit briefly at a time when grieving relatives weren't there. A question was raised as to whether relatives were allowed to look inside the coffins. The answer was an emphatic – NO! Arrangements for flowers were made, parent's wreaths to be placed with the individual coffins, and lists of senders to be kept for each recipient. The logistics were gone through in infinite detail, and two marquees were ordered to contain the floral tributes. The police had estimated that 2000 wreaths were expected. Croydon florists bought more and more flowers as orders mounted. Several really creative florists had innovative ideas. Throughout Croydon the stops were being pulled out, in order to equate the planned funeral with the depth of grief felt.

England Tuesday 15th August

A time of limbo existed for the parents and their families. Some managed to cope with the long wait, others did not. Tony Green noted in his diary that whilst his mother was *'bearing up well under the strain'* his father was *'very cut up about it'*. It seemed to Tony as though he was living in a bad dream yet there was so much tangible evidence that it was true. This day he wrote, *'We are still being flooded with letters from friends, relatives and absolute strangers offering their condolences. I posted 73 letters of thanks today.'* One of these was to a Nigerian student, Gide Arogundadi, who had recently arrived to study in London. A letter of thanks to him contained an invitation to Tea. Strangers were being kind, so it was a time to be kind to strangers.

Edward Prosper's parents were so overwhelmed by the public's sympathy that they wrote to The Daily Express 'Letters' column, expressing sincere thanks for all the letters they'd received. *'They have been a great consolation in our hour of stress. I am sure we speak on behalf of all the parents of the lost boys.'*

That morning, in the Town Hall, two things happened. A fund to provide a memorial for the boys was opened, and the Mayor had stated that the form of the memorial was to be decided in consultation with Lanfranc's headmaster Mr Fowle. Even before the fund was opened, collections had been held in offices and shops in many parts of town, and money for Lanfranc was now pouring in. A letter to all the parents was being typed, telling them of the lying in at Lanfranc School Hall, and of the funeral arrangements. *'May I again express our sympathy with you at this very trying time'*, wrote Ernest Taberner. The hard pressed, highly efficient Town Clerk hoped that he and the Council staff had planned everything to the last detail. Alderman Mrs Catherine Kettle, Mayor of Croydon, was expected back that day, and in her absence he had endeavoured to do a good job. Now it was a case of awaiting the coffins that were to be flown from Norway late that night, arriving in the early hours at Gatwick. The press were not to know any details in order to keep this 'home-coming' as dignified as possible.

Dignity was observed with a wordless tribute from 5,000 supporters of Crystal Palace Football Club who stood in silence, before singing 'Abide with me'. The Lanfranc boys would have liked that… although they preferred saluting the winning football team. With their sense of fair play they would have cheered Conrad Schumann, the 19 year old East German border guard, whose leaping figure, jumping over the barbed wire into West Berlin, became an icon for freedom. East-West relations had chilled further.

Norway Tuesday 15th August

On Tuesday 15th the coffins were taken from Stavanger Hospital to Sola airport, from whence they were to be flown to Gatwick Airport, in Surrey. Mr. W. D. Hiddleston, of J.H. Kenyon, Ltd., the London firm of Funeral Undertakers, arrived at the Hospital in Stavanger three quarters of an hour before the time planned to start, and found that everything was ready. Inside the Hospital grounds, the main part of the cortege, consisting of four hearses and nine military trucks, was drawn up ready to set out on the journey to Sola Airport. Outside the Hospital seven limousines waited.

Everybody was early, and while they waited Mr Hiddleston chatted to the Bishop of Stavanger and his Dean. He was introduced to the Mayor and other Civic dignitaries, and talked to the Police officials that he had already met, whilst everyone waited for the arrival of the British Ambassador, Sir John Walker. Outside the hospital a crowd had gathered in the streets, and Mr. Hiddleston was struck by their absolute silence. Inside the grounds everyone conversed in low tones: outside it seemed that nobody spoke at all, and being used to London crowds and public processions, he was deeply moved.

The arrival of Her Majesty's Ambassador was the signal for the procession to leave, and exactly at 8.15pm (as arranged at a conference he had attended the previous afternoon), the first hearse drove out and led the way to the Airport.

Two hearses led the way, followed by the Army trucks with Union Jack-draped coffins in each one. Then followed the final two hearses, and the limousines which carried the Bishop and his party, the Ambassador with British Army, Naval, and Air Force representatives, the Consul from Bergen, the Vice Consul from Stavanger, representatives of the Norwegian Government, Civic representatives from Stavanger, Red Cross, and Police. Mr Hiddleston travelled in the last car with Captain Sauvage and Captain Henderson of Cunard Eagle Airline Ltd, who had come to fly their deceased passengers and colleagues' home to Gatwick.

As they drove away, Hiddleston was struck by all the Norwegian flags flying at half-mast – not realising it was a familiar sight in the town since the accident. He knew that the population of Stavanger wasn't large, but felt sure that it turned out in full force that night. Before they had gone very far he sensed that the people had not turned out to witness a spectacle as normal crowds do. He could see no pushing, or clambering on to vantage points: no pointing: no lifting up of children or any thoughtless demonstration. The crowd was utterly quiet. Bill Cole and Roger Ives stood silently with them.

All the way out of town the same prevailed, and when the cortege left the city's streets behind, he found that this was not the end. From houses which bordered the twelve mile journey to the airport, the occupants had emerged to stand outside their gates. Cars had pulled right off the road, often on to the roadside paths, and their passengers stood alongside them. Norwegian soldiers and sailors stood to attention, and saluted as the cortege passed. And along the road alongside a lake about six miles out of town, two fishermen had drawn their boat up on the shore and stood to attention beside it.

Close to the airport the retinue passed a house where young mother Guro Skjæveland, her son and mother, had all been happily playing. Now they stood silent by their fence as the black cars and trucks slowly passed by. Guro's thoughts went to the families of the deceased, and to the tragedy of the many lives that were lost. She felt the sadness, and the solemnity of the occasion, and sensed that it was almost beautiful. They all remained silent long after the procession had passed.

Mr Hiddleston found the whole journey moving, and memorable.

It was getting dark when they arrived at the airport, and as the procession left the road and set off across the sweeping perimeter road, he could see the grey bulk of the hangar in the distance, and the wings of the waiting aircraft against the sky. By the time he had got out of his car and walked over to the hangar, the first ten coffins had already been taken out and placed inside the building.

He was aware that the Red Cross had requested that their young members be allowed to unload the coffins, and now Hiddleston stood in the doorway of the hangar and watched them, under the leadership of Kaare Hidle, perform this duty with the precision of guardsmen, and without a single word of command. Each coffin was carried into the hangar through a guard of honour of teenage Norwegian Red Cross boys and girls and lowered gently and precisely inside an enclosure which had been roped off in the middle of the hangar. Each traditional white coffin had a spray of red, white, and blue flowers from Stavanger Kommune on its lid, and eight small sprays of flowers from Strand Kommune fixed around the sides – the identical colours of Norway and Britain.

All arrangements at the Airport had been supervised by the Commander of the Norwegian Air Force, and Hiddleston watched with admiration for the efficiency with which these were carried out. He felt nothing but praise for them. He was also impressed by the silence which prevailed, for so much was being done but there was hardly a sound to be heard. Eventually all the coffins were laid out in the central enclosure. A dais had been built facing the doors and at the foot of this Hiddleston and helpers displayed wreaths with handwritten cards from the British Ambassador in Oslo, British Consul in Bergen, British Vice Consul in Stavanger, Norwegian Government, Local authorities and Education department, and the Red Cross. The British Club in Stavanger wrote *'Our deepest sympathy in this time of sadness. May God give you strength to overcome it.'* Mr Hiddleston's eyes were finally drawn to a simple spray of flowers with a card saying simply, *'From a Mother'*. He was considerably moved.

Through the open doors of the hangar he saw a stream of headlights approaching from the distance where the entrance of the airfield lay. Car after car drove up, and in a very few minutes the hangar was filled with people. They moved in quietly and crowded up to the rope enclosure, where they stood silently and waited.

The Bishop with his attendant Ministers led the procession from the back of the hangar, followed by the Ambassador with his Army, Naval, and Air Force attendants, and the Norwegian officials who took up positions on each side of the dais, facing the open doors where the waiting aircraft stood outside in the darkness. He read the service in English, and everyone joined in the Lord's Prayer. It was a short service but shared in its deepest sense by everyone there.

At its conclusion, the Bishop addressed the assembly, asking them to disperse as soon as possible, so that the coffins could be loaded on to the aircraft. Then he turned and led his party to a room at the back of the hangar. The crowd melted away almost immediately, and in a very short time there was no one in the hangar but the Red Cross bearer party and a few others, and the carrying out of the coffins went on diligently and quietly until the hangar was empty.

Outside the hangar, while the engines of the plane warmed up, Mr Hiddleston talked to the Bishop who said that on Thursday, when the mass funeral took place in Croydon, Stavanger's bells would toll throughout the service, and that afterwards all the flags would be raised again. As they talked the aircraft swivelled round and moved to the head of the runway.

Everyone in the small party waited silently while it remained poised to take off, its wingtip lights winking in the dark. When it eventually took to the air they watched the lights grow more distant in the night sky until they could see them no more. Only then did they turn away.

Mr. Hiddleston was so moved by this experience, and so vividly was it imprinted, that he made a written record so that Croydon's Council could know the incredible care and love that all in Stavanger, especially the young Red Cross members, had shown towards the Lanfranc boys and masters, and the crew of Papa Mike. Their mortal remains had been accorded every respect and dignity. Commendable in every single way, the people of Norway and of Stavanger and Strand in particular, had all shown themselves in their finest colours. They had shown compassion for complete strangers.

England Wednesday 16th August

In the early hours of Tuesday morning the Cunard Eagle Airways plane carrying the coffins landed at Gatwick airport. The tragic cargo was solemnly unloaded into hearses, kindly provided by numerous firms of undertakers whose men had willingly volunteered.

The journey of the coffins from Gatwick to Croydon was particularly moving. Although the media had been asked not to publicise it, somehow thousands of people heard about the cortege. They lined the roads in silent tribute all the way from the airport, through Redhill and on to Croydon, where the huge black cars moved through the sleeping town, past policemen at attention, and workers who removed their caps. The last part of the journey was along Mitcham Road and here, Patricia Reygate, from Lanfranc Girl's School, was awoken by her parents to see the procession pass their house. They left her younger brother Graham asleep, as it would have distressed him too much to have witnessed his old school friends passing by.

So 'The Lanfranc Boys' came home to their school that they had left so joyfully at the end of term, less than three weeks before. A policeman on duty at the gate stood smartly to attention and bowed his head. School caretaker John Hansford turned on the lights at 2.45 a.m. and one hour later the last of the coffins were set down. Tables from the school dining room became their biers, shrouded in dark cloth. The Vicar of Croydon, Canon Warren Hunt, together with two clergymen, received the coffins each of them prayerfully precessed to its place. A short service was then held. Together in death, each Lanfranc boy was nevertheless partly separated by a hospital screen of incongruously cheerful floral chintz. A vase of white chrysanthemums was placed at the foot of each coffin and, arranged alphabetically, each boy's place was named to make it easy for relatives to find. The flowers from Norway still adorned each casket, which had on its raised lid a simple cross, and a plaque with the name of the deceased. The Norwegians could not have treated the boys better. Now it was Croydon's turn. An altar with ornately embroidered altar cover stood at the top of the hall; on it a cross and two large candles; behind green foliage. Vases of gladioli stood at each side. Everything was made ready by Lanfranc's staff and the undertakers in a hushed hall which had last resounded to raucous voices and the dash of skidding feet. Now all was sepulchral, and helpers tip-toed quietly. Undertakers inured to sadness wiped away tears. Many, like Robert Powell and Mr. Ottewell, both Croydon undertakers, thought of their own children – who were the same age. This wasn't the way things should be… 'Three score years and ten' was what most people anticipated and deserved. Carrying 34 teenagers and two young masters home for burial wasn't what they were used to at all. They left for their homes after dawn, totally dispirited.

As the town awakened every shop and market stall put up a card saying 'Closed between 3 and 3.30p.m Thursday.' Croydon's florists had been to Covent Garden and their shops were overflowing. No one could find space to stand in, for all the buckets and boxes of flowers. Florist Mrs Rose Cuff had returned from her annual seaside holiday specially to help. Some wreaths had been made the night before, but orders kept coming, so one florist at Thornton Heath Pond stood their wreaths outside the shop – causing many a passer-by to reach for their handkerchief. People talked of nothing else, and the town bore signs similar to a mining community at a pit disaster.

At Lanfranc, meanwhile, the press who had waited patiently were allowed in to take photos before any parents arrived. In the foyer of the school, photographs of cricket and football teams adorned the walls. A keen cricketer with ambitions to play for Yorkshire, Michael Parkinson looked at the smiling young players in their whites and caps, and knew that some of them were now in the darkened hall. Trevor Condell, John Wells, Richard Lawrence… all hopefuls for Surrey Cricket Club. He decided to caption his story 'Hall of Sorrow'. Michael Parkinson was one of several famous journalists that came that day, absorbed the sad ambience, and left to write their stories.

Clive Grumett and other recent old boys of Lanfranc, plus the next year's team of prefects under new School Captain, Dave Keenan, had come to help. With guidance from Norman Cook they stood ready to open doors, act as ushers, and carry wreaths to the right location. In the 200-ft long marquee outside, hundreds of wreaths were to be laid in little plots allotted to each of the masters and boys. Then the wreaths began to arrive. A cricket bat made of flowers in memory of Trevor Condell came from 'the boys and girls of Greenside Road' his home. Lawrence Sims, who lived in Stanley Grove, West Croydon, was remembered by a bicycle made of flowers 'from local boys'. For John Wells, there were two cricket bats and a wicket. Dave Keenan carried wreath after wreath into the heady atmosphere of the marquee and felt himself enveloped by the mixed scent of all the flowers.

One of the first visitors to the school was the Mayor of Croydon, Alderman Mrs. C. P. Kettle, home at last, and already with a plan in mind to set up a public fund for the boys. She was greeted by a weary Canon Warren Hunt, who escorted her into the curtained hall. A constant retinue of parents followed. Each family had waited in trepidation for this moment but could scarcely believe it was happening. They had all been in this hall in happy times – so what were they doing here now? The coffins resting on their tables seemed grotesque. It was a terrible shock to see *so many* coffins together! Quietly each set of relatives were led to 'their' cubicle, where their loved one's coffin lay. They touched the casket, ran their hands over the smooth white-painted surface, stroking the wood as if they were caressing their dear one. How could they believe he was in there? Many found it hard to believe – or to accept.

Susan Green couldn't. How did they know that this was Geoff? She wanted to open the coffin to make sure because she felt sure it must be a terrible mistake. Her namesake Rosalind felt the same when her family visited in the next cubicle. They all stood by Quentin's coffin not believing he could be inside. Rosalind

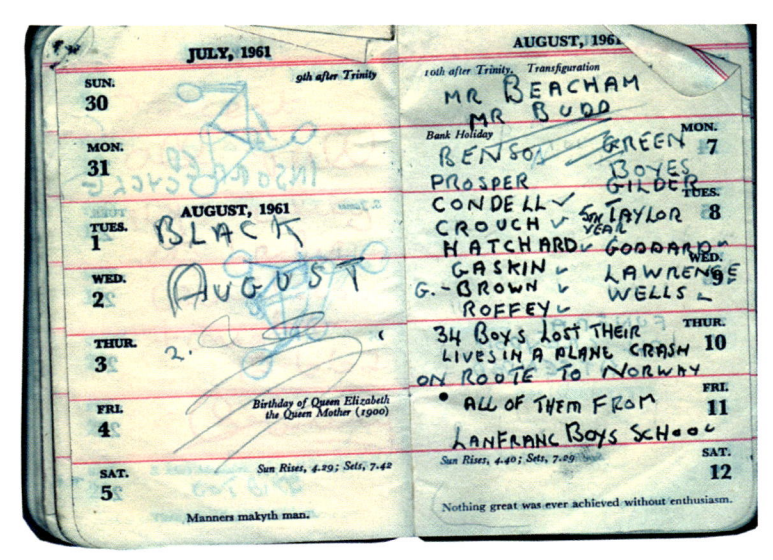

Leslie Bentley's Diary. 'Black August'.

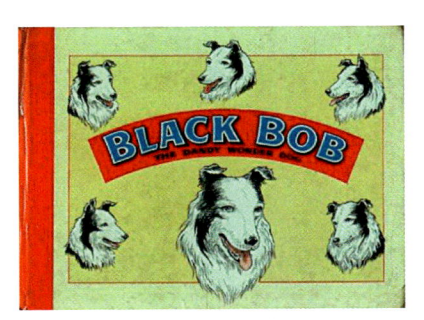

Black Bob, the last bedtime story read by Capt. Philip Watts.

A treasured memento – Gregory's ram

The Scout Jamboree first day cover that awaited collection.

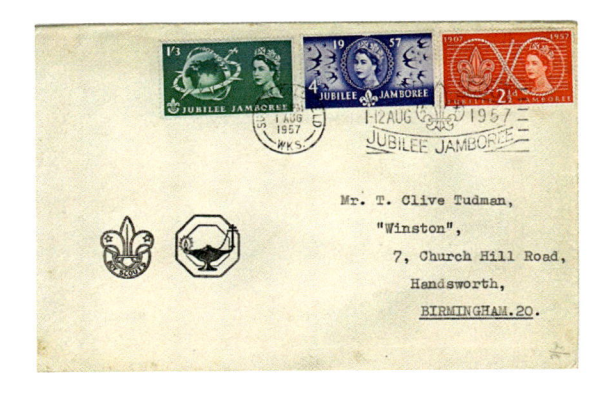

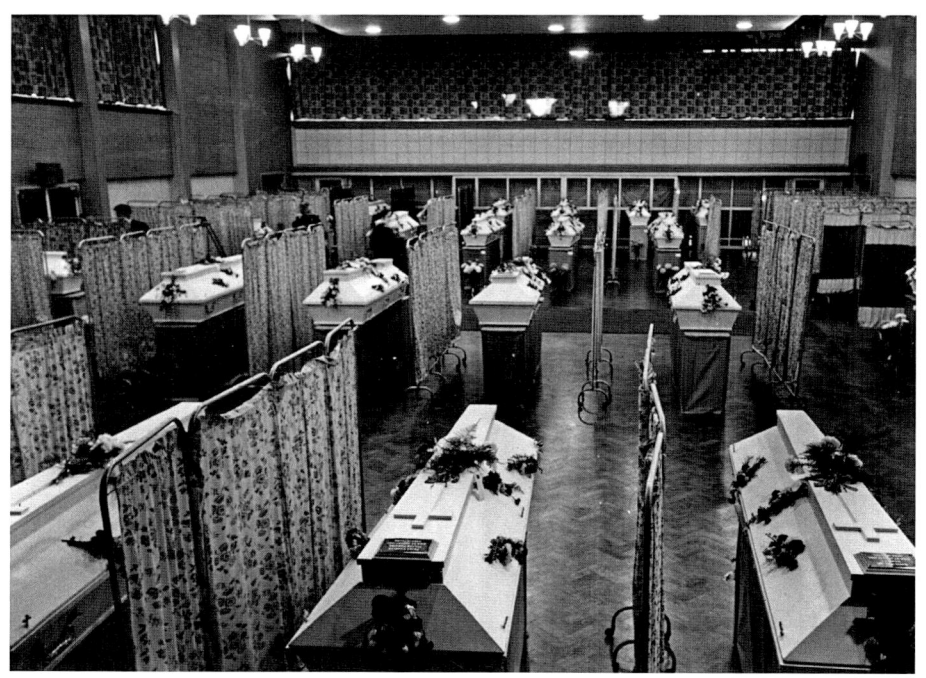

The Chapel of Rest – Lanfranc School Hall.

Hearses leave Lanfranc for Croydon Cemetery in Mitcham Road.

The coffins are taken into the decorated mass grave.

An official dignitary arrives at Croydon Parish Church.

Mr and Mrs Benson and other relatives arrive at Croydon Parish Church.

The Bishop, Vicar, and Mayor of Croydon, and other Croydon clergy leave after the service.

The Bishop, Vicar, and Mayor of Croydon wait at the mass grave.

Mourners and the Media gather at the graveside.

Relatives look for their loved one's coffin.

Surrey Street trader's floral tribute to the Lanfranc Boys.

Lanfranc boys and girls visit the grave.

Floral tributes

Mrs Catherine Kettle with the Mayor of Stavanger, Jan Johnsen, and the Mayor of Strand, Knut A. Jøssang, on their way to Holtaheia.

Mrs Catherine Kettle meets Norwegian Air Force Search and Rescue personnel. Left to right. Lt. Arnt Wangsholm, Lt. Jan M. Taarland, Sola Station Commander Lt. Col. Garstad, and Ops Officer Capt. J. P. Andersen.

The Bishop of Stavanger, Mayor of Croydon, Mayor of Stavanger, and Bishop of Croydon on the official visit in August 1961.

Christmas Day 1961. A service is held at the graveside.

Young Birds

by Ewan MacColl and Peggy Seeger

Summertime, the sun is high
The Earth is warm beneath the sky
The young birds try their wings
They're flying on their way
Now they're flying on their way
Schooldays done, it's time for play
Time to put your books away
It's time to say goodbye
We're flying on our way
Now we're flying on our way

The nest is cold, the young birds gone
Dove and Eagle, Lark and Swan
To Northern lands
Each one is flying on its way
Now they're flying on their way

Harvest time has come again
Young boys changed into young men
Impatient then
They must be flying on their way
Must be flying on their way

Summertime and winter sky
Storm and rain and winds are high
The young birds die
Their wings are broken, gone away
Wings are broken, gone away

Time of promise, time of dreams
Schoolboy's hopes and children's schemes
Are vanished now
The dream is ended, gone away
Dream is ended, gone away

Goodbye Eagle, Lark and Swan
Goodbye Jimmy, Frank and John
The song is done
Your journey ended, gone away
Journey ended, gone away

wanted to see him again but her mother said sadly that it wasn't possible. They stood whispering by the white pine box trying to imagine Quentin inside, touching the pretty flowers pinned there, not knowing what else to do. Other families walked quietly in, some noticing the other groups of relatives, some seeing little through blurred eyes. They were disparate strangers linked by tragedy. Whispers, sobs, and stifled wails punctuated the quietness. All Croydon's clergy were there to help and comfort; the Rev. Michael Percival Smith for one, threw his arms around a distraught couple who had lost their only child. Rosalind Green found it totally surreal. Her tearful six year old brother, on being told that his favourite brother had gone 'to be with God' replied angrily 'No he hasn't!' He was bewildered and wanted to know what the 'funny smell' was. Death wasn't a concept he could comprehend.

Julia Hendley and her parents visited the school hall together. It tore them apart to know that David was so close to them and yet so very far away. Julia wanted to open the coffin and see him again, to talk to David and to say all the things which were left unsaid when he was alive. It was awful and so heart-breaking for her, especially as her parents were shattered and helpless. They had turned to her for support, yet she realised there was so little she could do, except be there for them.

Margery Budd knew that George wouldn't have wanted any fuss over his funeral, but had gone along with the parents as she knew her husband would have wished to be buried with the boys, but John Beacham's family had faced a dilemma. John's mother felt that her youngest son's remains should be buried together with her husband's at her eldest son's church in Westfield Mid-Somer Norton in Somerset, where he was the vicar. Others in the family, including his sister Myrtle, thought he should be buried with George Budd and the boys, and that John would have wished this. His teenage nieces, Mary and Ruth, were devastated because 'Uncle John' was their favourite relative. One member of John's family who sensed the encompassing sadness, and who longed for his master to come home again, was 'Rusty', John's faithful dog. Rusty didn't know that there would be one less to 'round up' on family walks, and that his beloved master wasn't returning. Tommy Fowle had been informed of Mrs Beacham's wishes, and sympathetically understood. Croydon Council weren't including either John Beacham or Peter Boyes in the mass funeral. Theirs would happen later.

Outside, on the front football pitch, the vast marquee stood waiting. Wreaths from families were put into the school gym, whilst all others were placed in the marquee. Some of these floral tributes lay outside the big tent as boys and masters endeavoured to organise them inside. An incredible display, it was only the tip of the iceberg in terms of what was to come. A constant flow of people and delivery vans arrived with more flowers. More and more families arrived, their eyes downcast. Clive Grumett ushered them in, finding their raw grief hard for a sixteen year old to bear. One person he knew well was Mrs Boyes, his friend Peter's mother. Despite her grief she asked how Clive was, concerned for his feelings. Ivan Bignell was at the school and watched as the parents filed by. The experience was cathartic for him. On the road outside an old rag-and-bone man passed on his horse and cart, raised his hat and lowered his head. Younger schoolboys lingered at the gates feeling hopeless, half wishing they were allowed in, but only ticket-holders were admitted. Two policemen attended to make sure.

One Lanfranc boy who was admitted as a mourner was John Martin. His mother's friends Joan and Don Roffey had only one set of grandparents, so they requested a pass for John and his mother to accompany them. John couldn't believe the change in his school hall, and stood in awe of the spectacle. Slowly he walked up and down the rows looking for the names of friends and classmates. Curiosity made him wonder what was in the coffins. How had they died? What happens when a plane hits a mountain? Were they burnt, broken, had they found everything? He left accepting the true magnitude of the tragedy and knowing that his friends were not coming back.

Visiting parents left with a feeling of hopelessness and finality, but some also felt an inkling that they were not alone, that so many people cared. Croydon Council's organisation, with the help of Lanfranc' staff, had been amazing. Nothing had been left to chance. Everything ran like clockwork. But the Council's desire for uniformity and solemnity meant that parents who placed something special belonging to their son on the coffin lid had it quickly removed after they had left because it was deemed 'unsuitable'. Norman and Jean Cook thought this was disgraceful behaviour and put the objects back again as soon as the officials departed!

Anne Sharpely from The Evening Standard questioned Croydon Council's officiousness in her article, *'A Bouquet of Flowers'*. She wrote *'The organisation is dignified and well intended, but seeing these heartbroken mothers having to join in a public partnership in grief instead of in the privacy of their own parlours, one wonders if the arrangements have not been a little too prompt and well organised.* Were they consulted? 'No, it was decided by one or two members of the council', said the Mayor of Croydon's Secretary Mr. A. E. Apted. 'It was decided that nothing could be better than to take the boys back to their own school, and this met with the parents' approval.' Both were right. The parents *hadn't* been fully consulted, – but how could so many have been? The plans *had* met with parent's approval in as much as they were caught up in something so unexpected, and so big that they hadn't the capability, or the will, to act independently. Anne's feminine eye also took in for the record that a huge wreath from the Norwegian Government, made of red and white carnations and blue cornflowers, contrasted with a simple handful of sweet peas bound in straw, which had been placed in the plane with the coffins. Of the school hall she wrote, '*The sense of tragedy hung heavy like incense*'.

Although the general public were not allowed at the school, some Lanfranc boys were allowed in because they had money they wanted to donate for a memorial fund. The Police used their discretion. Bruce Guest and Malcolm Wright both had donations. Bruce had collected money from his school friends. Malcolm had 5 shillings from the 9 shillings he earned a week as a newspaper delivery boy. 'I thought somebody would like to have it,' he said sorrowfully, handing it over to a master.

Gordon Gregor, a columnist for The Daily Mirror, watched an old man walk up Lanfranc's driveway and noted that he had 'the mist of sadness in his eyes'. Later he wrote in his article, entitled *'Old George'* – '*He walked slowly in the sunshine. In his gnarled hands he carried flowers – huge lilies and chrysanthemums… For the past ten years boys of the school have helped cheer the life of the old man – retired bus driver George Durbridge… Two or three times a week he watched the boys playing games.* 'They have given me a lot of pleasure' said George. 'Coming here today with these flowers from my garden and saying a little prayer is the least I could do.' *George's flowers were added to a mass of blooms that lay in a huge marquee set up in the school grounds to house thousands of wreaths. Among the wreaths was one from the family of the pilot of the plane who was killed.*'

Fergus Cashin, an irascible hard-drinking journalist from The Daily Sketch, entitled his article, *'Our Mournful Tribute to Youth'*. He called Lanfranc's school hall, *'Hall of Tears'*, and wrote sensitively, *'Only a few yesterdays ago, easy laughter filled this hall, the smell of chalk clung heavily in the air, boys yelled innocent in their noisy play… And here today, death is laid out in neat white rows. Those 34 boys, who died so violently when their Viking crashed into a Norwegian mountain, have been brought back to school. Gently they were carried in their plain white coffins through the school gates into the Assembly Hall. And there on the desks where they studied and dreamed their coffins were rested. Each bore eight sprays of red, white and blue flowers from Norway. To each was pinned a type-written card – the uncomplicated statement of a name. All is silent. Two candles flicker against a varnished wooden cross. But no deathly hush fills this hall – for this is a cradle of life. And life will go on boisterous and gay in this very hall. Only we, who have grown old and slightly weary, stand silent and, perhaps, pray. That middle-aged man in a shabby black suit with tears in his eyes – who is he? One dare not ask. Perhaps he is a father. He is crying. Maybe for one particular boy, maybe for them all – as we all cry for them all. Outside it is raining, and through those gates come the relatives, each with individual sorrow, and each feeling the pathetic pain of their neighbour. Tomorrow, the day these boys should have been returning from their holiday, they will be buried in a mass grave near the school. And already 2,000 wreaths from all over the world fill a little white marquee. It is our mournful tribute to youth – sweet, gentle, adventurous youth …'*

The hardest of journalists were moved by the experience.

Returned from Cliftonville, young Shirley Bradbery sat alone at home in Livingstone Road. Her parents were away at work and she was amusing herself drawing and painting. As she sat at the table in her terraced house a chill, eerie feeling enveloped her, and she looked up to see a long line of boys walking past the table where she was sitting. They were in outdoor clothes and their teacher accompanying them tipped his head towards them as though listening to what they were saying. Shirley heard laughter and questions being asked, including 'which way do we go now Sir?' as though they were looking at maps. She saw their backs as they walked by her and disappeared through the wall into the house next door. Alone once more she felt drained and unable to understand what she'd seen. It didn't make sense, yet she knew she'd seen a long line of boys pass right by her. Through solid walls.

Norway Wednesday 16th August

In Stavanger on Wednesday 16th of August, an unreal feeling of emptiness hung over the city. It should have been an ordinary Wednesday but the aftermath of the tragedy that had occurred left a vacuum that slowly had to be filled. The people of Stavanger still felt mentally bruised and shocked by what had befallen them. They felt linked to a town in England that few if any had seen. They were joined, emotionally, to the families in Croydon who had lost their sons on Norwegian soil, in their mountains of Ryfylke. Traditionally family oriented, the good people of Stavanger were still dizzy from the tragedy. Their job, however, was over. They had risen to the awful occasion and given more than purely a good account. To Norwegians it seemed 'natural' behaviour, but in a world becoming politically frosty in the forbidding days of the Cold War, the warmth and goodness shown by Norwegians was a like lighthouse shining in the dark.

England Thursday 17th August
The Mass Funeral

On the day of the funeral the mass grave was lined with artificial grass netting, and the base thickly strewn with rhododendron leaves to hide the cold, damp earth. Early that morning, the foreman from Queen's Road cemetery visited Covent Garden market, and bought every blue and yellow flower (the Lanfranc School colours), that he could find. With two men, both old Lanfranc boys, they weaved hundreds of yellow dahlias and blue irises into the netting. The mounds of excavated earth were discretely covered.

It had been decided that the coffins would be taken from the school, and laid in the grave while the Memorial service was taking place in the Parish Church at 3.00pm. The original idea was that a gap in the hedge between the school playing fields and the cemetery grounds should be opened up to allow hearses through to the grave in relative privacy. At the last minute, at public request, the Mayor decided that the hearses should be driven along main roads, so that the people of Croydon could pay their last respects. This altered carefully planned timings, and police motor cycle escorts had to be drafted in at the last minute. Gloom hung over Croydon and everyone was possessed by the occasion.

Leaving from the front of their school where shiny black hearses, in pairs, backed up to the main entrance, each Lanfranc Boy, in his coffin, was led to the hearse by a member of clergy. Family flowers were positioned on its lid, and other flowers placed on the hearse roof. Then the hearses drove slowly to the school gates where two policemen stood at attention, and a solemn crowd waited to see the procession, with its motorcycle escort, leave. In the front rank were Lanfranc schoolboys, heads bowed in respect, but whose eyes were magnetically drawn towards each passing white box. The procession was in alphabetical order, and some boys murmured 'Goodbye Johnnie', 'Cheerio Eggy', 'Bye Micky', offering their own sad farewells until occluding lumps in their throats prohibited further speech. Police lined the length of Mitcham Road, and John Cooke and his mother stood silently with them. Keith Scotcher watched from the window of his house. Thousands lined the route, men and boys wearing black ties, heads bowed, as two by two the cortege passed. With the 33 boys travelled the remains of George Budd. Many parents in their grief had remembered Mr. Budd with floral tributes signed: *'From a broken-hearted mother and father'*, or from parents whose sons would no longer benefit from George's good teaching and endearing kindness. Beside each driver was a clergyman, for although it was mass funeral, each boy and man was treated individually. The coffins of John Beacham, and Peter Boyes, remained in the school hall.

The different arrangements meant that funeral directors had to change into mourning dress behind bushes in the cemetery, so that they could conduct the procession of hearses, over the last few hundred yards of public roads, with their usual solemnity. The police made sure that part of the operation was completed on time. Reg Searle and his cemetery staff, Chris Mitchell and others on duty, hoped they had thought of every eventuality, but they didn't know what to expect when the families arrived after the Memorial service. They had worked non-stop to manicure the flower beds, mow the grass verges, and brush the driveways; they had done their best. Now they just hoped nothing would go wrong.

Police leave was stopped for the day, and extra police were drafted into Croydon from other districts to cope with the crowds and traffic. They stood at attention as the hearses drove slowly by the hundreds of silent people lining the pavements at the approach to the cemetery gates. Each boy's floral tributes were removed and laid in their allotted plot on the immaculate lawns either side of the main drive. Then each coffin was carried on the shoulders of six men (hands clasped in front of them), preceded down the ramp into the mass grave by the chief undertaker. As each was laid in place a clergyman said the formal committal at the graveside. This clergyman then returned to the school to accompany the next coffin, whilst another took his place with the next to be committed.

Courtesy to the dead was observed all over Croydon. Flags flew at half-mast, men and boys wore black ties, women hats. Crowds which had gathered since noon had swelled into thousands. Rows of solemn silent faces watched as cars and taxis drew up outside the church, bringing relatives and friends of the dead boys. Clive Grumett and other Lanfranc prefects, representing the school, had difficulty finding each other but teachers Taylor and Hemmings shepherded them to their seats. Few members of Lanfranc's staff were able to attend as space was needed for all the relatives. Mike Spriggs had a place but Jean Cook sadly didn't. Outside, Eileen Puttick from Lanfranc Girls School, stood in her school uniform recalling happier days. The bells of the Parish Church tolled a funeral knell whilst the strains of Bach's cantata 'Flocks in Pastures Green Abiding' drifted over the crowds from loud speakers. At the stroke of three, as the funeral service began, the Town paused and came to standstill.

John Martin and his mother had a pass for the Funeral, and with many others were taken by bus from Lanfranc to the Parish Church. Crowds silently packed the streets, and Croydon seemed so unreal that John found it difficult to stay focused. There were crowds of people gathered around the entrance to the ancient church, and he saw some school prefects from both Lanfranc Boys and Girls schools handing out the order of service. There were huge loud speakers to relay the service outside, and there were Television and Pathe News film cameras. It seemed like a dream.

That was how so many others felt too. It felt like a crazy bad dream where they were acting in a play – although they didn't really know their lines, but they had an important role. Parents and relatives were brought to the church by shining black taxis that had collected them, on time, at their homes. Many had never travelled in such style. All were dressed in mourning, dark suits or dark coats, in spite of it being high summer. Many brothers and sisters wore their school uniforms. Some well-meaning parents, however, decided it would be better for their children not to attend and Geoff Brown's sister Janet and his girlfriend Maureen were sent away to the country, whilst Tim Budd remained unhappily in Haslemere. They all felt deprived of their right to grieve.

Rosalind Green felt strange attending her brother's funeral in her navy school blazer with its colourful badge of a crocus – symbolising Croydon's name. There hadn't been time, or money available, to buy other dark clothes. Inside the church, already very full, Rosalind was handed the Burial Service leaflet which stated starkly what had happened and listed everyone who had died. Within was the order for the Memorial Service in church, and the Burial at Mitcham Road Cemetery. Used to church services, this one felt very strange. She squeezed in to a pew together with her parents, three brothers, and other relatives, and couldn't really believe it was happening.

Shops in Church Street, Surrey Street, and other parts of Croydon closed their doors as organ music was relayed over loud speakers to the huge crowd outside. As the service began, across the North Sea in Norway the bells of Stavanger Cathedral tolled in memory of the men and boys who died near their town.

The organist from The Royal School of Church Music at Addington checked his organ stops and commenced the Memorial Service with the hymn *'Jesu, lover of my soul, Let me to thy bosom fly…'*. Normally the ancient church resounded to tuneful hymn singing, but this time the response was strangulated. Few could sing. Hearing the pathetic sound Rosalind felt determined to find her voice. All the boys deserved it! Others felt the same for wavering voices gradually increased their volume, although no one could do the hymn justice. Some distressed parents had to sit. It was impossible to sing with a lump in the throat.

Bishop John Taylor Hughes was a tall, well-built middle-aged man, with a rich voice whose modulating cadences commanded attention. He had confirmed some of the Lanfranc boys, and now he stood before their grieving families. First he assured parents that a similar service had already been held in Lanfranc School with a few Croydon clergy and members of the school staff present, and that it hadn't been necessary for the coffins to be present at the Parish Church. He also wanted them to know that few of Lanfranc's staff could be present with them in the church because relatives had taken precedence. Continuing he said he'd been moved by the care shown by the Church and people of Stavanger, and he expressed his gratitude towards these unknown friends. Speaking with calming deliberation, his voice had a soothing effect. His sermons always seemed simple, but they held deep meanings. He took his text from Hebrews 11, verse 40. *'They without us will not be made perfect'* – categorised as 'An exhortation to steadfastness and faith'. It seemed an unusual text in the circumstances, but Bishop Hughes had chosen it thoughtfully. Then he spoke from his heart.

'I want to speak simply and directly to each one of you here today who are carrying the burden of personal grief.' He paused, casting his mind back in time. *'One April afternoon, a woman and her teenage son had their tea together and then went back to their respective tasks about the house. Ten minutes later there was a call. The boy found his mother dying and within an hour she was gone. That was a memory of 40 years ago. I was that boy. It was the first great sadness in my life. Sometime during that evening there came a point when there was nothing more I could do to be of help to my father or young brother. The thought God gave me then was to go down and tell my vicar. He said nothing but quietly took me into the church then he knelt down and prayed before God. Many of you will know just what I mean. As you think of the volumes of prayer around you, you will also know of the strength that God has given you. That night for me was a night such as you will know only too well. In the course of it God spoke to me simply and clearly. He told me I must not worry about my mother or myself. Everything was being taken care of. There was work to do for each of us, so that one day we might meet together again.'* From this the Bishop said he had learnt two lessons. There was still love even if people were separated by death. He went on to say that all his troubles did not suddenly disappear from the night God had spoken to him. *'There have been times when struggles have reduced me to nothing. But nothing could separate me from the love*

of God or the knowledge that when my strength has come to an end God's power will sustain me. Everything depends on God and He will not fail to help us or our loved ones, provided we obey Him and trust Him and keep close by Him day by day.'

It was typical of Bishop Hughes to show the mourners that he knew how they felt. His sermon directly encouraged them to speak to God, and to listen to His voice. Indirectly he guided many who felt abandoned and 'betrayed', to place God *apart* from the tragedy, that God was not implicated. Some of those listening, in their grief, naively believed that God should not have allowed the terrible accident to happen. Instead the Bishop described, by his own experiences that God was there to be spoken to, to share one's grief with, and to take support from. Some quietly absorbed his message of consolation, but others were too distressed to comprehend.

The Vicar of Croydon spoke 'The Sentences' about life, death, resurrection, and eternal life. The 23rd Psalm was said, and then The Lesson: St John 14.1-7, 12. was read. Another hymn, *'Thou art the Way: by thee alone…'* followed, and was sung better. Then there were prayers, followed by The Blessing, and the final hymn, *'Jesus lives! Thy terrors now can no more, O death appal us.'* Everyone present did their best to sing this triumphant hymn, but *'Alleluia!'* at the end of each verse proved too much for almost everyone. It seemed inappropriate. Alleluia? No. No one felt they had anything to rejoice about.

The congregation of 700 waited as the dignitaries, including the Minister of Education Sir David Eccles, and the Norwegian Charge d'Affaires Mr. Knut B. Aars, were ushered out. Then the relatives emerged into the sunlight, where hundreds of melancholy people looked their way. A retinue of taxis bore some parents on to the cemetery, whilst Green Line buses provided transport for others.

At 3.50p.m. police out-riders led the cars containing the Bishop, the Vicar of Croydon, the Mayor, and dignitaries to the cemetery. At the cemetery gates Leslie Bentley's father, a sergeant in Croydon's Z division of special constabulary was on duty. Leslie was with him. Along the path to the grave were about 20 schoolboys in Lanfranc blazers. By the grave, a number of clergymen prayed silently as they waited for the mourners. Sergeant Bentley led Leslie through the crowd in a fatherly way, saying 'your place is in there, son, to say goodbye to your friends.'

The graveside committal service was also taken by the Bishop together with the Vicar of Croydon. Previously some cemetery staff had felt that deeply contemplative Bishop Hughes was a distant man, but he surprised them with unsuspected warmth and sympathy, exemplified when a major hitch occurred in their well laid plans. The taxis carrying parents and close relatives preceded the buses, and the taxi drivers felt obliged to park at the far end of the drive, whilst the buses parked close to the mass grave. Relatives had a long walk back to the grave, whilst others in the buses which parked much closer were able to congregate immediately around the grave. The order of precedence wasn't correct, and to make matters worse the press and television had taken the best positions with their tripods, and were reluctant to move. The diligent cemetery staff hadn't foreseen this, and with so much raw emotion all around the situation could have been calamitous. The crowd around the grave was 15 people deep. Realising the distress being caused, Bishop Hughes delayed the service, encouraging the families to come forwards, waiting until he was quite sure that parents and grandparents were closest to the coffins of their loved ones. Only then did he begin.

Before them lay a deep pit and in that pit were 34 white coffins in two rows of 17, heads placed inwards, toes outwards. All could see Norway's flowers adorning the simple caskets, whilst the stark grave was softened by the artificial grass and fresh flowers in Lanfranc's colours. Such tenderness had been shown to boys who had once raced through the cemetery on their bikes, late for school. Altruism had been shown by the cemetery staff to their relatives, whose grief was red-raw. One Lanfranc boy standing with them was Derek Meacher. Edwin Murray's parents had asked that he be there and Del's father went with him. Del was very sad, made more so by the uncontrolled grief around him. He wasn't very tall and so could only glimpse through gaps between people but he heard the Bishop of Croydon speaking and he looked up at his father and saw he was crying too – the first time he'd ever seen his 'Desert Rat' dad in tears.

When everyone was settled the Bishop commenced the burial with Psalm 103 verses 13-17 *'Like as a father pitieth his own children: even so is the Lord merciful unto them that fear him.'* This was followed by a short lesson from St John 6.37-40 which ended with the words *'...that every one which seeth the Son, and believeth on him, may have everlasting life: and I will raise him up at the last day.'* Sometimes the Bishop's words could not be heard for the wails of distraught parents. Then, finally two urns, one on each side of the grave, were used as the Bishop and the Vicar of Croydon symbolically threw handfuls of Croydon's soil on to the coffins with the words *'earth to earth, ashes to ashes, dust to dust.'* This was too much for one poor mother who tried to jump down into the grave. Mrs Eileen Adams watched the distressed mother being restrained, and felt nothing. Nothing at all. Eileen's only son, John, lay in the coffin at her feet, and she just felt… Empty.

The clergy and dignitaries walked sadly back to their transport, amazed at the numbers of wreaths. At their departure some parents climbed down to weep over their son's coffin, one father fell to his knees crying and had to be comforted by a relative, but most parents looked forlornly for a final moment and then walked dejectedly away. The day was hot, distressed relatives were wearing thick dark clothes, and numerous people had to be treated at a specially set up Red Cross centre. Feeling numb, John Martin walked around the grave with Robert Roffey's parents, looking at the name plates. At the coffin of Robert Martin, the edge of the grave obscured the name 'Robert', and just his second name 'John' and surname 'Martin' were visible. John Martin's heart jumped as he saw his own name in the grave!

The media observed everything and went away to write their stories. Some disgraced themselves by jumping down amongst the coffins to take an intimate shot. They were quietly but firmly escorted out. The Croydon Advertiser's reporter Betty Brownlie witnessed this, and was deeply shocked and upset. She knew from subsequently interviewing some parents, the depth of agony they were suffering.

Wreaths lined both sides of the entire length of the long cemetery drive, each boy's placed together. Parents walked down the avenue stunned at the length and breadth of the massed floral tributes, each family also having wreaths sent from Cunard Eagle Airways and Cunard Eagle Employees. Colin Smith's parents were impressed to see a floral ice skating boot sent from unknown friends at Streatham Ice Rink. Ronald Green saw an innovative floral cricket bat and stumps, footballs, even a bicycle made of flowers, and wept that he hadn't thought of such extravaganzas for his own son. Theirs was just a simple wreath, and he bitterly castigated himself for not providing something more appropriate. He wished he'd thought of a bicycle for Quentin. Feeling remiss and illogically shouldering the blame for allowing his son to go, Ronald Green was desolate with grief and despair.

One immense floral tribute dwarfed everything, and turned eyes in admiration and surprise. Eighteen foot long, it consisted of two emotive words – 'Lanfranc Boys'. Each letter was created from white and pink carnations, surmounted by long white feathers. The Surrey Street Traders had clubbed together and Joe Baker, the uncle of Lanfranc boy Bruce Guest, made it. Did Ewan MacColl and Peggy Seeger see this tribute with its unusual feathers? Did it make them think of bold migrating birds? Perhaps it did. Lanfranc School itself had a wreath intricately depicting the school badge in hundreds of small flowers. An inscription on it read *'From the boys of Lanfranc School in remembrance of those who were here with us in our work and play.'*

Margery Budd had been daunted at the thought of such a large funeral. The service had felt unreal for her because it seemed a civic occasion, too large and impersonal. Now standing at the graveside where 34 coffins lay so neatly the reality came home. One of the coffins was that of a husband and father. *'Why me?'* she asked herself. *'What have I done to deserve this?'*

Clive Grumett, who had stood with other Lanfranc boys on top of a mound of earth, waited until the relatives departed, then said goodbye to the masters and other boys. As he walked home he felt an overwhelming sense of anti-climax. He felt empty, now that he'd said 'farewell' to so many good mates. He had always thought they'd remain friends long into adulthood.

Far away in Norway the flags that had remained at half mast were now hoisted back up their flag poles.

The people of Croydon were finally allowed in, to pay their respects, and to marvel at the ocean of flowers. Eileen Puttick was staggered at the numbers drawn there – she had never seen so many people in her life. She tearfully recalled Roger Taylor from the school plays at Lanfranc in which she had acted. In Michael Benson's plot was a wreath from 'Smudge'. Janis Wilding, the girl who had envied Michael as he left the newsagents in Aurelia Road laden with sweets and comics, explained the significance of 'Smudge' to the puzzled lady next to her. 'It's from his tortoiseshell cat' she said sadly. Since Michael's death, Janis had decided she would never, *ever*, feel envious of anyone again.

The grave was left open. The intention was to close it by about seven o'clock that evening. The cemetery staff knew there would be many members of the public who would want to pay their respects at the graveside. They were right. A senior policeman reported that the queue of people waiting to visit the grave stretched back to Thornton Heath Pond, and was likely to get longer that evening as people returned home from work. Three people who waited to file by were young Shirley Bradbery and her parents. Shirley had been agitated and upset since witnessing a ghostly retinue of boys walk through her terraced house in Livingstone Road. On visiting the grave, and seeing all their flowers, she felt relieved and more at peace. Were these her boys? At rest now? She felt grateful that her parents had taken her.

On the six o'clock news that evening, a full coverage of Croydon's mass funeral was broadcast. John Martin watched it with the Roffey's in their front room. As the news report moved to the service at the Parish Church, grandfather Roffey said, 'Well, if you see an old codger with a walking stick – that's me!' Immediately the news film showed him, with his stick, followed by the others going into the church. Everyone in the room started laughing! It was the first time they had laughed in a very long time, and an unexpected way of relieving the stress of a day which had been very hard to endure.

At the Budd household, Margery Budd and her sons Geoff and Tim turned on their thirteen year old 9" Bush television with its Bakelite casing that George had bought in 1948. They watched the BBC news report of the Lanfranc funeral and then the television broke down. It was the last programme it ever showed.

The gates at the cemetery remained open, and thousands more people filed past the grave in silence. The queue extended beyond Thornton Heath Pond into London Road towards Norbury. At eleven o'clock the gates were closed but those unable to pay their respects in time were told that the cemetery would open again at eight o'clock the next morning. The cemetery staff had worked non-stop for seventeen hours. It was the longest day anyone of them could remember. It felt strange for them to leave with the grave unfilled, but two policemen guarded it that night in lonely vigil.

The funeral of Captain Philip Watts took place at Brookwood Crematorium, Woking, on the same day as the Lanfranc funeral.

On the evening of the funeral a special meeting of the Town Council convened. There was only one item on the agenda – the sympathies of all members of the County Borough Council were voiced to the families of those that had perished on the mountain near Stavanger. A vote of thanks to all those who had been involved in the funeral, including the staff of the Cemeteries and Crematorium Department, was passed. Those attending felt that there was something very moving about a town mourning its dead, because arguments and old enmities were forgotten.

Anne Sharpley of The Evening Standard meanwhile, wrote her news story from a mother's viewpoint. She wrote: *'For Mrs Eileen Adams today remains strange. For eight years she has lived near the cemetery gates at Croydon with her son John taking no more than a child's passing interest in the great hearses and their burdens that passed their door. Mrs Adams stayed dry-eyed and calm when something which still has no reality for her occurred this afternoon. The body of John, her only son, in a gleaming hearse, his simple white coffin of Norwegian pine pinned with the posies, now withered, that the Norwegians had fastened to it, led the procession of 34 such hearses to the cemetery.'* She went on to describe the special wreaths. *'Some has sent cricket bats and others sailing boats. Another boy's parents had sent a bicycle wheel. And strangest and most touchingly stiff-upper-lipped of all were the parents who had sent a large fish of orange dahlias and on the accompanying card "A reminder of happy days and 'tight lines' at Frensham. May your ground bait bring its own reward – Good fishing lad!'* Anne Sharpely captured the doleful bizarreness of the day.

It seemed, for many concerned, that that was the end of the 'Lanfranc Boys', who had departed so happily for Norway eight days earlier.

Norway Thursday 17th August

On the day of the funeral in Croydon, Stavanger's church bells tolled and, at the same time as Croydon's Memorial service, a service of remembrance took place in Stavanger Cathedral. At the end of the service, flags were raised from half mast. But the people of Stavanger couldn't instantly forget.

Normality was hard to find for those who were intimately involved. Counselling as such didn't exist, and people exposed to traumatic stress were expected to take it in their stride. Some couldn't. Stavanger didn't feel the same for Kaare Hidle and he decided to leave and move to Oslo, to get away from haunting memories. Red Cross members found that only those who had been on Holtaheia could understand what they had been through. They couldn't discuss it with others. Sofus Tønnessen became their leader and many talked over the experience with him. Kare Østerhus who had driven the lorry with some of the stretchers, had no one to counsel him, and nightmares followed. He wasn't alone. Anna Nordland had nightmares of children, arms outstretched, crying for their mothers. The RNoAF Rescue Squadron officers had to look upon it as a job, but it was a job like no other, and whilst dealing with it professionally, emotionally it made a mark. They all had to get on with variously blighted lives. Few received the understanding due to them. There was no such diagnosis as Post Traumatic Stress Disorder and no one realised what cost it had been to the rescuers, least of all the bereaved relatives in Croydon. They had absolutely no idea.

England Friday 18th August

Thousands more filed past the open grave, in Croydon, the next morning, and a count of the wreaths finalised the total at 1,750. (More visitors brought flowers in the days that followed when it was estimated that over 100,000 people came to pay their respects.) By three o'clock that afternoon, the numbers had lessened, and the Medical Officer of Health decided that the grave must be closed. Bulldozers from the nearby building site moved in and completed the work. Then cemetery workmen made sure that the site was left tidy when the heavy machinery was moved away.

As Chris Mitchell witnessed the mass grave being closed he had another Lanfranc funeral to organise that day. Peter Boyes was to have a fitting send off, especially as his grandfather had worked at the cemetery. One cannot imagine what exceptional grief Mrs Boyes bore that day as her son's remains were added to those of her late husband's. Peter should have been starting work at Philips Croydon Works in Purley Way in a few days. Now she was totally alone in the world. Clive Grumett and his friend Bob Edmeads, good friends of Peter's, were to discover that, altruistically, she always inquired how they were both doing.

For nine days Croydon's newspapers had focused on her victims and the editor of the Croydon Times had run more off the press in order to send 1,000 copies to Norway for sale in Oslo, Bergen, and Stavanger because people wanted to see photos of the Lanfranc Boys. Now on August 18th 1,500 'Times' papers were flown out again, so that Norwegians could read about the return of the Lanfranc Boys and their two masters, and of their funeral. On the front page were messages printed in Norwegian from the Mayor and the Vicar of Croydon, captioned 'TAKK TIL NORGE' – Thank you Norway. Letters of thanks were sent from Croydon Town Hall to twenty-two named personnel that Stavanger's mayor had advised were involved. The typists had difficulty ensuring both Norwegian military and civic titles and names were correctly spelt. These all important letters were scrutinised for any mistakes and lines were pencilled in through Norwegian Ø's. The letters had to be correct as they had a lot to thank everyone for. In Stavanger the pall gradually rose from the city. They had done all that they could. Recovering from the shock and sadness at what had befallen them, they tried to get back to normality.

England Saturday 19th August

With the immense preparations for the Lanfranc Boy's mass funeral, several other funerals had been postponed until Saturday. John Beacham was also to be cremated that day and his ashes taken away to Somerset.

When the Beacham family followed his coffin to the Chapel at the Crematorium in their car that Saturday, his sister Myrtle heard someone remark 'Whose funeral is this?' She was mortified when someone answered loudly 'Oh it's one of the Lanfranc masters – probably too posh to be buried with the rest!' Incensed, Myrtle longed to jump out of the car and say how very untrue that was! *All* except his mother had wanted John buried with the others, as they believed he would have wished. The comment hurt her deeply because the close knit Beacham family hadn't wanted John's funeral to be a separate ceremony. A chance and unnecessary bigoted remark left an added scar on top of one that went very deep. John was Myrtle's 'baby' brother for whom she'd cared since his birth. He'd been her real live 'doll', and had grown up to become her children's favourite uncle, who, very adept with his hands, made them toy doll's houses and farm yards. It wasn't just the boys at Lanfranc who would miss John.

Across England in Warwickshire, Nina Smalley, widow of Murray Smalley, Papa Mike's First Officer, was to bury her husband at St. Nicholas Church, Kenilworth. Nina had only been married for two years, whilst her parents in law were devastated at the loss of their only son, especially as they had lost their only daughter as a child. Now their hopes were focused upon their small granddaughter Karen.

Susan's mother was inconsolable. Although she had her daughter Ann, who did her utmost to cheer her mother up, poor Jean Endicott was inconsolable. Susan's funeral took place in Paignton Parish Church, South Devon, on Saturday 19th, and the church was packed with mourners, including ex-Croydon Council employee, Charles Cooper, representing Croydon. The service was arranged fittingly for Susan with *'The Lord's my Shepherd'* sung to the tune *'Crimond'*, the Lesson from Revelations 21 *'And I saw a new heaven and a new earth'*, followed by the hymn *'All things bright and beautiful'* – just as Susan had been in her life – bright, and beautiful. Her burial took place in the tranquil graveyard at Stoke Gabriel overlooking the River Dart. Chris Moysey, her heart-broken fiancé had to leave her there and somehow get on with his life. Jean Endicott's heart nearly gave up. She collapsed after the funeral and might have succumbed if a doctor hadn't reached her in time.

In Croydon and elsewhere, several people felt moved to write poems as it helped express the sorrow they felt.

Poetry inspired by the Holtaheia Air Crash

The Papa Mike Disaster
by Janet Sawyer 1961

Lives that England ill could spare;
Hands of skill and hearts yet brave;
Fine thoughts fled in mountain air,
Driven to untimely grave.

Flushed the glowing heart with joy;
Filled the mind the flashing sun:
Light the eye of man and boy,
Recked not of the end to come.

Silver soared the Viking's wings,
Streaking upwards to the blue.
Spirits proud as those of kings
Thirty Croydon schoolboys knew.

Now upon the mountainside,
Still and dumb on foreign strand,
Lie the remnants of our pride,
Scattered o'er the sombre land.

Plucked from manhood's threshold light
While youth's fervours scarce yet burn;
Sped to meet death's scalding blight;
Parted, never to return.

Hushed are now the tones of joy
In the towns of those that know
What it is to lose a boy
Hardly yet begun to grow.

Fly the flags here at half-mast:
Mothers weep and sisters sigh,
Gaze on liners flying past
Seeing careless days gone by.

Think no more upon the dead,
Hopes that were and might have been:
For the living pray instead,
Left behind to live again.

'My boy should have been there too,'
Thankful now a mother said.
Sighed again, for wept anew
Those whose boy had gone instead.

Bid the youthful souls to rest,
Happy as in childhood's prime,
In the gardens of the blest
Through the syllables of Time.

God will watch and understand
Why we sit and weep.

The Lanfranc Boys by Angela Stanford

It was the ninth of August
Nineteen sixty one
The Lanfranc school disaster
When parents lost their sons

On a flight to Norway
A trip planned months ago
Their plane hit a mountain side
Then ploughed into the snow

There were no survivors
The search was all in vain

Even hardened rescuers
Couldn't hide their pain

They brought them home to Croydon
We mourned out bitter loss
Now on that mountain far away
Stands a monumental cross

Time hasn't dimmed the memory
Of all those young loved ones
A sad day in our history
When Croydon lost its sons.

In Memoriam by G. E. Manning

The news transfixed us. Like a searing pain
It crucified the workings of the mind,
And let a horror of imagination
Raise up a torment of a shattered plane
Impacted on a rain-swept mountain-top;
And broken bodies, torn and blasted there,
To make a sacrifice to cruel Death.
An anguished cry burst from bewildered lips,
Searching in vain the hidden ways of God:
'Why, for Thy tender mercy's sake, Lord, why?'
No man can answer. Grief is comfortless.
And yet there comes a lifting of the soul
When, with compelling power, compassion spreads,
All harshness and all jealousies forgot,
And in a wide communion of grief
Unites a town, a country, a world,
In a vast brotherhood of pitying hearts.
And then a certain knowledge springs
       from sorrow's roots.

Strange paradox. Because they died,
       God gave them all
A power they never knew while still they lived.
The Lanfranc School will be a finer school
Because an aircraft crashed beyond the sea.
Out of their graves the silent dead will speak
To every living master, every boy:
'You who remember us will always be
Our rich memorial of living souls.
We had our future snatched by sudden death;
But we live on in you, our purpose served,
If when you turn your thoughts towards the crest
Of that high peak where part of Lanfranc died,
You lift your hearts to pledge yourselves anew
To live the better, for our memory's sake,
And make us, by your striving, proud
That we were members, too, of such a school
Until His hand removed us from the roll.'

Comfort Ye by J.H.

Pound! Storm flash! Hushing retreat,
    questioning event.
Event? No! Nightmare! Let us wake from this sleep.
Dreams, storms, life ends with the memories we keep
Living the life out, rejecting the pain sent
That returns, flooding the heart out, taking the sleep.
With pictures. No — not pictures —
    eyes that have smiles sent,
Bringing the pain back, remembering the event.
Those we have life-sucked why can't we keep?
In the deep twilight our surrendered bodies are lent
To uneasy movements as mist-memories seep
And we support the pain-pressure packed deep.
Leaving our lasting lives unbroken, but bent.
When the light failed, violence-doused with the sands,
And we who were left had to suffer,
    who held our hands?

Poem by T. A. Walker

What might you have been,
If God had let you stay,
Why so soon to silently steal away?
So short, so brief, the tune to know your ways,
The Sadness and Grief can never be erased,
When the shadows of the moon, silently creep,
Across the bed of flowers,
Where you and others sleep,
God will watch and understand
Why we sit and weep.

The rest of 'Black August'

In the days following the funeral all the parents had to try to get on with their lives. Fathers had jobs to return to, many wives had jobs too. Life had to carry on for the sake of the rest of the family, but for a few parents this was impossible as they had no other children, the light had gone out of their lives, there was only emptiness and total despair. The wife of Captain Philip Watts maintained that she also 'died' on August 9th.

Part of Ronald Green's heart had died too, as he now tortured himself for letting his son go on the trip. It was his decision and he felt he must bear the terrible consequences, but like others in post-traumatic situations he threw himself into related work to bring order out of chaos. Although not a natural leader, Ronald was a City businessman, used to speaking at important board meetings, and this ability was to come to the fore helping the other parents. Alan White was another father who needed to throw himself into closely associated post-tragedy work, in order the fill the terrible void. They were to become the spokespersons for the Lanfranc parents.

Before this happened though, Ronald Green was determined to complete a task he'd promised Quentin he would do, namely finishing off some roughly made storage space in his bedroom. No expense was spared in buying the best materials and he worked alone, with tears rolling down his cheeks. Ronald was desperate for forgiveness for letting Quentin go; bitterly regretting he hadn't told him he was going to give back all the instalments he'd repaid for his bike. This was to have been a surprise on his return. Now Quentin would never know.

In other boy's bedrooms in Croydon everything was left exactly as before. Some beds were left unmade, others were tidied. Bedrooms became shrines and doors closed on them, never to be used by others. Despite the funeral, despite the publicity and letters of condolence, some parents found it impossible to believe that their son had gone. Mothers and siblings expected to see their loved one walk up the road and through the garden gate, and some stood watching for them at their windows. Some fathers helped create and perfect the 'shrine' to their son, never wanting to forget him. Other fathers dealt with their grief very differently. Broken-hearted, and believing that death was absolutely final, the only way they could cope was to lock it all away. Their son had once lived but was now dead. They kept their emotions behind a shut door inside them and wouldn't allow anyone to open it – for fear of unleashing the terrible pain all over again. Mr. Adams forbade his wife Eileen to talk about their son John. A few fathers started to drink to numb the torture. Those with a strong Christian faith, although their hearts ached, were able to proceed stoically. Those without such a backbone had little to keep them upright. Now that the event had ceased to be big news, although public sympathy remained, the parents found that the only people who really understood what they were going through were the other parents involved. Gradually, they were to turn to each other.

Carol Storey, Richard Lawrence's girlfriend travelled over from Reading with her family to pay their last respects. The vast carpet of flowers still covered the damp earth of the mass grave and a breeze gently lifted the fading petals. She knew she would never forget this day – or her first sweetheart, Richard.

Ex-Lanfranc boy Ian Bell cycled to the cemetery and was amazed at all the flowers. Remembering his old friends who had died, he realised that Quentin, with whom he'd shared a desk, wouldn't have died if only he'd passed the 13+ exam.

In Kennard's cosy Arcade the Stamp shop owner felt sad. He had recognised the face of the boy who had reserved the special Scouting Jubilee stamps from his photo in the newspapers. Now another good customer, Peter Willis, had come in and wanted to buy it. He turned the small stamped envelope over in his hands, unsure whether to part with it. Sorrowfully, he told Peter the story about the Lanfranc boy who had reserved it. Peter handed over half a crown in payment and treasured the envelope, never forgetting its poignant significance.

Artistic, spiritual, soulful people were moved to record their feelings. Almost certainly having visited the cemetery, Ewan MacColl and Peggy Seeger wrote the lyrics and score for their song 'Young Birds'. G.E. Manning (Headmaster of Ashburton Secondary Boys School), Jim Hemmings (English teacher at Lanfranc), and Angela Stanford (sister of a Lanfranc boy), and Janet Sawyer (a complete stranger) articulated their grief in poems. So too, at a later date, did Ragnvald Honganvik, with his poem 'Runer i Stein'. Sculptor George Musgrove created a small bronze cast of a boy cricketer and presented it to Lanfranc.

August 21st should have been Quentin Green's 14th birthday. It was, however, the Mayor's 66th birthday and she was busy at the Town Hall, prior to an official visit to Stavanger. Geoff Brown's father Ernest, a member of St Stephen's Church, composed a letter of thanks, writing *'It is a wonderful example to all other corporate bodies seeing that they can act with utmost consideration and humanity in times of distress.'* Certainly, much humanity had been shown. Rupert Wearing King for Croydon Education Committee wrote that same day saying that the school meals staff at Lanfranc (who loved all of Lanfranc's cheeky lads) had offered their services voluntarily and didn't want to be paid.

Ernest Taberner was much concerned with questions of payment that day. Conversations between him and the underwriters for Cunard Eagle had resulted in them waiving their claim to the victim's death benefits, which, in the tragic circumstances, Croydon Corporation's insurance brokers were also willing to do. The balance of John Beacham's salary had to be paid to his estate. These sad formalities were easy to deal with, what he didn't expect was a bombshell.

On August 22nd Mr. Wearing King wrote to ask John Beacham's solicitors a question put forward by some parents – namely would they be refunded any of the travel money they'd paid? Also, more importantly, what was the situation regarding insurance? The solicitor was requested to immediately send him any documents relating to insurance, handed over by his family. Mr. Wearing King enclosed a cheque for John Beacham's August salary of £61.1s.7d for his estate. In the office outside, Fiona Mantle a 16 year old clerk, had found his salary details and that of George Budd. She removed them from the ring binder, and when all was completed, instead of tearing up their papers (as she did with others who left the pay of Croydon Education Committee), and dropping them unceremoniously into the bin, she sadly folded them, lent down, and placed them gently into the waste paper basket.

That morning Croydon's Aldermen received letters from Ernest Taberner advising that both Cunard Eagle and Croydon Corporation were waiving their claims to death grants which was £18.15s.0d. per victim. As the bill to Croydon from the Cemetery alone came to over £680 this was a generous gesture. The hard working Town Clerk (now en route to Norway with the Mayor and Bishop) had left correspondence to be dispatched in his absence.

Airborne and en route for Stavanger, the three felt somewhat discomfited flying to Sola Airport where Lanfranc's boys had never landed. Mrs Kettle hadn't flown before. Ernest Taberner had prudently paid £3 to insure them all. Any nerves felt landing at Sola, were quickly dispelled by the warm reception accorded by Mayor Jan Johnsen, the Bishop of Stavanger, Dean of Stavanger, and other officials. At a dinner that evening, attended by the British Vice-Consul, members of Stavanger Town Council, and the clergy, the envoys from Croydon were made welcome and told that their visit was much appreciated. With them was young Croydon Times reporter Christopher Reynolds.

The Mayor had asked to see Holtaheia, so at 8.45 a.m. on Wednesday 23rd they all visited Strand, accompanied by Civic, Church, and Police officials. It was a beautiful day, and on the speedboat from Stavanger Mrs Kettle, dressed in black, stood on the open deck spellbound by the beauty of the mountains and fjords. She had never visited Norway before. Ernest Taberner told her that it was even more beautiful inland. Arriving at Tau they met Strand's Mayor and other Civic and Church officials, Harald Brekke of the Red Cross, and other volunteers who helped in the recovery operations. Taken by car to Holta they were introduced to farmer Lars Hoftun, who, after Ola Lekvam, had been one of the first locals on the scene. Continuing their journey on foot they climbed Holtaheia, where they saw the devastation and witnessed the impact mark on the cliff face.

Wiping tears from her eyes Mrs Kettle emotionally voiced their gratitude for what had been done, adding 'It is a terrible thing that such a dreadful tragedy had to happen in such a wonderful place.' Her words were translated by the Bishop of Stavanger. The party from Croydon could see just how difficult it had been for the Red Cross to carry the bodies down. Heather growing near the summit caught her eye and Mrs Kettle asked if she could take some back with her for the boy's grave. It was a touching request, and specimens were collected for her. They spent twenty minutes at the site and reporter Chris Reynolds felt that the tragedy was made even worse because the Lanfranc Boys had never seen the beautiful countryside, and that the mountain hostel in which they should have stayed was only a few miles away. On their way back down they visited Holta farm, and Mrs Kettle talked to the farmer, his wife, and daughter who had helped when their home had been made into a rescue headquarters.

Later that afternoon the Commissioner of Police, armed with maps and documents, described to them all in detail the course of events, from the time the plane flew over Sola Airport, until the next morning when it was located on Holtaheia. It was obvious to the Croydon party that no time had been lost before the search began, but that bad weather had forced it to be abandoned that night. They were impressed that telephoned sightings had helped the police pinpoint the likely crash to Holta.

Arrangements were then made for all the helpers from Strand to attend a reception given by the Mayor of Stavanger at their Hotel. Not only was Mrs Kettle made an honorary member of Stavanger's Aldermanic Council but the dinner given in their honour included lamb chops with mint sauce (a taste not to Norwegian liking but especially made for their English guests). They met over 60 people who had been engaged in the work of recovery, the Vice-Consul, Civic heads of Stavanger and Strand, the helicopter crews, airport officials, Red Cross workers, telephone operators and others including the ladies who had decorated the coffins with flowers. In a dignified silk dress, and wearing her regalia of office, Catherine Kettle thanked all the gathering for *'the wonderful things the people of Norway did for us in our great time of distress.'* She then described in detail all that had ensued when the bodies of the boys and their two masters had been flown home. The memory of the mass funeral brought tears to her eyes and those present could see the tragedy had taken its toll on her. (A Norwegian present confided to the 'Times' reporter, *'Your Mayor's face is jerking. She feels this tragedy in her heart'.*) Mixing with their guests they talked with the leaders of the different operations. Mrs Kettle presented the Mayors of Stavanger and Strand with albums embossed with Croydon's arms, containing photographs taken in Croydon on the day of the mass funeral. They then presented, for Lanfranc School, a magnificent 9ft tall photograph of the 'Pulpit Rock' a special attraction the Lanfranc Boys should have visited.

The reception was followed by a service in the Cathedral, which was so packed that many people stood. Christopher Reynolds had learnt from Bishop Birkeli that he shared the same surname as the Cathedral's first bishop – a Roman Catholic English monk named 'Reinald' from Winchester. The 'Funeral March' was played, tugging at Catherine Kettle's heartstrings. The Bishop of Croydon preached in the pulpit side by side with the Bishop of Stavanger, who interpreted sentence by sentence. Bishop Hughes said *'This tragedy has brought our two countries very close together and it has shown our two branches of the Christian Church to be united in a practical love of God and God's children.'* According to the young reporter it was 'a sermon of out-standing beauty'. Linked by its founder, then by The Reformation, Lutheran and Anglican bishops shared an historic service.

The next morning, Thursday 24th, the Croydon party were taken to a sculptor's yard where they met the anonymous donor of a half-ton carved granite Norwegian Cross. Too heavy to be carried, it was to be flown by helicopter to Holtaheia. The Red Cross had provided a brass plaque to be affixed to it. At midday the three envoys left for England, taking with them the huge photograph and the heather from the mountain. Mrs Kettle felt that the visit to Norway had forged a link between Croydon and Stavanger which she believed would not easily be broken.

Whilst they were away, letters were mailed from Croydon Town Hall to all who had sent flowers and wreaths, saying that a full list of donors had been given to all the families, and that Croydon Corporation hoped they would understand why an individual acknowledgement could not be sent. A letter was also sent to Kenyons Funeral Undertakers, of 45, Edgeware Road, saying that parents had asked if there were any personal effects belonging to the boys recovered from the crash. And if so, what happened to them? W.D. Hiddleston replied the next day that he had the boy's effects. They had been handed over to him by Police in Rogaland. He cautioned that although most consisted of papers and articles removed from the boy's clothing, – all required careful attention. Regretfully he finished *'I'm afraid that in some cases there might be nothing to return to the parents…'*

The Town Clerk in his absence had left instructions with the Borough Treasurer to collect details of the mass funeral expenses, and asked 'Are the Council going to claim back money from Cunard Eagle? If so – we must tell them as early as possible.'

On their return to Croydon a meeting was held at the Town Hall, at which the three told the parents of their mission, and answered their questions. The next day the Mayor received letters of appreciation from the parents, who also expressed their gratitude to all involved with the funeral, and for the meeting which had enabled them to discuss points troubling them. They were grateful to the Mayor for making a room at the Town Hall available to them when needed.

Meanwhile in Norway the accident investigators had been drafting their findings for a preliminary report. Inspector John Michelson had painstakingly prepared an analysis of the flight of Papa Mike for this, whilst investigators at the site of the crash had gathered evidence there. The preliminary report was released in Oslo on August 25th and was seized upon immediately by the press. On reading newspaper reports the parents felt side-lined, angry, and indignant. This was about their loved ones – so why did they only get to know about it by reading newspapers?

There were many matters of concern for Croydon Corporation too. One matter for the Mayor was that letters of thanks should be sent to all who had helped in Norway – and she had a very long list. The Finance Department wanted to know the funeral's full cost, and what could be reclaimed from Cunard Eagle, or from Croydon Corporation insurance policies. A vexed question that worried R. Wearing King was how Margery Budd would cope without her husband's salary.

On the evening of August 30th the parents, plus Mrs Budd, all met at Croydon Town Hall for a meeting convened by Ronald Green. There were many questions they needed answered. Why hadn't they been given copies of the accident report? And what was the position about insurance? Margery Budd went home and searched through her husband's papers. The next day she wrote enclosing a policy relating to the Austria trip, saying 'I think you will find that similar coverage for the Norwegian trip was arranged at the time through the Education Committee.'

Insurance arranged through the Education Committee? No insurance documents had been forthcoming from John Beacham's solicitors… Alarm bells rang at the Town Hall.

SEPTEMBER – DECEMBER 1961

Mrs Catherine Kettle empathised with the parents, some of whom she knew from her Councillor work in Upper Norwood. Promising help, on September 1st she composed a difficult letter to The Rt. Hon. Peter Thorneycroft, M.P. She commenced with the parent's troubling lack of information about the incident, and that despite addressing some of their questions since visiting Stavanger – parents otherwise *only* gleaned information from newspaper reports. She insisted it should be the British Government's *duty* to tell the parents the findings of the Norwegian Commission. Requesting a translated report for each family, she said they needed assurance that the Norwegian Commission's findings were accepted, or that a Commission of Inquiry would be appointed in Britain. Concluding, she related their concerns about crash details published in newspapers, insisting that any reassurance would be appreciated. She sent a copy to Ernest Taberner.

Her Town Clerk had his own problem. Crash details weren't his concern, but insurance was. Questions had been raised at the recent meeting, and convenor, 49 year old Ronald Green, the only person to have insured his son, had offered his help. Enclosing a copy of the Mayor's letter, Ernest Taberner wrote to him that Mrs Budd had just supplied an insurance policy from the Whitsun trip believing it to be similar to one for Norway. Confirming that *nothing* had been done through the Education Office, he asked Mr Green to check with the Insurance Company or with the Tourist Agency. Ernest Taberner frowned. Where was the Norway trip insurance policy? Surely there was one?

On September 2nd, W.D. Hiddleston sorted the scorched, personal effects he'd brought back to London from Stavanger. Amongst them was a burnt Hugo's Language Institute pocket-book, 'Norwegian Simplified', issued from Croydon Library. He wondered who had taken it out. Removing the tattered front page he posted this to Croydon Central Library. All the other possessions he parcelled up for the headmaster of Lanfranc to assign to various parents. He wondered whether receiving these oddments wouldn't simply cause more misery…

Many parents, however, were pitifully thankful for *anything* that related to their loved one. Mrs Eileen Adams wrote thanking Mr Taberner for recounting his Stavanger visit so vividly that she felt she had almost been there herself. London businessman Mr Alan White was concerned that the parents should appoint their own solicitors, and not use the same solicitor at Cunard Eagle. Writing for advice on this point, he suggested a chat by telephone. Based in London's Fleet Street 46 year old Alan White needed to be involved. He praised the Council officers for their wonderful organisation, but realising parents had differing views on a Memorial Fund (now standing at £2,677.5s.6d.) he suggested a committee be formed – and he asked to be on it.

Tommy Fowle returned to Lanfranc on Monday Sept 4th to find Royal Academy of Arts certificates awaiting him – months early! A sympathetic letter enclosed with them said they'd dealt with Lanfranc's examinations first. He looked with trepidation at the certificates of those who would no longer collect them at Speech Day. They were results their parents could feel proud of, if that was any consolation. Just back from a holiday where he'd tried to relax and forget, his vacation's good effects evaporated and responsibility descended like a weighty yoke. He decided to deliver the seven certificates personally, and talk about their boy's success. Tommy Fowle looked at the sad pile of relics he'd unpacked on his desk … two penknives, a cine camera, a pocket chess set, a fountain pen…, personal effects returned from the scene of the crash. He put his head in his hands. He was back in harness again; his maxim was 'Life must go on'; but he needed superhuman strength.

On September 5th, in Stavanger, Sofus Tønnessen, somewhat restored, wrote his report of the rescue work of the Red Cross Hjelpekorps during August 10th and 11th. Collectively they had worked 648 hours. He ended with a small, final comment. *'There is only one thing to say about the crew after this terrible task that was inhumanly strenuous both mentally and physically – they were excellent!'* He filed the report away – but he knew he could never forget.

On Thursday 7th September Lanfranc School commenced its Autumn Term, and it wasn't a usual beginning. Photographers took pictures of returning fifth formers (trying hard to conceal their feelings) entering at the front. Keith Scotcher saw Peter Crouch cycle in and noted the brave face that he put on. Len Dee and 'Carthorse' cycled in at the back, an awkward twosome without 'Eggy' – who should have been riding with them on his new bike. Inside, the school hall was cleared and cleaned, yet imagined spectres made the boys shiver. All had seen news photos of the 36 coffins, and realised they would eat off the tables that had borne them. The gloom that had permeated the school in August remained. The boys needed time to mourn their friends and masters. Lanfranc wasn't the same, yet the head's maxim 'Life must go on' was the only way forward. Accordingly their first assembly was a memorial service, taken by the Vicar of Croydon, Canon Warren-Hunt. This allowed the whole school to pay their respects. They tried to act like men and not cry. Then Tommy Fowle bravely spoke to them, and his 'Rough-Tough' school couldn't take it. Fifth form boys shed secret tears, whilst younger lads didn't care a jot that anyone saw them.

Surprisingly, at many other schools, it was the same. The boys and masters of Lanfranc were remembered at the first assembly at Dunraven School in Streatham, where pupil Roy Brown witnessed his normally 'stiff upper lip' headmaster, many staff, and girl pupils, in tears. At Susan Endicott's school in East Ham, girls stood remembering their late biology teacher, guiltily wishing they hadn't been so unruly.

The loss of two teachers at Lanfranc necessitated new replacements, and Colin Jones from South Wales had been selected to teach Physical Education. In trepidation of his posting, the 21 year old wondered how he could possibly replace a 'Budd or Beacham'. That first day he found Lanfranc in turmoil, staff and pupils still traumatised. Realising his presence should be low key, as no one had the time to welcome him, Colin wandered around until the school secretary rescued him, and ushered him into the staffroom. He watched activity up and down the school drive for three lonely hours until noon, when he was introduced, briefly, to the headmaster. Welcoming him, Tommy Fowle asked to be excused from staff introductions and the normal school tour. At the end of what was the longest day of his teaching career; Colin Jones gratefully exited the school premises. Everyone had long faces. No one had spoken. What *had* he come to?

It hadn't been any easier for the boys. In one class the register hadn't been changed to delete the names of boys who had died. Mr Taylor, who had stayed to help rather than emigrate to Australia had called out surnames without thinking and was surprised at the silence. His pupils were shocked and angry – how could he not realise? 'Mighty Mouse' was mortified, but the truth was that everyone was unnerved by the unimaginable events and initially Lanfranc was like a car trying to run on one cylinder. Soon these boys, including Clive Grumett, discovered their strict physics teacher had a kind heart, and an ear to listen to them, just as other staff also did their best to cheer up their unhappy pupils.

Not all were so lucky. Boys who had left Lanfranc in July felt in limbo. Their friends had died, but now engaged in jobs or training, they had no framework of understanding to bolster them up. The only way some could cope was to shut the door on their memories. To pretend it hadn't happened and 'bottle' it all away. Very few boys now wanted to fly. The prospect was terrifying.

Tommy Fowle, who had always run a 'tight ship', had much to attend to, in order to keep it afloat. And now he had a thorny problem thrust on to his plate. More questions about insurance for the Norway trip! He had sent the Town Clerk a copy of The Phoenix Assurance Company's policy covering George Budd and John Beacham from personal liability whilst in charge of the Norway trip, but nothing had been found regarding the *boy's* insurance. Now the matter was with the Education Office. He felt sure his colleagues, used to taking school trips abroad, would have made sure that everything was covered. He wiped his brow, wondering what compensation the parents would get for their son's deaths. Nothing that compared to the love that they had put into their young lives, or commensurate with the fine adults they would have become. It hurt him to think of them all. He had the rest of his school to think of too.

On September 8th certified copies were issued from entries made in the Air Register Book of Births and Deaths by the General Register Office. With official finality, each parent received their son's death certificate. That day Ronald Green received a letter from a firm of chartered accountants in London saying that, as spokesperson for the parents, he should urge them to choose a solicitor to act for them for several different matters. One was that money found on the body of George Budd, and waived by Mrs Budd, was probably the boy's pocket money. Parents, such as Brian Mitchell's, were not concerned about getting 'pocket money' back, preferring to give it to the Memorial Fund. Their prime concern was to be informed, in which exact plot, was their son buried.

Sir Peter Thorneycroft replied to the Mayor on September 11th, enclosing copies of the interim statement of the Norwegian Aircraft Accident Commission, and commended the Norwegians for their full cordial cooperation. Parents were sent three typed pages, but many found it impossible to analyse, whilst others could not bring themselves to read it. Emotions were too raw. Their son's weren't coming back – and the report didn't offer an explanation as to *why* they had died. The Report *did* say that further facts coming to light could change conclusions already drawn, whilst some media 'theories' were dismissed. One was the technical fault which delayed the flight five hours, another bad weather. Weather conditions were deemed 'satisfactory for landing with aids which were available at Sola at the time under consideration'. The criticism that the Royal Norwegian Air Force GCA (ground control approach), at Sola, wasn't employed by Air Traffic Control to bring in British aircraft, was demolished. The report stated that weather conditions at the time negated any necessity for Air Traffic Control to call for the use of radar. Furthermore, that afternoon other planes were brought down at Sola by use of the same aids and methods. They also stated that the pilot *could* have requested GCA. Interference between various radio beacons, or atmospheric disturbance, together with the aircraft's ambiguous response to a question regarding a marker beacon was, it was thought, possible contributing factors. Various parts of Papa Mike had been removed, including propeller blades and radio equipment, to determine the course of events during the critical moments prior to the crash – but these were seriously damaged, and it was uncertain whether tests will provide any information of importance. The report was starkly academic. They couldn't take it all in. Their sons were dead. DEAD! Some had lost their *only son*. Some had lost their *only child*! Many fathers were very bitter. Some with other sons could only focus on the son who had died. Many parents suffering depression found it worsened by a string of bad world news – a French plane crashed in Morocco killing all 77 on board, the United States exploded a 2.6 kiloton nuclear bomb, and Dag Hammarskjöld, Secretary General of the United Nations, died in a 'mystery' plane crash in the Congo. Everything seemed gloom and doom.

Mrs Kettle officially set up her Mayor's Trust Fund for a Lanfranc memorial, to be a wooden sports pavilion, which would cost £5,000. Her fund grew rapidly helped along by donations from schools and businesses and fund raising events, such as a concert given by Croydon Youth Orchestra and Choir. Meanwhile in Norway another memorial, the granite cross, was to be transported to Holtaheia's peak in October. (Unknown to the parents, the Red Cross boys and girls were working on Holtaheia, clearing wreckage.) Some parents wanted to attend the unveiling and to see where their son had died. None had seen their son's body and omitting this essential stage in the bereavement process had left an unfilled void. Letters regarding dates for a ceremony shuttled between Magne A. Paulsen of the Red Cross, and Alan White secretary of the Parents Committee. A date in May 1962, when the weather would be better, was fixed. Plans for a parent's 'Pilgrimage' to Holtaheia were initiated and its announcement was well received, but many felt heavy-hearted with the news of another plane crash. On October 7th a Derby Aviation Douglas C47 Dakota 4 crashed on Mt Canigou in the Pyrenees killing all 34 aboard. It was crushing news. A brighter note was that all the population of Tristan da Cunha, their island threatened by volcanic ash and lava, were evacuated to safety by H.M.S. Leopard.

On October 12th Croydon's finance department announced that associated funeral costs, plus the Mayor's official visit to Norway amounted to £628.6s.0d which together with cemetery costs of £680 totalled over £1,300. Whatever some may have felt about Croydon Council's paternalistic actions, no one could fault their generosity. Mrs Margery Budd was a concern for them because George Budd's teacher's annuation scheme didn't provide for a widow. Ernest Taberner scrutinised their policies, discovering a means by which Margery could receive a small pension. It was a seismic shock to be a widow and Margery knew she would have to be the bread-winner now. Geoff Budd had returned to university but she had the welfare of young Tim to consider, and Tim, like other youngsters affected by the tragedy, faced having his world turned upside down.

The pain of loss was felt by an unusually wide section of society in Croydon. Friends dreamt of their dead school mates. Diana Murphy lived behind

Mitcham Road cemetery where she and her friend Brenda Ireland had so often played with 'Beanie' and 'Micky' – Geoff Green and Michael Benson. Their four sets of initials were carved on the cemetery wall together. Around this time Diana had a vivid dream. Geoff and Michael came through her bedroom window to see her. Diana wasn't frightened at all. She was happy to see them. Susan Green on the other hand was scared of passing Geoff's bedroom because he used to tease her by putting a sheet over his head and pretending to be a ghost. His bedroom was closed now – but she was terrified he'd appear as a real ghost. (Two years later his bedroom was redecorated and given to Susan. She kept being disturbed by tapping at the window until one day she shouted 'Go away Geoff!' – and she never heard tapping again.) Lady Edridge school girl Denise learnt that 'Brian', whom she'd met off the bus, was Brian Mitchell, a victim of the crash, and she wished she'd known him better. Her school contemporary, Barbara Whiffen mourned for her boyfriend Eddie Prosper. Now Barbara took a longer route to school to avoid passing his house because she couldn't bear to meet Eddie's inconsolable mother.

The Town Clerk meanwhile, addressed the insurance question. A.I.R. Tours had sent him their brochure and Ernest Taberner had sent their insurance details to the parents. Their personal accident insurance covered children aged 8 to 15 years for £250, whilst those aged 16 qualified for £1000 on death. The parents probably regarded this with disgust. No amount of payment could replace their sons – any sum was derisory, but to discover that if a boy was one day *younger* than 16 he was 'worth' three quarters less – was horrible. On October 18th, the parent's solicitors enquired whether the Lanfranc boys were insured with A.I.R. Tours for these sums. They were in for a shock. So was the Town Clerk.

That day Sir Peter Thorneycroft made a flight to Norway to investigate the crash at the same time that the *'five times worse'* accident rate of independent air firms, versus scheduled flights, was discussed in The House of Commons. Meanwhile, on the flight deck of an R.A.F. Comet, the Aviation Minister followed the route of Papa Mike. During the six hour round trip, (which cost £2,000), he discussed the hazards and problems of the route to Stavanger. But why were charter flights *five times* as risky? Was it due to cost-cutting short cuts? Around this time, Harold Bamberg decided to scrap two of his remaining four Vikings, and sell the others. Cunard Eagle Airways Ltd. had taken a blow with all the adverse publicity. His old Vikings had to go. (G-AJPH, was withdrawn in October. G-AMNX, was withdrawn in December.)

On October 20th, solicitors in Accrington acting for A.I.R. Tours replied to solicitors engaged by the parents. They wrote saying that John Beacham had not completed their Insurance Proposal Forms as he stated that *'the Insurance was already in hand from the Insurance Company of the local Education Authority...'* This was a bombshell to all the solicitors. The Lanfranc boys were *not insured* – how could they explain to the parents that their boy's lives were worth – effectively, nothing!

Ernest Taberner and Catherine Kettle held private discussions. Unaware of this bombshell, many parents wanted their son's remembered with a lasting memorial. Trevor Condell, John Bradbery, and Geoff Green's parents bought silver sports cups in memory of their sons. Mrs Green, in floods of tears, awarded Geoff's cup to young Ian Greest for being Lanfranc's best all round junior sportsman. Some parents gave gifts in their son's memory to their churches. Alan White and his wife Elsie wanted Martin remembered with a wooden seat placed at the top of their road, and with a marble tablet at Lanfranc to commemorate all the boys – and the Red Cross.

Many parents threw themselves into voluntary work. Brian Mitchell's and Derek Goddard's parents worked hard for the Scouts, others with youth or sports clubs. Although friends and neighbours were kind, no one understood exactly what they were going through, except the other Lanfranc parents, so they stuck together and sought mutual comfort. Elsie White and other mothers visited the mass grave together each week to replace flowers, and to feel close to their sons. Mr and Mrs Hatchard gave their son David's model aeroplane collection to Ron Cox's son, also a David. Other parents with only one child did the same, sadly hugging the lucky recipient. A depressing month, October culminated in a stand-off between American and Russian tanks at the Brandenburg Gate in Berlin, followed defiantly by the detonation of 'Tsar Bomba' a 58-Megaton Hydrogen bomb (an unbroken world record). Comrade Khrushchev, who had autocratically ordered that 'Comrade' Stalin's body be removed from the Lenin Mausoleum, heightened escalating Cold War stakes.

With the sword of Damocles hanging over the World, Tommy Fowle still had to carry his school forward whilst bearing the deaths of 34 'sons', two good friends, *and* having to deal sympathetically with grieving parents. Lanfranc wasn't the same anymore, despite his staff working hard to raise the spirits of the boys. On the evening of November 10th, he had Speech Day to get through. Several of the boys who had died had won prizes, and adding to the agony there were new prizes given by bereaved parents. All eyes were on Mr Fowle as he spoke, lauding those who had died, and applauding those who had helped the school during the tragedy. Of the 'unknown friends in Norway' he said, *'Could a greater contrast be imagined than that of the cruel awe-inspiring magnificence of the Norwegian landscape and the warm-hearted sympathy and generosity of the people who shared our distress?'* He thanked the bereaved parents for not blaming the school for organising the trip, and everyone who had expressed sympathy in so many ways. *'Such a wave of spontaneous sympathy must be experienced to be believed. I had no conception of the effect of such a tragedy on the public generally, not only on people of our own island, but in all parts of the globe. In a world so beset by the forces of evil, this is both reassuring and comforting.'* The Speech Day programme listed Edward Gilder, John Bradbury, Geoff Brown, Peter Boyes, Derek Goddard, David Hendley, Brian Mitchell, Roger Taylor, Reggie Chapple, Geoffrey Crouch, Robert Martin, Robert Roffey, Clifford Gaskin, David Gore, Alan Lee, David Higgins, Trevor Condell, Richard Lawrence, and John Wells amongst the prize and award winners. Prizes were given out by Mrs Kettle (who had developed an enormous empathy with Lanfranc), but unlike the previous year, applause was muted with so many 'winners' dead. Nevertheless, when the guest speaker, Mr. Arthur Rowe, manager of Crystal Palace Football Club stood up, he received a tumultuous reception. Released from their pent up emotions by their love of their football team, the boys responded with cheers and whistles. They desperately wanted to feel happy again.

Mrs Kettle was impressed with Lanfranc, its staff and especially its 'stiff-backed' headmaster, and since their trip to Stavanger she and Ernest Taberner felt ever more personally involved. Together they addressed the Finance Committee for a Town Memorial for the boys. Local stone masons, some of whom were Old

Lanfrancians, had offered to build a memorial but architects 'Scherrer & Hicks', already working on new buildings at the cemetery, were engaged instead.

On November 19th the Daily Express announced *'Scientists at the Royal Aircraft Establishment, Farnborough have been called in to help find the cause of the Stavanger air disaster… Parts of the Viking charter plane … have been flown to Britain and are being examined by experts at Farnborough.'*

On December 6th, at a Parents Meeting, they were told that proposal forms for insurance for the Norway trip had *not* been completed by John Beacham. It was an *'unfortunate technicality'*, despite payment for insurance cover being included in the A.I.R. Tours price, paid by the parents. John Beacham had believed that similar insurance was covered through the Croydon Education Authority. No fortune could have compensated for the loss of their sons, but to learn that they weren't insured due to a 'technicality' was a huge psychological blow. Solicitors were, however, working for compensation from Cunard Eagle Airways. At the same meeting it was announced that a group of Lanfranc boys, together with Mr. Fowle, would accompany the party of parents, by boat, to Norway for a 'Pilgrimage to Holtaheia'.

No bereaved family had a happy Christmas, but many hoped for a better New Year. Whilst his family were at church on Christmas Day Ronald Green attended a private service by the mass grave with other relatives. Vases of fresh flowers stood over individual plots in the cold foggy air. Whilst they all stood at one side of the grave, Ronald stood, head bent, by Quentin's plot. A news photographer captured an image of the plaintive scene, Ronald alone in the foreground. Returning home, he insisted that a place for Quentin be laid at the dinner table. Christmas dinner was eaten in miserable silence, the empty place a haunting reminder. It didn't feel like Christmas, and it was Ronald's last.

1962

One week later on January 1st, Ronald Green suddenly died. Doctors said it was a heart attack but his family knew his heart was broken. His was the first 'collateral' death associated with the air crash. That New Year's Day, whilst other parents wondered what 1962 would bring, the folk song 'Young Birds', about the Lanfranc Boys, was released by Ewan MacColl and Peggy Seeger – but no parents knew.

On February 10th, the Daily Mail published 'FREAK WIND KILLED CROYDON BOYS'. *'The airliner …, appears to have been blown off course by a freak wind. This is stated in the Anglo-Norwegian commission's report on the crash of the chartered Cunard Eagle Viking, code named Papa Mike. The report says it is certain the Viking's crew made a navigation error of about 20 miles. But it adds that the investigation has been unable to find a complete explanation for the accident. At Sola, just before the crash, the wind was only about 25m.p.h. But there was a strong depression just to the north, near the plane's approach route. This could have caused sudden, rapidly veering winds of up to 60m.p.h. The report rejects criticisms made at the time that the airport should have been guiding Papa Mike by radar 'talk-down'. The report is now being studied by Ministry of Aviation officials. The joint report is to be published next week. Mr. Peter Thorneycroft, Minister of Aviation, is expected to make a statement in Parliament after it has been published.'* Was the crash due to a 'freak wind'? Reading the newspapers the parents didn't know what to believe.

Two days later they all heard from their solicitors who had won a claim against Cunard Eagle. They were all to receive £600 in compensation (except the son's of widows who would receive £1000), whilst miscellaneous expenses and their fare to Norway would be repaid. Croydon Council also eventually paid the 'insurance' for the boys. Many parents had never owned so much money but the payments were a bitter compensation. Who wanted money? They all wanted something that no amount of money could ever buy.

On Saturday May 5th, whilst 12 East Germans escaped to freedom in a tunnel under the Berlin Wall, Lanfranc Secondary School Memorial Garden was dedicated. Rain threatened as the relatives assembled around a beautifully finished stone built garden, landscaped, paved, and planted. Michael Benson's builder father and uncle had helped build the monument, whilst Lanfranc boy Charles Ella's uncle, Bill Brayford, a lorry driver from Yorkshire, had transported special York stone. A cross, of Norwegian blue granite, stood at the far end, and an inscribed plaque, to be unveiled, at the other end. Masons had carved names into smooth cream-coloured limestone blocks pin-pointing the position of each boy, and George Budd. Peter Boyes and John Beacham's names were included. Once gloomy, dank earth, now the mass grave was light and uplifting. As the B.B.C. News camera team commenced filming the ceremony for 'Town and

Around', the Salvation Army Citadel Band played. The guest of honour was Mr. Jan Johnsen the Mayor of Stavanger. Rain fell as Croydon's Mayor, Mrs C.G. Kettle, spoke for the citizens of Croydon. The Bishop of Croydon, The Rt. Rev. John Taylor Hughes, assisted by the Rev. Harold J. Edgeler of Croydon's Free Church Federal Council, commenced the Service of Dedication by remembering all those who had died. A reading from I Corinthians 15, 51-58 and the hymn *The King of Love my Shepherd is* followed. The Mayor then asked the Bishop to dedicate the ground. This was followed by more prayers and an address and blessing by the Bishop. Finally Mr. Jan Johnsen, Mayor of Stavanger, spoke. All eyes were on the slim, bronzed, fine featured man, who had done so much to help at the time. The speech he had prepared, besides greetings from his fellow countrymen and women in Stavanger and Strand, and especially the Red Cross, contained a heartfelt plea that young people must be allowed to travel across international frontiers in order to form 'a new and better world'. It was a message of friendship and peace between nations.

He then unveiled the tablet at the southern end of the Memorial Garden – revealing the inscription – *'This garden is DEDICATED TO THE MEMORY of the MASTERS AND BOYS of the LANFRANC SECONDARY SCHOOL, CROYDON, who lost their lives in an aeroplane accident near Stavanger, Norway, 9th August, 1961.* 'There is nothing in death or life, in the world as it is, or the world as it shall be, in the forces of the universe, in heights or depths – nothing in all creation that can separate us from the love of God in Christ Jesus our Lord.'*

It was a beautiful service and very fitting to have Stavanger's Mayor to unveil the inscribed tablet. Many present were to meet Jan Johnsen again, soon, in Norway. But some parents, however, had decided against going. They just couldn't face seeing Stavanger, and especially not Holtaheia.

The Pilgrimage to Norway

On Saturday May 12th, a party of 65 relatives and close friends representing 25 of the boy's families, plus a party of 25 boys from Lanfranc school accompanied by Mr and Mrs Fowle, Mr Harper and Mr Barlow, all caught the train to Newcastle from London's King's Cross station. Half of the parents nearly missed the train when the coach booked to transport them broke down and a substitute only arrived after an agonising one hour's wait. They stepped aboard the train, pulled by a steam locomotive, in the nick of time. No one, of course, had wanted to go by air. The Pilgrimage was a sad adventure for brothers and sisters, and the Lanfranc school boys, but the parents felt it was something they were compelled to do – even though they knew it carried a high emotional cost. Some parents simply had not wanted to go as they felt that they would not be able to cope. The largest family group consisted of Kathleen Green, her elder sons Tony and Martyn, daughter Rosalind, and seven year old son Nigel. Tony and Rosalind kept detailed diaries whilst Martyn was intent upon making a 16mm film of the Pilgrimage.

The party boarded the Bergen Line M.S. Venus at Newcastle, casting off from the quayside at 6.00pm. The sea was calm within the Tyne estuary, but as soon as the Venus left its protection they felt a rolling motion. The lumpy North Sea was in a foul mood, a north-easter was blowing, humping the ominously green expanse into white-topped crests and dark wallowing troughs. Dinner in the cafeteria was only eaten (and retained), by those with strong 'sea-legs'. Party members quickly realised why their Bergen Line ship was known to all former passengers (many of whom had crossed the Bay of Biscay in her) as 'Vomiting Venus' – she didn't have stabilisers. As most of the party retired to their cabins, Rosalind went on deck where Norwegian youths, and a few Lanfranc boys, were enjoying staggering around, leaning exaggeratedly into the wind which inflated their coats and supported them from falling. Not the least bit sea-sick she loved the excitement as 'Vomiting Venus' pitched and rolled, its juddering metal plates creaking. It was her first time on any boat and she thought M.S. Venus very handsome with its shiny black hull, bright white superstructure and horizontally striped funnels. She would have been surprised at its history, for M.S.Venus was built for the Bergen Line in1931, seized by Germany in 1941, bombed and sunk by the Allies at Hamburg in 1945, but later salvaged and restored, and returned to the Bergen Line! As she watched seabird acrobatics in the buffeting wind, and relished salt spray on her face, Rosalind thought of how much her father had wanted to go on this Pilgrimage. Yet like almost every one of her companions she felt odd to be going to Stavanger. The name of the city had made a cold shiver run down her spine for months. She'd hated the name, and its association. Yet since meeting Jan Johnson, Stavanger's Mayor, somehow the terror had been removed from *'Stavanger'*. Reading newspaper cuttings her mother had saved, she knew how affected by the tragedy the people of Stavanger had been, and Jan Johnsen had said so himself. So perhaps Stavanger wouldn't be too much of a trauma to visit. But she wasn't at all sure about Holtaheia! Photos she'd seen of the mountain had shown a dark, sinister, totally forbidding place. Music from Grieg's 'Hall of the Mountain King' thrummed in her head. No, Holtaheia was clearly a horrible place – but she *had* to go there. She wanted to see for herself. She wanted to find answers as to why her brother and his friends had died. Sea spray masked tears as she thought of them and she was finally forced inside when a capricious gust whipped her tightly tied head scarf away, playing with it like a wind-battered sea bird before a wave licked up and swallowed it.

The next morning she rose early and went out on deck again. Her cabin mate had been ill all night. The Venus was still rolling and the wind was strong. Most of the party stayed in their cabins although some enjoyed a little breakfast before lying down to await quieter waters. Impeded by the rough sea, at 3.00 pm M.V. Venus docked half an hour late but the disembarkation was further delayed when the gangway refused to swing into position. On the quayside in Stavanger crowds of people waited to greet them all. Proud of her 'sea legs' at sea, on encountering terra firma Rosalind was amazed to experience the ground going up and down! Those who had retired to their bunks appeared unaffected. Customs formalities over they were taken by coach to Sola Strand Hotel close by Sola Airport, but weren't there very long before a coach transported them to Stavanger Cathedral. Just turned sixteen, Rosalind had been bought a scarlet raincoat for her birthday. She wore this to the service in the Cathedral – and wished she hadn't. The soberly dressed congregation were already assembled when the party from Croydon were ushered in. They turned around to look, and Rosalind saw shock and surprise in some eyes. She was instantly and embarrassingly aware that she was wearing bright red, when everyone else was wearing black! Her blushing face matched her coat as she took her place and studiously contemplated the massive stone columns and medieval architecture. She felt doubly discomfited because the stone floor and the seats in the cathedral appeared to being rolling up and down. At the end of the service, taken in Norwegian and English, she walked out gingerly as the floor was still rising and falling. This Pilgrimage to Norway, she thought, was full of surprises.

Monday 14th May was a surprise too. The North Sea depression which should have brought bad weather to Stavanger unaccountably stopped. Instead the day was fine, warm, and sunny. After a Smorgasbord breakfast (another experience), the party were soon on the ferry to Tau, and thence by coach to Holta farm. All had come prepared with jumpers and anoraks, but rainwear wasn't needed so these were left at Holta farm. Red Cross members, in aquamarine jump-suits and dark berets, were there to greet the party from Croydon. They stood out from the crowds gathering to make the ascent. Those from Croydon were each given a bunch of flowers to place by the Cross. This kind gesture continued an invisible process which had begun the previous evening at the Cathedral, which metaphorically, was like a chrysalis's gradual internal 'reorganisation' before metamorphosis. No one in the party realised it then, but the compassion of strangers was going to help heal wounds.

A long procession set off up the rocky track and Kathleen Green wished she hadn't left Nigel behind at the hotel. She'd thought 'a mountain' would be impossible for a seven year old, yet there were younger children there. Martyn, loaded down with a heavy camera and tripod, took every opportunity to stop and film, whilst Tony forged on ahead enjoying the sunshine and blue skies. Red Cross girl Evy Smith offered her assistance to Kathleen, leaving Rosalind temporarily alone, until Captain E. L. Endicott, the father of stewardess Susan, joined her. His wife and daughter Ann walked sadly together, and as it wasn't possible for three to walk side by side he'd decided to talk to the lonely sixteen year old, as something about her reminded him of his late daughter.

Now that this epoch making day had come, Rosalind felt doubly melancholy. She was sad for her brother Quentin, and she wished her father had been there – as he'd so wanted but being joined by Susan's father jogged her from reverie, and the two conversed as they scrambled up the path; strangers glad of a companion. Captain Endicott asked her about school and her ambitions for the future. He said that Susan had studied Zoology at London University, taking a Masters degree as well. Rosalind said she hadn't a hope of going to university because she hadn't worked hard enough at school, although she was working hard now – as she had a promise to keep for her father – who had died. He commiserated, saying it wasn't too late to try. An aspiration was quietly seeded.

They followed a route marked by sticks with pale blue ribbons. The ground was snow covered higher up, and they traversed a mountain torrent via a stepping stone bridge nick-named 'Marian's bridge' after an English Red Cross helper. A 'soup' tent offered sustenance to any in need, but they bypassed this, pausing to drink melted snow at a rest stop higher up. Hundreds of people of all ages were walking with them in a long, colourful crocodile. The frost shattered cliff loomed closer and from below she could see two tall standard bearers, one holding the Union Jack, the other the Norwegian flag, on either side of a white draped shape at the cliff edge. Following a narrow track around to the back and up to the plateau top they joined crowds already gathered. Captain Endicott rejoined his wife and daughter. Talking to the father of the stewardess had made climbing Holtaheia, a place she had envisaged with dread, an interesting, pleasant, experience. Now, having scrambled to the top where it had all happened, she looked around and was amazed.

Whilst climbing, she'd been so deep in conversation and careful where she placed her feet that she hadn't looked back. The uneven route had banished her residual sea motion, and now as she stood firmly on Holtaheia's summit, she beheld an incredible panorama of rocky peaks, mountain lakes, fjords, and islands. People snaked up the slope below her, and a monstrous helicopter landed nearby, but the view took her breath away. She could scarcely credit it. *This* was the dreaded mountain where her brother and his friends, their masters, and the crew of Papa Mike had died – yet it didn't seem horrible. Holtaheia seemed an innocent, craggy sentinel in an awe-inspiring landscape. She had never seen anything like this before. It was a revelation.

Around 500 people gathered on the weathered summit. The Red Cross standard bearers stood ram-rod straight, their swirling flags creating a visible and an invisible message. Identical colours but different crosses linked yet distinguished the two countries. Symbolically Norway 'held hands' with Britain, or more particularly, Croydon. Behind the six foot high veiled monument, close to the cliff edge, stood the Tau Band; young school children in smart blue uniforms, yellow bow ties, and peaked caps. Microphones had somehow been set up. Dignitaries, including Sir John Walker, Mrs Kettle, and Ernest Taberner, arrived with the helicopter, and shortly a huge semi-circle formed about the monument to be unveiled. Relatives, clutching bunches of flowers, stood at the front. Standing next to those playing a role in the ceremony was a young man in traditional rural dress. He looked unhappy and out of place, even though he knew the area best of all. Ola Lekvam saw crowds of people around him but was haunted by what he'd seen, alone, nine months previously. The two standard bearers, focusing on the distance, felt the same. Everyone spoke in whispers.

On a huge rock members of the RNoAF Rescue Squadron, at home with aerial views, stood overlooking the whole assembly. They too recalled the shattered bones of a Vickers Viking and other sights they preferred not to recall, and they now marvelled at what the young Red Cross members had achieved. Sofus Tønnessen stood apart from his assembled brigade, blocking out hideous images from his mind, overlaying them with what he now saw. So many who stood on Holtaheia's peak knew what it had looked like in August 1961, and these people now had to control painful recollections. Egil Eriksson was at least distracted by taking photographs this momentous day. For members of the Red Cross 1st and 2nd rescue teams, little was erased. They couldn't forget what they had experienced. But for the grieving parents and relatives, now at the very spot where their loved ones had died, the place was washed clean. There were little signs of wreckage, because the Red Cross had sympathetically cleared and buried most, sinking parts in a bog, or piling rocks over immovable pieces. The relatives were spared the true horror. Few could have imagined what it was that the rescuers had witnessed. They were not haunted by images that could never be erased. For the relatives 'The Lanfranc Boys' rested in Croydon. They had simply come to see where their loved ones had died; to put into place what had happened; to say 'goodbye' where their souls had departed; to sense whether any essence of their collective joie de vivre remained, and to see a memorial cross unveiled.

As the ceremony began the atmosphere was heavy with grief. Collectively the Cunard Eagle representatives, Lanfranc headmaster and school boys, and relatives from Croydon were outnumbered four to one by friendly, sympathetic Norwegians. Tau school band evocatively played 'Green-sleeves' then Sofus Tønnessen, now leader of the Red Cross, spoke with compassion, inviting the headmaster of Lanfranc to unveil the cross which he said was – *'a memorial to the deep interest and sympathy shown by the Norwegian people.'* Until then the relatives had no understanding of the Norwegian Red Cross organisation. It was an eye-opener to see so many young people, and such a young leader. Many had been accompanied up the mountain by friendly Red Cross members, and felt the stirrings of friendship. Kathleen Green had already invited Evy Smith to visit her home for a holiday in England.

Tommy Fowle stood forward to speak. His wife was there with him. It was hard for him to speak without tears, but he managed. A long serving church warden at All Saints Church in Shirley, he spoke of the cross dedicated in Croydon, saying that the two crosses would remind future generations of the link established between two towns in tragic circumstances. *'It seems impossible,'* he continued, *' during that unforgettable night and the anxious hours of the following day, that we should ever recover from the stunning effect of the shock, but companionship, warm-heartedness and spiritual guidance have, in some measure, brought comfort and hope.'*

Then as cameras clicked he removed the white sheet, revealing a fresh granite cross standing as a permanent reminder of what had happened at that spot. On its upright stave, a bronze plaque commemorated the tragedy, the words in Norwegian stating – **'*In memory of those who lost their lives here on August 9th 1961. Thirty-four English schoolboys, their two teachers and the crew of three*'**. It was a poignant moment for Tommy Fowle as he paused, head bowed, before the cross. The faces of 'his' boys flashed through his mind. What might they have become, but for this? They'd had their lives before them… It was tragic… Then collecting himself he officially handed the safe-keeping of the cross into the hands of Herr Vasstueit, the Mayor of Strand, before solemnly standing aside.

Tau school band played *'Nearer my God to Thee'* and as the music drifted away on the light breeze Bishop Birkeli told those mourning, *'if you are still carrying your burden, lay it down at the cross. Leave it here and God will give you new hope and happiness.'* He dedicated the cross to *'the dear ones who found their complete salvation on this spot'*. *'Abide with Me'* was played, and then as the service ended Sir John Walker stepped forward to place a wreath at the cross. A second wreath, from Lanfranc School, was placed by Mr Fowle, followed by ones from the Stavanger Red Cross and Cunard Eagle Airways. Finally the parents, wiping tear-streaked faces, placed bunches of flowers at the foot of the cross.

Heart-breaking for all, it was particularly sad for those parents who had lost their only child. Unimaginable grief was felt by them, and they had no children to comfort them. Rosalind Green saw her namesake Susan being comforted by her father and wished her own father was there. She needed his protective arms about her. So did her mother. They hugged each other instead, and followed others being shown the second bronze plaque, affixed to the cliff wall at the point where Papa Mike had impacted. A narrow rock ledge led down to the cliff face where a circular impact scar had bruised the rock and smashed to oblivion all lichen growth there. They saw the Norwegian inscription, which translated read, **'Against this mountain wall the British plane Papa Mike crashed in the evening of August 9th, 1961 – a stormy day with low clouds. The plane got lost in an inexplicable way a few minutes before it should have landed at Sola. All on board perished.'** Like 'doubting Thomas' they touched the blasted rock and tried to comprehend. From their hearts they sent messages of eternal love.

They were not alone in doing so. The Lanfranc boys present were moved. Dave Randall had been shocked to see scraps of wreckage, and to see an old duffle bag hidden under a rock, but the ceremony had been a relief for him. Every relative and those from Lanfranc left thought-messages for their departed loved ones. Across the North Sea in Croydon, those relatives who hadn't come on the Pilgrimage tried to envisage Holtaheia. They imagined a horrible scenario. They were wrong. What they could not know at the time was that love is a great healer, and that love shown to the visitors from Croydon by everyone on Holtaheia, had added to the Pilgrimage's unique process of healing.

The sad but uplifting ceremony over, the parents were guests of Strand Kommune at Tau church hall. Lanfranc boy Dave Randall, used to rowdy school meal times was surprised to find himself seated next to the Ambassador's son for a sumptuous dinner, including reindeer steak. Dave was on his best behaviour. During 'second' helpings of courses more speeches were made, including one by Alfred Hauge, Norway's famous novelist, poet, and historian. Hauge was the expert about Ryfylke in Rogaland, pronouncing that what had happened on Holtaheia had added to the region's history. He told how the monuments had been donated; flown in by Royal Norwegian Air Force helicopter; and erected by the Red Cross. Croydon's Mayor replied, remarking optimistically that – *'this showed the kind of love and friendship she hoped to see spread across the world.'* Tommy Fowle spoke, recalling his night of *'black despair'*, saying – *'Yet, shining like a beacon through our desperation and unhappiness came the messages of concern, crystallised, as it were, by the warm-hearted sympathy and tenderness which you, our friends in Norway, showered on the remains of our lads, unknown to you, but so dear to us.'* At the end of a long day the relatives returned to their hotel tired but strangely uplifted after a roller-coaster day of sad-happy emotions. All were deeply impressed with the sincerity and kindness they had collectively and individually been shown.

Rosalind took back with her a small juniper bush which Captain Endicott had dug from the mountain and entrusted to her, in case it was confiscated when he flew home the next day. The gift of the dwarf bush and its association meant a lot to her. That night, with her G.C.E. O-levels approaching, Rosalind wrote notes for an English essay entitled *'Mountainous Country.'*

'As I looked around me on the sunny day I could see mountains, lakes, fjords and dotted around, tiny farms. I was standing on the very top of Holtaheia Mountain where 39 people lost their lives, one of them my brother. But somehow the mountain looked beautiful; – rugged, yet serene and lonely, not like a mountain of death at all. Looking down 2000 feet I saw the sea glinting in the sunshine and the tiny islands had changed from a verdant green to a misty grey. Mountain lakes, fed by mountain torrents streaming from yet un-melted snow fields, were a vivid blue and on this warm day were as calm as an English mill pond.

Standing at the top of Holtaheia I could see the Cross, unveiled in memory of the boys who lost their lives last August. But through my tears I looked around me to capture the scene. The mountains rising high into the cool clear mountain air were rugged, but this ruggedness had an indescribable beauty of its own, even Holtaheia (which many people had imagined cruel) was a mixture of beauty and mystery. It is a mystery which will haunt me, forever. Running down the mountainside, first in small drips and then trickles, the water from the melting snow gradually collects together in surging torrents recklessly pursuing the last drop of water, leaping over rock and waterfalls determined not to be left behind. The water is crystal clear, ice cold, and very refreshing to drink. Near the water and in fact over the lower slopes grows wiry mountain grass, and if you search carefully you will find delicate white flowers….'

It had been cathartic. Her feelings for Holtaheia had completely changed. She had discovered the wonders of the natural world. Besides memories and photographs, she had also carried back a piece of rock to give to her friend Denise Schröder (in memory of Brian Mitchell), and a small angular piece of plexi-glass she'd found, for herself. A fragment of smashed window it had some small indecipherable letters scratched into it. She wondered which Lanfranc boy had looked through the window from which this shard came.

On Tuesday 15th May, a cloudy day with rain, the party were taken to see 'The Pulpit Rock' aboard '*M.S. Clipper*'. Despite it being bad weather there was a holiday atmosphere aboard the launch which nine months previously had transported Red Cross rescuers. Now some of these Hjelpekorps members chatted happily to the relatives. The cloud hung low in Lysefjord and only the first few feet of the famous monolith could be seen. They were accompanied by several of Stavanger's and Strand's officials. Svein Hole, Strand's Town Clerk did his best to teach one linguistically challenged girl some words of Norwegian. Back in Stavanger again, each family was presented with a souvenir commemorative plate of Stavanger.

Wednesday 16th was a day when party members could choose to do what they wished, and several couples paid a final visit to Holtaheia, including Ed Murray's parents. Violet Murray recalled Edwin triumphantly planting a Union Jack in a castle of sand before he left home, now she touched the cross against which another Union Jack had waved bravely in the wind. Mr and Mrs Murray had been apprehensive about making the trip but were very glad that they had. They thought the Norwegians were wonderful and didn't know how to thank them enough.

Thursday 17th was Norway's National Day and the party spent the whole day in Stavanger at The Atlantic Hotel, watching parades of mock defiant school children thrash teacher's canes. Each had the symbol of their school, an animal silhouette, sewn on to their coats. The Lanfranc boys came as the parent's guests and watched the parade from the second floor windows highly amused at the 'rebellious' pupils and itching to buy themselves a souvenir cane to swish as well. When the Red Cross were spotted marching towards the hotel, Mr. Prosper and Martyn Green impulsively dashed outside and held up the parade. From the windows above everyone shouted *'Two – Four – Six – Eight – who do we appreciate? RED CROSS!!!* Sofus Tønnessen stopped his brigade, turned, and saluted the cheering crowd from Croydon, before marching smartly on again. When the Mayor of Stavanger marched by he was loudly cheered as well. The gradual metamorphosis, invisibly transforming the Croydon party, culminated in a celebration at their hotel that night. It hadn't occurred to any of the parents or their children to think that they would feel really *happy* in Norway. Or that anyone would actually *let their hair down*. But they did. After a farewell dinner, at which animals sculpted from ice were a table feature, there was a dance. To the British teenagers waltzes seemed too tame, so they requested some modern music and were rewarded by Chubby Checker's 'Let's Twist Again'. Hauling bemused Norwegian partners on to the dance floor the youngsters in the party taught their new friends 'The Twist' and 'The Method' as their parents clapped and then joined in. It was an undreamt off last night. They all *laughed* and *danced* together.

The next day, no one wanted to go home. Everyone bought souvenirs and gifts for family and friends who didn't come. Mrs Wells gave Dave Randall the rest of her Norwegian Kroner and told him to enjoy himself. Susan Green's father bought a huge fresh salmon, slinging it over his shoulder before climbing the gangway of M.S. Venus. As Venus pulled out from the quayside by Stavanger old town, everyone from Croydon cheered and waved to their new friends, the Red Cross, who had come to see them off. Some in the party pretended to dive in, to swim back! The Pilgrimage to Stavanger had changed strait-jacketed chrysalides of misery into imagos of hope. Friendship and love are antidotes to loneliness and despair, and the relatives on the Pilgrimage had received a powerful injection of both. Resilient youngsters in the party had their lives ahead and it was up to them to make the most of them, and to live their lives remembering their brothers who had lost their own. Restored parents realised that whilst they would never, ever forget their lost son, they had other children to focus on, and a future to contend with. Those tragic parents who had lost their only child, however, and who were the worst hit, had made lasting friends who were to provide future consolation in their blighted lives. The Pilgrimage had given something different to each one. And it had eased the pain, and cured the ignorance, they'd felt about Stavanger, and Holtaheia. The Norwegian people had won their hearts completely. A line had now been drawn and they could move on from August 9th 1961.

Compassion, the 'Golden Rule' had initiated healing.

The Lanfranc school party stayed for a further five days. They were to do all the activities that their lost friends should have done. Geoffrey Parr had been determined from the trip's inception that he must go – to remember them. Leaving Stavanger they stayed at The Preikestolen mountain lodge and the next day walked to see the vertiginous Pulpit Rock. On the way back, some were so excited by the experience that they rushed down the steep path too fast for safety and Doug Kerr fell and hurt his back. Whilst his friends engaged in further adventure pursuits Doug was an invalid, cared for jointly by Mr and Mrs Fowle. Whilst teachers Harper and Barlow supervised the other lads, Tommy Fowle had some rare free time to contemplate what had happened to his 'lost' boys, and to recall them all. Visiting Rogaland and meeting the people had helped him move on a little. He liked the young Red Cross members and he already had plans for them to visit Lanfranc with their leader Sofus Tønnessen. They were fine young men and women and admirable role models. His visit to Holtaheia had been a partial release, but he'd also been on duty for Lanfranc. Though there had been happy moments, the Pilgrimage to Holtaheia wasn't a holiday. It had taken a toll on him and he still had two further ceremonies associated with the disaster to prepare for.

The Mayor of Stavanger Mr Jan Johnsen unveils the memorial wall at the Lanfranc Memorial Garden on May 5th 1962.

The Mayor of Croydon followed by the Mayor of Stavanger and Bishop of Croydon after the service of Dedication of the Lanfranc Memorial Garden.

Young and old walk up to Holtaheia.

Lanfranc boys and relatives pause at a refreshment tent.

Holtaheia, May 14th 1962

Mr. A. T. Fowle unveils the Cross. Tau School band stand behind.

Bishop Birkeli speaks after the unveiling.

Holtaheia after the Cross has been unveiled.

Relatives at the ceremony, holding bunches of flowers provided for them.

British Ambassador Sir John Walker speaks to parents.

Relatives add their flowers to the wreaths already laid.

> MOT DENNE FJELLVEGGEN
> GIKK DET BRITISKE FLYET
> „PAPA MIKE" I KVELDINGEN.
> DEN 9. AUGUST 1961 – EN
> STORMFULL DAG MED LAVT
> SKYDEKKE. FLYET BLE UFOR-
> KLARLIG BORTE FÅ MINUT-
> TER FØR DET SKULLE LAN-
> DE PÅ SOLA.
> ALLE OMBORD OMKOM.

Against this mountain wall the British plane Papa Mike crashed in the evening of August 9th, 1961 – a stormy day with low clouds. The plane got lost in an inexplicable way a few minutes before it should have landed at Sola. All on board perished.

Red Cross standard bearers and others at the end of the ceremony.

The Cross on Holtaheia.

Sofus Tønnessen and the Red Cross salute the parents at Stavanger's National Day Parade.

Reconstruction of the last part of Papa Mike's flight, from the Report of the Royal Norwegian Commission 1962.

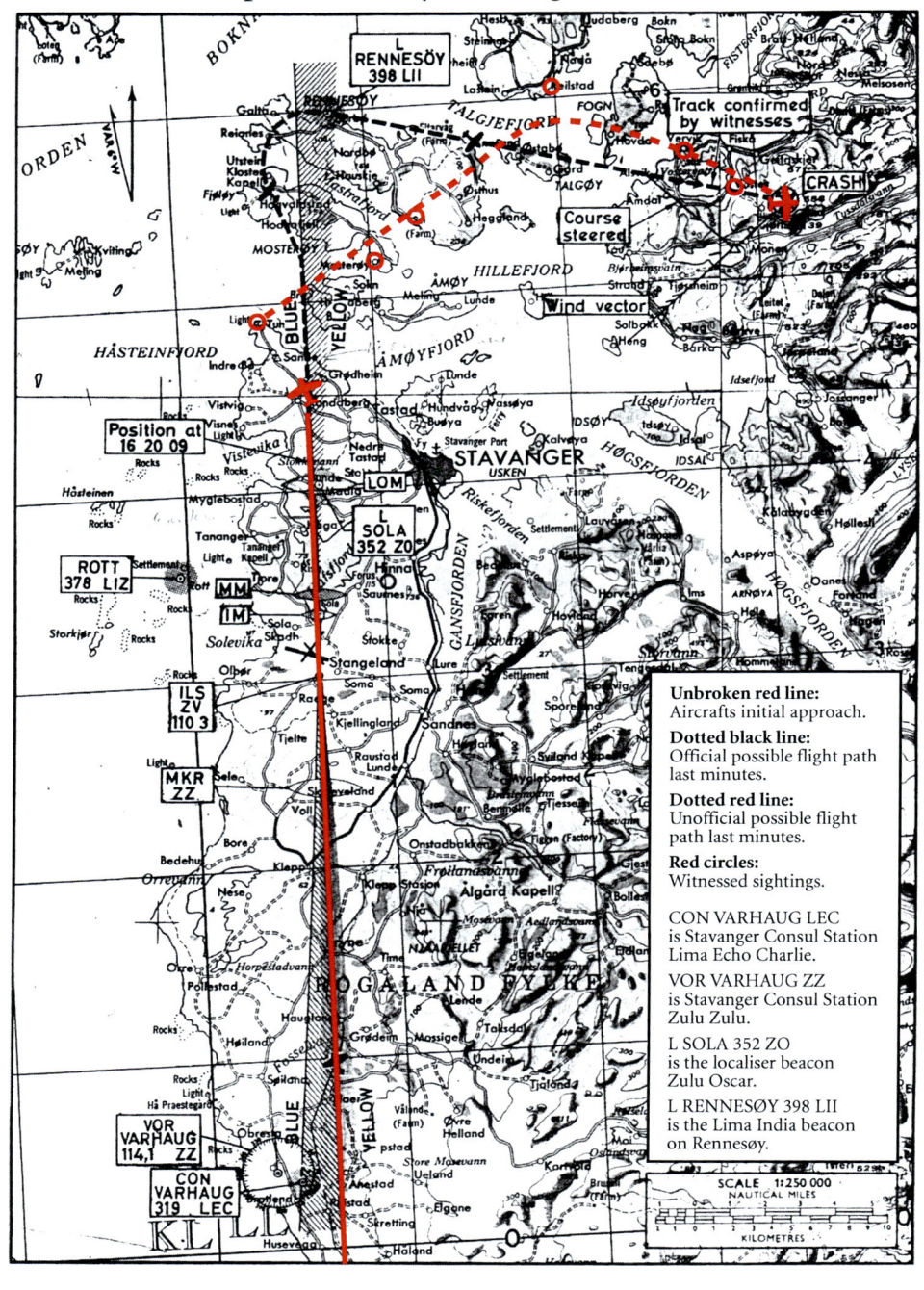

Wasted Lives

On May 22nd a memorial plaque commemorating the Lanfranc Boys and teachers, and the role of the Norwegian Red Cross, donated by Mr and Mrs Alan White, was unveiled in the foyer of the school. Parents who had been on the Pilgrimage met again for the occasion, a little happier now than they had been before the trip. A week later, however, the Report of the Royal Norwegian Commission for the Investigation of Civil Aircraft Accidents on the Accident to Viking G-AHPM near Stavanger, Norway on 9th August, 1961 was published by Her Majesty's Stationery Office. Whilst it didn't extinguish their new spark of happiness it did fill them with frustration and despair. During June all the parents received a copy of the Ministry of Aviation Civil Aircraft Accident report. They read it with trepidation.

The lengthy technical report apparently left no stone unturned. It concluded with 18 points, almost all of which were positive. The aircraft had valid Certificates of Airworthiness and Maintenance. It had been maintained in accordance with an Approved Maintenance Schedule and all documents were in order and properly signed. The Crew was properly licensed and within prescribed limits in respect of maximum flying time and minimum rest period. The possibility was excluded of the crew having been affected either by alcohol or carbon monoxide. The aircraft weight at take-off was below the maximum allowed, whilst the centre of gravity was the prescribed limits. The operator's Standard of Compliance with the relevant Regulations of the British Air Navigation Order, 1960, was satisfactory, and adequate in respect of this particular flight. The delay to the aircraft prior to departure from London Airport had no bearing on the accident. The instrument approach procedures at Stavanger Airport, Sola, were similar to those with which the Captain was familiar. On the basis of the Flight Forecast the estimates given by the pilot on radio telephony to the ground services were considered to be accurate. During the flight from the LEC Consol Beacon to the Outer Marker Beacon the crew had the opportunity to assess the angle of drift. There was no reason to suspect electronic interference with the aircraft's navigation aids by portable transistor radios (none were found at the crash site). The Captain attempted to carry out an ILS approach to runway 18 at Sola. The Air Traffic Control Organisation functioned properly, as did all ground navigation and communication aids. The wind speed at the 1600 ft. level in the Sola area was considerably greater than indicated by the Meteorological Information given to the pilot. The weather, although somewhat unusual for the season, was not of a nature to cause serious difficulties to a pilot of Captain Watt's experience. Other aircraft landed before and after the accident. At the accident site it was estimated that the aircraft struck the mountain ridge on a heading of approximately 135 to 140 degrees. With the wind speed and direction at that time its track made good would have been about 111 degrees M. No evidence was found of pre-crash mechanical or structural failure or defects in the aircraft or its equipment. Findings indicated that the engines were under power and the propellers in the constant speed range. Wheels and flaps were retracted. At the moment of impact the aircraft was flying nearly level or slightly port wing down and was probably in a horizontal or slightly climbing flight, but the evidence for the latter was inconclusive. It was noted that it was significant that the heading of the aircraft at the time of impact was one that would be steered by a pilot who, for some reason, thought he was on the Western side of the Localiser beam. At the end of these factual conclusions the cause was finally given. *'The cause of this accident was a deviation from the prescribed flight path for reasons unknown.'* It was signed: J.K. Christie (President), Gullbrand Nyhus, Nils K. Jørstad. Oslo 28th May 1962.

Apart from a map, some diagrams, and some dark photos, that was the end of the report. The crash had happened 'For reasons unknown'. So nobody was any the wiser as a result of the accident? Nothing could be learned from it? It seemed utterly incomprehensible. Surely there was an answer? Some parents felt that the report was a whitewash. It wasn't, but the sad conclusion that many parents came to was that there were lots of little things that weren't quite as they should have been and collectively they contributed to the disaster. The unbearable truth, however, was that nothing could be learnt from the tragedy of Holtaheia. Their sons and brothers, the 'Lanfranc Boys' had died and NOTHING positive regarding future aviation safety could be learnt from their deaths. It seemed that they were wasted lives.

MEMORIES OF ALL WHO DIED

Papa Mike Air Crew of Cunard Eagle Airways.

Captain Philip Guy Watts – age 40

'My father was the pilot of the Viking airplane Papa Mike on 9 August 1961. His real family name was 'Karginoff' but it is a Jewish Russian name and in 1939 he had to change it to his mother's maiden name in order to fly in the RAF. He received lots of medals from the war including a Battle of Britain clasp which goes with either the France & Germany Star, or the 1939-45 Star, which he was awarded. My father was a Spitfire pilot in WW2 and was later in the First Jet Squadron flying Gloster Meteors (1944-45). In Mike Cooper's book of that time it is recorded that Dad shot down a 'doodlebug'. He flew all through the war aged 18 to 23 only to be killed in a civilian plane crash. My mother never got over his death. After the accident some of my Dad's wartime chums wrote to my Mum. One wrote "Phil was a very experienced pilot and I know that he would have tried to do everything humanly possible to have saved the plane". My mother continued to receive letters and cards from the families of the boys and the air hostess up until she died in 1998. It all broke her heart, and sad to say the grief blighted her life. She was a widow for 37 years. My mother kept the many letters written to her after the accident. Some of them were from fellow 'Sprogs' and all wrote affectionately of my Dad. He was exonerated of all blame when the official accident report was published 18 months after the crash. Perhaps this knowledge provided some small amount of comfort to my Mum. My father used to say that "we have to learn to take the rough with the smooth.'

As a five year old I remember him carrying me on his shoulder at the seaside. I remember being in the car (a Triumph Roadster) with him and my mother, and being in the dickie seat with my Auntie Nance. I remember my Dad taking off the guide wheels of my bicycle and taking me to Watchetts Park in Frimley to ride on two wheels for the first time. Dad held the back of the seat and ran as I cycled and then me being unaware he had let me go as I rode unassisted for the first time. I remember him reading me 'Black Bob' about a black sheep dog the night before he died. I remember being in a toyshop with him at Christmas 1960 when he bought me soldiers, and going to Billy Smarts Circus and he held my hand when the Lions were in the Ring. I remember being sick in bed with mumps and measles in the summer time and hearing him mowing the lawn through the open bedroom window and seeing him going past, up and down, as he cut the grass (we lived in a bungalow). I remember feeling safe. He drove me to London Airport and took me up in a plane; we circled over our house and I saw my Mum in the back garden waving. I remember watching him shaving. I can close my eyes and smell him. He was a kind man and was often laughing. The day he died it changed all of our lives forever. I know that at the age of 55 I still miss him. He would have loved my children – his grandchildren. I have a photo of my father in 1939 aged 18 in his RAF uniform, and my son Peter is the spitting image of him.' Son **Dr. Simon Karginoff.**

First Officer Reginald Leonard Murray Smalley – age 30

Reginald Leonard Murray Smalley, known as Murray, was the only son of Councillor Dr Leonard Smalley and Claire Smalley of Kenilworth, Warwickshire. Born in 1932 he had a very happy childhood and was a very gifted artist. He was educated at Malvern College where he was a boarder. He hated boarding, however, and vowed never to send his children to boarding school. His only sister, Pamela, died aged 13. After leaving school he joined the RAF where he served with 605 Squadron Royal Auxiliary Air Force, leaving in 1953. Thereafter he had various jobs in and out of aviation until he joined Cunard Eagle Airways on March 15th 1961.

Murray Smalley loved amateur dramatics and worked as a stagehand at the Priory Theatre in Kenilworth. Here he met his wife Nina. Their daughter Karen was born in 1960, and the family moved to Lightwater, near Camberley, in 1961. Murray was very well respected and had a wide circle of friends. He was a very loving husband and he adored his wife and young daughter, missing them both very much when he was sent by Cunard Eagle Airways to fly commercial flights from Cyprus to North Africa and on to Malta, during June 1961. He found his free time lonely and boring without Nina and Karen. He had just bought a new home and was very pleased to return to England to fly from London Airport instead during July, and then into August 1961. Whilst working in Cyprus he bought Nina a special present of a ring – which sadly, she received after his death. Their daughter Karen treasures this ring today. Information supplied by Daughter **Karen Haugh, nee Smalley.**

Stewardess Susan Endicott – age 22

'Sue was slim and petite with blond wavy hair. She was kind and caring, vibrant and fun, bright, with a great sense of humour, and loving. When she left school she went to South Devon Technical College, Torquay to study science subjects for entry to University and she had a tutor for Latin as she wanted to study Medicine. She was good at Tennis and joined Paignton Tennis Club, and also the Royal Torbay Yacht Club, where she made many friends and crewed in races. She loved sailing. She also loved riding, especially galloping on Paignton beach. Sue had a friend who died of cancer and so she decided to go into Cancer Research once she'd graduated from London University. Just before becoming an undergraduate Sue met Chris Moysey who was starting officer training at Sandhurst Military Academy. During her undergraduate years she went to some wonderful Sandhurst Balls. They were both so happy together. Sue passed her final exams; was presented with her degree by the Queen Mother and then went on to obtain a higher degree at the London School of Hygiene and Tropical Medicine. Chris was posted to Germany and Sue decided that as a stop-gap she would teach biology until he returned, they could marry, and she could get a job researching Cancer. But her teaching job at Burgess Manor Secondary School in East Ham (now Newham), East London, was very tough; the girls played her up and wouldn't take her lessons seriously. Finally, frustrated and unhappy with teaching she applied to become an air hostess. Also good at languages, this new job was one she loved because, although hard work, it involved meeting people and travelling abroad. She sent home postcards from all the different places she went to. Bermuda and Hong Kong in particular she loved. Sue went to all the 'Proms', loved jiving and dancing to Chris Barber, and enjoyed 'Stomps' in the Albert Hall. She loved the London fashion scene too and went to Vidal Sasoon to have her hair cut in super short cuts that suited her. Sue was always great fun to be with, she had charisma. Sue was very, very special.' Sister **Ann Turner (nee Endicott).**

'I met Sue at a beach party in Torquay a year or so before the accident. I remember very well Sue's kindness to a rather shy young man of 19! She was a lovely vivacious young woman, full of high spirits but generous and gentle as well. I saw Sue one or more times afterwards. I've carried memories of her and that day ever since and never forgotten the wonderful Sue who died so tragically along with the other crew and school boys and teachers of Lanfranc School.' Friend **Peter Hamilton**.

'Sue was part of our lives in so many ways. She was wild, effervescent and so much fun. We met through mutual friends when she went to London University. We had many fun times together including a sailing holiday on The Broads one summer and once memorably, barefoot at a dance in Devon she cut her foot badly on some glass, only to find a handy Vet to bind her up and stem the blood. She quite simply cheered us all up with her *joie de vivre* and kept us constantly amused. We shall never ever forget the shock of the plane crash. We had just married and the pain of losing Sue seemed unbearable after our carefree happiness. She will live in our hearts forever. Unlike the rest of us Sue will be forever young.' Friends **Mary** and **David Brockett**.

We knew Sue from our home area in Devon and later when we were all working or studying in London. Sue was petite, blond, glamorous and highly intelligent. She had a great sense of humour and was always the life and soul of any party – a larger than life character. She had a great zest for life but this did not prevent her obtaining high academic achievements of which both she and her family were very proud. Her untimely death in such a horrific and sad accident was a terrible blow to her family and her many, many friends. **Michael** and **Anne Davidson.**

Lanfranc Masters and Boys

John Beacham – age 32

Birdhurst Rise, South Croydon. He had been a master at Lanfranc for nearly 9 years the whole extent of his teaching service, he devoted his time to school. He was brought up in Bath he was an old boy of City of Bath Boys School.

'John was my youngest brother. I was nine when he was born and when he started school I started as a nurse. We were very close and when I was at home he would develop a 'stomach ache' (to get off school) because I was there! After doing his National Service he went to Teacher Training College – St Marks and St John. He enjoyed teaching at Lanfranc.' Sister **Myrtle Foster.**

'John was a wonderful uncle and it was great fun having him around. He spent hours building models with me and constructed extensive model railway layouts. He was always very generous to me and my sister, particularly as he had a television which he let us watch. We always eagerly anticipated his many school trips which he and colleagues organised as not only would he come back with lots of photos, but always presents! He always had time to play with us kids. He was really great.' Nephew **Ian Beacham.**

'My uncle John was an inspirational teacher and he profoundly influenced me. His subject was geography, and I was fascinated by the way he was interested in environmental agenda. He used to stay with us in the vicarage my father had in his North Somerset parish, and he would take us three boys out for days exploring the countryside around. He was very committed to his teaching and spent days in Somerset preparing material for his lessons. He loved his profession and was a great explorer of the world: he wanted his students to share his enthusiasm and open their eyes to all that was around them. It was a natural development of his enthusiasm that when the concept of overseas educational visits became a possibility in the late 1950s/early 1960s he would be a pioneer. As I recall, his students considered his field trips to be the high point of their schooldays, so the tragedy of Stavanger was all the more devastating for everyone. My memory of the mass funeral is, of course, indelibly etched in my youthful memory, and something I shall never forget.' Nephew **Peter Beacham OBE.**

'John Beacham was in charge of the school prefects. A slim, tall man with a direct approach to life, especially discipline. He had to deal with some of the more rebellious schoolboys. He was unmarried but I believe he had a girlfriend. Head boy **Clive Grumett.**

'Billy Beacham was a nice bloke even though I got the cane a lot from him and it was called (in my class), 'The Generator' – after me.' Pupil **Anthony Jenner.**

'Mr Beacham's epitaph has to be his unerring aim with a piece of chalk!' Pupil **Ray Cattle.**

'Johnny Beacham was a disciplinarian. If you were naughty your name was written on the top left hand corner of the black board. When the next boy was naughty then his name replaced the first one and if a third boy was naughty then his name replaced the second. The boy whose name was left on the board at the end of the lesson got the detention!' Pupil **Mike Green**.

'I got the slipper from Mr Beacham and it was the biggest slipper you'd ever seen! It was done in front of the class and it hurt! He was very well respected. I can remember his face very clearly.' Pupil **Bill Tarbuck**.

'I liked Mr Beacham. He was like John Alderton of 'Please Sir'. A pleasant teacher, we all liked him. He was smart, fairly tall and slim. He was straighter and more serious than Mr Budd. I warmed to him.' Pupil **Dave King**.

George Budd – age 47

Mead Way, Old Coulsdon. He had celebrated his 24th Wedding anniversary three weeks before. George Budd taught at Portland School and Benson Junior in Croydon before joining Lanfranc. Head master of Portland School, Mr C.R. Butt, said 'He was a very good fellow. Very keen on his job, he got on well with the boys. He was what I would call a boy's man. He will be a great loss to the teaching profession.' George Budd's neighbour, Mr C.J. Swaine said 'He was extremely fond of children. He was a nice man, a quiet, neighbourly type, who would always help if he possibly could.' Another neighbour said: 'We knew him as one of the kindliest men you could meet. He was so kind, so quick to help anybody else in trouble.' One of Mr Budd's pupils said: 'He made us work hard, but he was kind to us. I liked Mr Budd, all the boys did.'

'When the new Lanfranc School opened he was appointed Head of Science. As a family we became quite part of the school. Mother and I always attended speech days and enjoyed coming to the annual Shakespeare productions. We knew many of the staff and these relationships were cemented by mother's involvement in helping with the school trips abroad which John Beacham and Dad started in 1957. I went with them on that first trip to Seefeld in the Austrian Tyrol, and again to Bolzano in Italy in1959. Tim also joined the school parties on two occasions. My father had a family to support and a mortgage to pay, this having been extended to provide a sum on which the family could live whilst he was training as a teacher. This meant that he was not home from work until quite late two or three days every week. Towards the end of the fifties, he was appointed head of the Addington Evening Institute.

Dad was an active member of the National Union of Teachers and attended the Union's annual conference each Easter. He became Assistant Secretary of the Croydon Branch of the NUT, working with Jack Jones, the then Secretary. Dad was very much a family man. We had days out together, to Chessington Zoo, the Natural History and Science Museums, the Tower of London and London Zoo. From home we could walk out of our garden over Happy Valley and Farthing Downs and often as far as Chaldon Church and we enjoyed these country walks. We had a fortnight's seaside holiday on the south coast each year.

Tim inherited dad's scientific bent and Dad was happy to answer questions and encourage exploration. He showed Tim round his science lab at school and on one occasion he found an injured rabbit and Tim watched as dad 'put it down' using chloroform. He recalls that it was typical of dad to treat him as an adult and he had talked it through what he was doing. On the way home he said 'better not tell mother'. Son **Geoffrey Budd**.

'George Budd was a very generous man. He drove me to school when I lived near Redhill. He was an affable man, nothing fazed him. He never raised his voice.' Colleague **Jim Towers**.

'Mr Budd was short and a little rotund with a gentle disposition. He had rather a laid back attitude to teaching and he was difficult to make angry but he had the ability to make his subject interesting.' Head boy **Clive Grumett**.

'Mr Budd was one of the 'old school'. He would instil discipline and politeness and was a most respected member of staff. I cannot remember a bad word being said of him. He made science and biology exciting.' Pupil **Peter Moore**.

'Mr Budd was my form teacher. He had more humour about him. He was friendly to the kids and a lot more open. His was banter rather than sarcasm. My memories of him are very good. He was livelier and allowed us to go on a bit. He was always relaxed.' Pupil **Dave King**.

'George Budd had a nice personality and was very helpful to all the pupils. Although Science wasn't one of our favourite subjects he had a way of getting your attention and holding it throughout the lesson.' Pupil **William Hall**.

'Mr Budd stuck up for me when other teachers took against me – I wasn't an easy child at times – apt to 'push it'.' Pupil **Ray Cattle**.

Fifth Year Lanfranc Boys

John Edward Henry Bradbery – age 16
Ockley Road, West Croydon. A promising scholar who was good at sports.

'John was a boy with a lot of energy and drive. He was involved in the school play each year and if I remember rightly played a woman's part one year. He was one of the school prefects. Won the school prize for geography on both the 4th and 5th years and did well academically.' Head Boy **Clive Grumett**.

'John could have gone into accountancy as he was very bright. He was tall and loved sport, cricket, football, in fact all sports, and his ambition was to play golf. He loved cars. At the age of 12 he had acquired a keen interest in old vintage and classical cars including American automobiles. He wanted to own a Jaguar. On seeing his favourite car, 1936 vintage Jaguar, he would casually remind me that one day he would own such a car, of course albeit in a more modern format. He grew up in the image of his mother and with a high IQ. He always showed extraordinary respect for his parents, he was extremely close to his father who was an all-round sportsman and loved cricket. As he progressed through his young life John seemed to walk in his father's footsteps in respect of all forms of sport and athletics and he had the potential to become a county cricket player – which was always his aim. At quite an early age John developed confident communication skills and mixed well with his peers, male and female alike. He loved a good chat, especially about cricket or sport in general. From the beginning of his middle teens during his holiday periods he worked with his mother at the headquarters of J. Sainsbury, Blackfriars. It was indeed most noticeable that young John on such occasions was always smartly dressed and walked upright, "bubbling over with youth and pride". John was a well-balanced, likeable, rather mature for his age, full of life and interest with an easy smile. Although still in his teens it was a pleasure to be in his company especially when the season's county cricket came into focus and the Test series with Australia, New Zealand and Pakistan.' Family friend **Bill Smith**.

Peter George Boyes – age 16
Thornton Road, Thornton Heath. He was quiet and self-confidant.

'He was tall, slim, and had blond hair. If you didn't know Peter you'd assume he was a bit shy and introvert, which he was, but he was also a gentle soul and was just getting round to girls. He was a good football player and played for the school sometimes. Peter had a good brain, proven by the fact he got the 4th form prizes for Maths and Metalwork and obtained his RSA Technical Certificate in six subjects in his final 5th year. His passing was especially sad as his father had died the previous year and Peter was an only child. This is why I believe that Mrs Boyes did not want Peter buried in the mass grave. I remember meeting Mrs Boyes at the school before the funeral and afterwards, when with a mutual friend I visited her at her home. Considering the grief she must have been going through she was nothing but kindness, concerned about how we were feeling and how we were doing.' Head Boy **Clive Grumett**.

'Peter was a quiet lad who liked school and passed all his exams. He was due to start working for Phillips Electrical Company on his return from Stavanger. It was a very sad time for the family especially as Peter's paternal grandparents, to whom he was very close, died two years before the trip and his father, a fireman, died one year before. The holiday was to be a new start for Peter. A private funeral was held for Peter to enable him to be buried with his father.' Godmother **Mary Jamieson**.

Geoffrey Graham Brown – age 16
Norbury Crescent, Norbury. He was a good sprinter and rugby wing three-quarter. He was training to be a chef and awaiting the results of his RSA exams.

'Many happy times were spent working on our grandparents' farm together during the school holidays – building and playing in 'camps' and I remember trying to stay standing on the trailer as it bumped along the fields whilst he or our brother Ian was driving the tractor. Geoff liked fishing – on holiday in Scotland the year before, he fished whilst Ian, Dad and I walked in the mountains. I remember that Geoff didn't like drinking tea. I enjoyed being 'baby sat' by Geoff and Maureen. They were fun and kind to me.' Sister **Janet Mann.**

'My boyfriend, Geoff Brown, with whom I was very much in love, was on that flight and I knew many of the other boys as well. Geoff and his best friend Derek Goddard had actually left school but had gone on the trip as helpers. Geoff was a truly lovely person. He was born in January 1945 whilst his father was serving in the RAF at Forres in Scotland, and he always retained a great fondness for Scotland and wanted to visit it often. He was old for his age (probably because he was the eldest in his family), and he often worked on his grandfather's farm in Gomshall, Surrey during the holidays. Geoff was really close to his family. He was also a very capable babysitter for his uncle's baby son at times. His parents, Marian and Ernest, ran the youth club at St. Stephens so Geoff was always there, as was I. Geoff cycled everywhere and we used to cycle to Gomshall, Boxhill and many other places. He enjoyed camping, walking and most outdoor activities, and he was a great Buddy Holly fan. Geoff had just left school and was waiting to go to Westminster College to become a chef. Some holidays he and I stayed at Shoreham by Sea in Sussex which a friend's parents owned. We had a great time there and Geoff was there for the week before he went on the ill-fated trip.' Girlfriend **Maureen Kay.**

'Geoff as very grounded and sensible, extremely pleasant and friendly to everyone, he had a younger brother Ian, and a sister Janet, the whole family were members of St Stephens and extremely well liked.' Friend **Ann Lewis.**

Edward Arthur Gilder – age 16
Denning Avenue, Waddon. He had a pleasing personality and was a conscientious worker. He played soccer and was awaiting the results of RSA exams.'

'Ted was born on the 9th October 1944 in Withington Manchester. We believe this was because the family were evacuated during the war, due to the V1/V2 flying bombs. Later the family returned to Waddon where Ted grew up. He went to Duppas Junior School and then on to Lanfranc Boys school where he played in the football team. He excelled in art and technical drawing, and went on school trips to Switzerland and Italy. Although Ted had actually finished school in July 1961, he wanted to go on the trip to Norway. He was due to start a job in an insurance company in London on his return. He was a regular member with his family at St George's church, Waddon where he was a Server and sang in the choir. In his memory there is an engraved candlestick in the church which has been dedicated to Ted. He was a great Crystal Palace fan and went with his father to see every home game at Selhurst Park. Ted was a school prefect in his last year. He had a special walking stick that he always took on school trips. He has metal badges of Italy, Austria and Switzerland and he took it to Norway. We always had family holidays together and I had a lot of fun with Ted, swimming etc. We had a lot of pets. Ted was closest to me. When I look back on his 16 years I think he had a full life having been to Switzerland, Austria and Italy.' Sister **Christine Phillips**.

'Edward Gilder was in the church choir at St George's church Waddon. He took a solo part in 'We Three Kings'. When he was slightly older he was in the post-voice breaking choir – up with the men. He became a server.' Friend **David Randall**.

Derek Frank Goddard – age 16

Virginia Road, Thornton Heath. He was a popular pupil, obtaining a school Merit prize in his first year. He played a Citizen in 'Romeo and Juliet'.

'My son Colin and Derek were cousins and went to St Stephen's youth club – which they enjoyed. Although Derek wasn't brought up to be very church going, they were confirmed together and were great pals. Derek loved swimming. As a youngster he was late in learning to talk, but he had a happy smile. My son Colin and Derek went camping together.' Aunt **Joan Shannon**.

'I knew Derek Goddard and Geoff Brown, both of whom were in St. Stephen's Church youth club. I have photos of Geoff & Derek on various youth club activities, mainly walks in pouring rain.' Friend **Chris Meyer**.

'I was good friends with Derek Goddard. He was a great insect-collector and kept stick insects. He let me hold one on my hand – it was fragile and wobbly. He was a really nice lad, but an only child and his parents never got over his death.' Friend **Graham Edwards**.

'I was a very close friend of Derek Goddard (and Geoff Brown). We all were members of the St. Stephens Church Youth Club. We had been friends for several years and spent most of our teens together.' Friend **Ann Lewis.**

'Derek and Geoff were no saints they were the usual teenage boys and had the occasional cigarette and booze! I remember being at Derek's house when his parents were out. There were six or eight of us and Derek raided their drinks cabinet. His mother came back and we hid our drinks behind the sofa – but she went ballistic! Derek was a good friend and he was very keen on Buddy Holly. We all used to go round together with another friend David Heyden. He told me that losing his two best friends had a really profound effect on the rest of his life too'. Friend **Maureen Kay.**

'Derek Goddard was a prefect. He used to stand at the gates on Mitcham Common and he'd report you if you were late. You could get into school the back way from the cemetery. Derek would have caught me coming in late!' Lanfranc boy **Bill Tarbuck.**

St. Stephens Church, Norbury held a Remembrance Service and the Church was packed. It's something I'll never forget. There are certain memories that are still very strong in my mind. Losing two of our close group of friends was dreadful and things were never the same after that. Friend **Allan Mott.**

'Derek was one of my very first friends when he and I were at 'Aberdeen House' a pre-school in Norbury. At break times in the garden playground, the boys all played 'bumper-cars' together and I played with them. With folded arms we rushed around 'bumping' into each other – hard! Derek always had a huge grin on his face. Infant school friend **Rosalind Jones.**

David William Hendley – age 16

Lucerne Road, Thornton Heath. He was a member of the Air Training Corps and liked everything to do with flying, making model aeroplanes in his spare time. David played the part of an Officer of the Watch in 'Romeo and Juliet'. In 1960 he was awarded the 4th year prize for Technical Drawing and Maths.

'My brother, David had just left school that summer, but returned for the trip. He was about to start an apprenticeship as an aircraft draughtsman. He was thrilled to bits as he had always been so interested in aircraft and flying from an early age. His room was full of model aircraft, walls covered with pictures of designs, and books on all aspects of design and construction. Ironically he had never flown and had never been inside an aircraft until that fateful trip. David was a calm gentle person, loved swimming, was in the choir of St. Oswald's Church, and he supported Crystal Palace football club.' Sister **Julia Giles**.

Brian Robert Mitchell – age 16

Norbury Avenue, Thornton Heath. He had left school to attend an arts and crafts school in London to train as a silversmith, but attended evening school at Lanfranc to take GCE and RSA examinations. He had been to Italy, Austria, and Switzerland. Brian had a keen sense of humour, and liked modern music.

'Brian Mitchell was my uncle but was 4 years old when I was born. With two grown up, married siblings I was like a sister for him. Every weekend would be spent together. As we grew up Brian joined the Cubs and then the Scouts. He created exciting times for me in the large garden where we had a rope swing from the huge plum tree, a tent, a tree-house, and even a dug out underground hide-away with nooks for candles. We played tracking, found dead trapped butterflies under the redcurrant bushes, and caught tadpoles in the pond. At the end of the day we cooked dough on sticks to eat with jam. In later years music took over as a shared interest. Every Christmas we would put on a performing music show. As we did not share a home we never argued. Brian was a kind good natured person who was full of fun and he was my best friend. The Scout movement was a very important part of Brian's life which his parents remained involved with after he died. I believe it was their life line…my Granddad ran the Scout football club which Brian had been in, and every week my Nan would have the uniforms hanging on her washing line. Monthly dances were held in the Scout hall "The Endeavour" in Melfort Rd, which I also went to. Brian made me a necklace of my initial for my birthday which he was to finish when he returned. It was never polished and finished, but I wore it every day for many years.' Niece **Shirley Waller** nee **Mitchell**.

'Until shortly before this tragedy, I was the senior Patrol Leader in the 67th Croydon Scout Troup where Brian Mitchell had been my Second for some time, and we got on really well. In August 1961, I had just joined the Rover Crew and had nominated Brian to take over the Patrol from me, fully expecting him to re-join me a year or so later, when we would be able to enjoy working together in the most senior branch of Scouting. Brian's death taught me to always do the best that I could and to treat everyone as I would expect to be treated, ethics which I feel were in Brian, even at that young age. At a Scout Camp together where a patrol member had an accident Brian proved he was a resourceful, reliable, and hard-working Second. He also had a delightful sense of humour!' Friend **Paul Fairweather**.

'Brian and I were great friends. I lived near him in Highbury Avenue. Most school days we would meet on the corner, him with his bike, me walking. He would give me a lift on the crossbar where it wasn't hilly, otherwise we would both walk. The best part of the route to school was Galpins Road which was downhill all the way to Mitcham Common. We used to cut across diagonally from Galpins Road into a side entrance to the school. As the school was quite new then, there were gaps around the perimeter. Brian and I used to go through one of these gaps at break or lunchtime and have a fag! I have a mental picture of Brian, I see a very young Roy Orbison the singer, probably because Brian used BrylCream and he had black hair with a wave. We were great mates.' Friend **Peter Muncey**.

Roger Morris Taylor – age 16

Foulsham Road, Thornton Heath. School Vice Captain. He was keen on science research and making transistor radios. Roger won the 4th year History prize.

'Roger was always smart and he carried himself well. He was a very good school ambassador. He had a high profile and was one of the school 'tops' and would sit up with the headmaster.' Lanfranc schoolboy **Dave King**.

'I was brought up at 15, Foulsham Road and although I was only two at the time of the tragedy I can recall the horror and sadness in the street at the time. Roger Taylor and his parents lived a few doors away from my family. As I grew up we often used to speak to his parents and my father would come away from these encounters filled with emotion. The sadness of Roger's parents remains with me to this day and as a child I could hardly contemplate what it must be like to lose a son in such a terrible accident. I believe Roger was an only child. I wanted to add this memory to reassure anyone who knew him that he and his family were always remembered by mine, and will always be in our thoughts and prayers.' Neighbour **Mary Marsh**.

I was in the same class as Roger and was a good friend of his. My parents were also good friends of Roger's parents, Fred and Ruby Taylor. My Dad and Fred worked together. As soon as he was informed about the crash, my Dad was one of the first people Fred telephoned. I can still remember that moment. All Fred was able to say before putting down the telephone was: "Roger was on that plane". We were all devastated. I too would have been on that plane but for the fact that I was a keen cyclist and had been to Norway the year before for a cycling holiday with my cycling club. Roger was a lovely boy. He was very talented and I am sure he would have done well at whatever he was planning to do with his life. He was Fred and Ruby's only child and they were devoted to him. I don't think they ever got over his death.

In 1976 Fred and Ruby decided to move from their house in Foulsham Road, Thornton Heath to Cheam. At that time my wife and I were looking to buy a house in Thornton Heath and we bought their house. It was a lovely home and we had 18 very happy years there. One very sad moment for me was when I went up into the loft and found some of the scenery from Roger's model train set. Friend **Paul Chapman**.

Fourth Year Lanfranc Boys

Reginald Thomas Chapple – age 15
Denning Avenue, Waddon. Reggie was a Surrey boxing champion. He was interested in acting and was keen on travelling abroad.

'Reggie was the 'blue-eyed boy' with very, very, blonde hair and blue eyes. He was the apple of my parent's eyes. He had a stick with metal badges and it survived the crash. Reggie was very sporty. His father was into boxing, so Reggie boxed and played tennis and became a black belt in Judo/Jujitsu. He had a very square jaw and quite a strong face. He was studious in many respects so he wasn't a boy up to mischief. He gave up boxing to concentrate on Jujitsu. He was quite a good actor and was in a school play. He always wanted to be out playing tennis yet he was quite shy and not into girls, yet when my friend Mary came round he always wanted to talk to her. He was a good looking boy.' Sister **June Brown**.

'Reggie Chapple was a nice chap. I liked him. He was a blonde haired kid and he was good company. Reggie was a really nice person, even though he was a boxer. A 'Tommy Steele' type.' Friend **Anthony Jenner**.

Trevor Condell – age 14

Greenside Road, West Croydon. Trevor played several times as wicket keeper for Surrey Schools and had just joined Streatham Colts. He also played football for Croydon under 13's. He obtained school cricket colours in 1959.

'The last thing that I recall about Trevor is that when we took him to catch the coach for London Airport he suddenly remembered he'd forgotten his camera and we had to rush back home to get it. We got back just in time to give it to him.' Mother **Mrs Condell**.

'Trevor was the youngest in the family and the apple of my parent's eyes. They followed his school and sport's career with great interest, particularly his efforts on the cricket pitch. We used to live in Addington and Trevor was a choir boy at The Royal School of Church Music. When we moved to Croydon Trevor became a mad keen Crystal Palace supporter and he and Dad collected all the scores which Trevor always wrote in his diary. He also loved watching Norman Wisdom films and would roll around on the floor in helpless laughter! He was very proud of his bike which his Nan bought him. Trevor had left school when the accident happened. He was due to start as an apprentice electrician on his return from holiday. My parents donated 'The Condell Cup' for the most improved cricketer, in Trevor's memory.' Sister **Pat Chase** nee **Condell**.

'I knew Trevor Condell very well. We were in the Lanfranc Cricket Team together. He was the wicket keeper. Trevor was a lovely chap, a nice boy.' Friend **Patrick Wilson**.

'He was a lovely lad.' Friend **Keith Rhodes**.

'Trevor was a very able and agile wicket keeper and capable batsman. One of my enduring memories of Trevor was that after five minutes into any game he would look totally dishevelled, covered in dust and mud from head to foot, and the tops of his cricket pads flopping over his knees and his shirt un-tucked. This because he flung himself enthusiastically all over the pitch in order to stop the ball. One skill that he tried to keep secret was that he could bowl leg-spin – virtually unique and probably devastating at age 11, but I could never get him to forgo his wicket keeping gloves! He was always cheerful and even at that age extremely supportive.' Friend **David Lewsey**.

'Trevor was a superb wicket keeper and played for Surrey Colts.' Friend **Graham White**.

Geoffrey Crouch – age 15
Chapman Road, West Croydon. Geoffrey loved mathematics. Before deciding what he wanted to be he was concentrating on getting as many subjects in GCE as he could. Geoffrey won the 2nd Year Progress Prize in 1959.

'My brothers Geoffrey and Peter were three years younger than me, Geoffrey being the eldest by 20 minutes. They were not identical twins but they did everything together. Geoffrey was the quiet, academic one, and Peter was the boisterous, practical one. Peter was very much the leader, where he went Geoffrey followed, and any scrapes they got into were invariably at the instigation of Peter. They had been put into different classes whilst at Lanfranc because their abilities were different, Geoffrey was studious and Peter was more interested in how things worked by taking them apart and putting them back together again.' Sister **Pauline Hogan**.

'Geoffrey and myself were quite opposites. He was a quiet, studious boy and very academic like my dad. Following me he sometimes found himself in trouble (but not in a bad way) doing things that boy's of my type did – like scrumping and playing where we shouldn't – like the sewage farm. One time he fell in playing tag with me and Bobby Martin. On that occasion my mum had to burn his clothes as they smelt so bad! Our family, like a lot of the Lanfranc boys were not well off but we had a happy, loving, and eventful childhood. Our playing grounds bordered on Factory Lane, so the gasometer, the Council tip, the plastics factory, Waddon and Beddington Parks, and the coal tip were places where we spent our free time. Our activities varied from catching newts, tadpoles, fishing for red-throats, collecting and playing conkers, and generally doing 'boy things' which Geoffrey was dragged into by me. Geoffrey was destined for better things in life and I am afraid his death broke my dad's heart. In fact the light went out of his eyes right from the night of the crash and although he did sometimes laugh again it was not the same.' Twin brother **Peter Crouch**.

Clifford Victor Gaskin – age 15

'Grecian Crescent, Upper Norwood. He was especially excited at the thought of flying as his ambition was to go into the RAF. He was a member of the Crystal Palace Model Flying Club and he designed and made his own models. Clifford played the part of Second Capulet, in 'Romeo and Juliet'.'

Sadly, no one from Lanfranc was found to supply memories of Clifford, so these facts about him were gleaned from 'The Lanfrancian'.

'19th December House Drama Festival – This year for the first time, the Drama Festival was placed on a House competitive basis; each House, with the exception of Livingstone, presenting a one-act play. The trophy, a newly-purchased honours board, was decisively gained by Caxton. The producer of the play 'Shivering Shocks', was Clifford Gaskin, and he is to be commended on this first time effort.'

'Clifford Gaskin passed in two subjects in the City and Guilds Preliminary Course Exemption.'

'I knew Clifford Gaskin from my junior school years at Rockmount Junior mixed where Clifford was in my class. As I recall Clifford was a slim boy with a mop of curly hair and was very jovial. He also suffered from a lot of nose bleeds. As he lived not far from me I played with him sometimes outside his house in Grecian Crescent.' Junior school friend **Laurence Kingston-Lynch**.

David John Hatchard – age 15

Hambrook Road, South Norwood. David was interested in marine life, kept tropical fish in two large aquariums, and had a small pond in the garden. Model railways and 'Sally', his Terrier dog, also claimed his time.

'I was a friend and neighbour of Mr and Mrs Hatchard. David was a nice boy, quiet and well behaved. When he was younger David used to play with my son.

Mr and Mrs Hatchard were very nice people and were heartbroken after the accident. They had already lost one child as a baby.' Neighbour **Lucy Marlow**.

'I knew both David and his family very well, he lived in South Norwood, S.E.25 with his parents and was an only child. I introduced him to Croydon Korfball Club where he started to learn the game as a junior, on his death his parents arranged for a trophy to be presented annually by the Club in his name.' Neighbour **Mary Turner**.

'I was a mate of David Hatchard – he lived in South Norwood like me. I had a paper round and delivering all those papers was pretty emotional, especially when I got around to David Hatchard's road. I felt so sorry for his mum and dad, it totally broke them.' Friend **Michael O'Rourke**.

'On the night before David died he turned up at my place on his bicycle. At that time I was about to jump on mine and go and see friends not far from where he lived. I remember chatting to him outside my house and he told me how excited he was to be going on a school flight to Norway the following day. One thing that for some unknown reason stuck in my mind was the fact that he was so proud of the new sandals that his mum had bought for him and these were going with him. We cycled down to South Norwood and chatted on the way as best as one can on a bike on a main road and at the point where we went our own ways we came to a stop. I have to say that I once again envied him as I had never been on a plane and he was so excited about it. I remember seeing him cycle off. For some reason I can still to this day see those sandals as he left.' Friend **Jon Bowerman**.

Richard Michael Lawrence – age 15

Spa Hill, Upper Norwood. Richard was interested in drama and photography.

'Richard was very much a 'chip off the old block' and followed Dad's engineering interests by building a soap cart and the like. Although I was very much the little brother and a 'pest' I remember times when he stood up for me as my big brother. On holiday the girls always liked Richard as he was a good looking boy and was the one seen to be the 'adult' of us three in the eyes of mum and dad's friends. For Celia, being two years younger, Richard was the big brother who was quite 'acceptable' to the girls and she was never short of friends who wanted to come home for tea. Richard was fairly studious but preferred the engineering side of school. He would have been the 'son and heir' to Dad's business. Richard was in the school cricket team and he and his team friends seemed like young men to us. But he was also quite a practical joker. I know that dad was very proud of him and looked to him to continue the business. Richard was a good son who didn't shine at school but got on well, didn't go off the rails and Mum and Dad were proud of him, as we were too. As our elder brother he was responsible, serious, not academically gifted but very practical and a really good person.' Brother **Harry** and Sister **Celia**.

Robert James Martin – age 15

Campbell Road, West Croydon. Robert liked modern music, swimming and rugby. He belonged to the Army Cadet Force. He was known for entertaining young friends with 'magic' tricks. He had been abroad several times. An only child he won the School Progress Prize for Form 2F during 1959.

'I spent most of my childhood with Robert but he was always called Bobby.

Geoffrey and Peter Crouch were very good friends of Bobby and we all used to go dancing together, as well as just spending time together. He was an only child. We used to go over to Wandle and Beddington Park catching sticklebacks and hanging around with Peter and Geoffrey Crouch. Bobby came dancing with me as I was mad on ballroom dancing and as he was such a kind and thoughtful person I always got my way. Bobby always spent the evening with my Nan. Bobby and I were going to buy a white sports car when we got older and drive around Europe.' Cousin **Patricia Ward**.

'According to an article that Robert Martin wrote for the 'The Lanfrancian' he was also interested in Trokarts – a small version of racing car with no body but a roll bar. Costing around £50, made of welded tubular steel, Trokarts gave 'all the thrills of big time racing' at speeds of 25-35 m.p.h.'

'Robert was such a wonderful young man who died on what was to be a great adventure with his friends.' Aunt **Lilian Martin**.

Edward Albert Prosper – age 15

Penrith Road, West Croydon, Edward worked his way through school from D-stream to B-stream in his fourth year. He was not afraid of hard work.

'Eddie Prosper joined our junior section of the Boys Brigade, The Lifeboys, in 1955. He was at Beulah School and also went to Beulah Baptist Sunday School. In 1958 he was promoted to our company section and donned the pill box. Eddie was a keen Boys Brigade boy and hoped to become a member of the band. He won perfect attendance prizes at Boys Brigade Bible Class and Drill Parade from 1958 to 1960 as well as doing well at sport. After his death our Pipes and Drums used to stop outside his home on Church Parade mornings and play a tune in his memory. His parents ran flower shows for the Spa Allotments Society at Downsview Church and they presented a cup for the best Fuchsias blooms, calling it the 'Eddie Prosper Cup' in memory of their son. Eddie was a bright, promising boy. **Denis Finch**, Hon President 5th Croydon Boys Brigade.

'I lost a very dear friend in the crash, Edward Prosper. I used to go to his house after school to play and in those days we did not have the electronic gadgets that are available today to entertain us. The television was our main source of entertainment from 5.00pm onwards in those days. I can remember Fridays, as being special when visiting Eddie after school, as his father was a butcher and Friday was meat day for their household. We had an adventure cycling down to Brighton together once! Eddie's Mum and Dad made the journey to Stavanger in the following May to commemorate the unveiling of the memorial to the Lanfranc School for Boys and both were presented to Sir John Walker the British Ambassador to Norway at this sad occasion.' Friend **Peter John Moore**.

Robert Donald Roffey – age 15
Addington Road, West Croydon. Robert loved animals, reading, and had won a bronze medal for ballroom dancing. He had made other school journeys.

'My mother worked with Robert Roffey's mother and as she had sent Robert to ballroom dancing classes my mother thought it would be a good idea for me. So I went with Robert and found I enjoyed it – especially as there were so many girls and hardly any boys! After a Saturday morning dancing we then spent the afternoon ice skating.' Friend **John Martin**.

'My closest friend was Robert Roffey as I was at Infant and Junior school with him – Christchurch School Longley road Croydon. We first met when I was four and a half. He often came to my house for tea after school and I went to his every couple of weeks or so. We were at Lanfranc together although not in the same class.' Friend **B. Orford**.

'I helped run the 57th Croydon cub-scout group between 1956-1961 and one boy who died in the crash was a neighbour Robert Roffey, a friend of my brother. I have a cutting from the Croydon Advertiser of Robert's parents presenting a lectern Bible for the chapel of Queen Mary's Hospital for Children, Carshalton, where the Robert was once a patient.' Cub Mistress **Sylvia Binelli**.

'I was older than Robert, by 2/3 years, and although he wasn't in my immediate circle of friends, we did play together sometimes. Robert was quiet and appeared sensitive to me. One memory that sticks out is that many of the neighbours and children crammed into his parent's front room to watch the Coronation on what was possibly the first and only TV in the street. I also went fishing with Robert at Hampton Court.' Friend **Jim Knight**.

'I biked together with Robert and we stuck together in the gymnasium for a game that Mr. Cook organised. We played in shorts and shirts and we sat on the floor back to back. When Mr Cook blew the whistle we had to jump up and be the first to slap our partner on his back. Robert and I made a pact not to hit hard. He was a dark haired, dark eyed, gentle boy.' Friend **Mark Cottington**.

Third Year Lanfranc Boys

John James Adams – age 14

Thornton Road, West Croydon. John wanted to join the Merchant Navy. He loved fishing.

John was a very quiet, shy lad. I think he is still in our midst. He was a lovely baby – all 'giggly' and 'kicking about' and he was a wonderful son. He was not academic though he did well enough at both West Thornton Junior School and Lanfranc. John always accepted and took life in his stride, – almost as if he had been here before. He had a strange sense of humour too. Coming in one day from school he told us that a teacher had asked him if his father was Indian. 'Yes I think he might be!' he'd replied, leaving everyone bemused! John was kind, forthright, and honest. He was thrilled to be going to Norway.' Mother **Mrs Eileen Adams**.

Michael John Benson – age 14
West Croydon. He had been a keen stamp collector since the age of five and had over 7,000 stamps. He had a job waiting for him in the printing trade.

'Michael was a very good elder brother. He failed the 11+ but he was bright. He was a very keen stamp collector and had built up a meticulously well-kept collection. Michael was a keen angler, fisherman, and he was also very good at painting and drawing. He wanted to be a commercial artist. There was a 'gang' of kids in our neighbourhood, and Michael and his friend Geoff were leading lights. Although he was three years older than me he always treated me as an equal, and was always supportive and inclusive. Known as 'Micky' and 'Mick', he organised great outings to such events as the Boys and Girls Exhibition at Earls Court, Science and Natural History Museums at Kensington, and other London sites. Bonfire Night was also a big event, we all made 'guys' and sat outside the various workplaces, particularly the 'Acc and Tab' at the top of our road. The resulting funds enabled terrific fireworks on 5th November. Mick was keen on fishing and we spent many hours at Mitcham Common Pond and Norwood Lakes. We also went swimming a great deal, Micky was a strong swimmer and hardly a week seemed to go by without him bringing home another certificate for swimming ever longer distances. Another sport he was involved in was judo and he was rapidly progressing through the various 'belts'. Micky was also keen on Rock and Roll, particularly Elvis Presley and Little Richard, and had a good record collection.' Brother **Derek Benson**.

'My friend Brenda Ireland and I loved Michael and Geoffrey Green even at an early age, and always hung out with them at West Thornton Junior School. They were best buddies, and in my girlish way I used to think I would marry one of them one day. We used to run home with Michael and Geoffrey and a lot of the time we were actually chasing them! Michael was very good at drawing – horses in particular. Michael and Geoffrey were very good at sliding on the ice in the winter on the playground, they never lost their balance. I remember engraving our initials on the cemetery brick wall on Mitcham Road M.B. (Michael Benson) G.G. (Geoffrey Green) B.I. (Brenda Ireland) and D.M. (Diana Murphy). They are most likely still there, just weathered a little.' Friend **Diana Johnson** (nee Murphy).

David Charles Gore – age 14

Mitcham Road, West Croydon. David's hobbies were photography and aircraft. He spent hours at London Airport taking pictures and aircraft spotting. His home was full of beautifully made model aeroplanes. He was a member of the school quiz team which reached the semi-final of the Croydon Civic Quiz.

'I recall David was a studious, thoughtful, quiet lad, who was very keen on gardening. His mother was a widow and his only brother, Jim, was ten years older and married, so David looked after the garden for her. He was always asking gardening questions. David loved aeroplanes and anything to do with flying! He made a lot of model aircraft – on the dining room table.' Sister-in-law **Valerie (Gore) Barratt**.

Geoffrey Michael Green – age 14

Mitcham Road, West Croydon. He had a cheerful disposition, was form captain, and had progressed from C-stream to A-stream. He was a good footballer.

'Geoff was so full of life. Nothing seemed to worry him; everything was an adventure to be had. My undying picture in my mind is of him coming home from school, always with his cap on the back of his head, smiling with his satchel flung over his shoulders. He was confident and full of mischief. Before Guy Fawkes Night he came home with burns on his chest because some boys had stuffed a banger in his shirt – but he never revealed who had done it. He loved fishing and used to spend many happy hours by the pond on Mitcham Common or further afield by the River Wandle catching tadpoles. He was naturally sporty, good at most things, but football was the game he most loved. Geoff was extremely good at art. There was hardly a scrap of paper or inside cover of a book that did not have one of his sketches. He particularly liked pen and ink drawing and his dressing table always had bottles of ink and nibs lying in the tray. Geoff had an enquiring mind and had started to teach himself Russian. At the last school open day his class master said 'what can I say, he is good at almost everything and if he applies himself now the world would be his oyster.' But, of course, that wasn't meant to be.' Sister **Sue Hayes**.

'My friend Brenda and I used to chase Geoffrey and his friend Michael Benson home from school. Geoff had to run across Mitcham Road to his house, but he always got away because he was a fast runner! I called him Geoff Green Bean or 'Beanie' – he was such an adorable looking boy. He was my sweetheart and I thought I'd marry him one day. Geoffrey was an intelligent boy. I always knew he was extremely intelligent. And he was a gentle boy who would have become a most wonderful man.' Friend **Diana Johnson** (nee Murphy).

Quentin Raymond Vincent Green – age 13
Hill Drive, Norbury. He was an A-stream pupil. Nicknamed 'Kew Green', he had a dynamic personality. He won a place on the plane by a tossed coin.

'The day I took the shot of Quentin used in the newspapers we were on a breakwater at Brighton. I photographed him at a low angle against a dull sky – but moments before we could have come a cropper on slippery seaweed and fallen into the rough sea. Once before Quentin had a real close call with water – on the Norfolk Broads. He was running up and down the bank to amuse Nigel and had slipped and fallen in between the boat and the bank. He couldn't swim then, and went down three times before father grabbed his hand. Quentin enjoyed singing so much that he didn't mind spending time at choir practises, nor singing twice in church on Sundays. He enjoyed acting too and played 'The Page to Paris' in Romeo and Juliet – an impressive production by Mr Jim Hemmings. Even though he was the fourth child he wasn't going to be 'overlooked' and could be quite assertive claiming to me more than once 'I got you interested in photography!' You could say that the photo I took of him which was published in so many newspapers confirmed my interest in photography. I went on to make it a profession.' Brother **Martyn Green**.

'I used to sit next to Quentin when we were at Winterbourne School together. He was such a lovely person. He loved to sing and he was always asking me to listen to him singing *Blue Moon*. He was bubbly and popular and I was so upset when I heard about the crash. I was in Luxembourg on holiday at the time and I remember the picture of Quentin on the foreign newspaper as the boy who should not have gone on the trip.' Friend **Keith Alford**.

'I was 14 when the accident happened. My teacher was Mr. Budd and I was going on this trip. I filled in all the paperwork, but at the last minute my parents couldn't afford for me to go so I had to cancel. I remember Quentin and another boy tossing a coin. At the time I envied Quentin because he was going instead of me. I was on holiday with my parents at the time and saw the awful news in the paper. I lost a lot of friends to that accident.' Friend **Roger Culley**.

'I remember his red hair and rosy face.' Friend **Linda Jones**.

'Quentin and I were in the same year and by the merest of chances I would have been on the plane as well, but a feeling that I had cost my parent's more than enough on school holidays made me choose the less costly option of a trip to Austria. Quentin had a bike that had been sprayed in a particular shade of green by Allen's Cycles in Broad Green – and I copied it.' Friend **Roy Cattle**.

'Quentin was in my class and I remember him as a reflective, bright and serious boy with a mischievous twinkle.' Friend **Alan Foster**.

'My best friend was Quentin. He and I looked after the School Pets which were kept in hutches next to the school vegetable patch and gardens. We took it in turns to go in during the school holidays. I was also down to be on that trip in 1961, but had to pull out before the trip because my father couldn't afford the balance of the cost. I can't remember who tossed the coin with Quentin, but I was sad when Quentin went and I did not.' Friend **Geoffrey Parr**.

'Quentin was a dear boy; small for his age, and quite vulnerable, but our little group did our best to protect him from some of the rough and tumble of Lanfranc.' Friend **Michael O'Rourke**.

'Quentin was very polite, well spoken with good manners. I liked him because he was his own person and not one to be miss-lead by stronger contemporaries.' Friend **Graham White**.

'Quentin was short but sophisticated and eloquent. I was fascinated by him. He felt like my elder brother to me. He was very talkative but never noisy. He was always reasoned and pleasant. He had the quality of leadership. He seemed more grammar school. Everyone liked him. His conversation was always deliberate and reasoned. He was always comfortable with himself. He had his own group of friends. His size didn't bother him.' Friend **Dave King**.

'I was in Mr Gubby's class for woodwork with Quentin and I remember an incident involving him. At the time we all thought it was funny… it concerned Quentin's cycle, his pride and joy, a top of the range drop handled bar racing bike. It was stolen and we were in woodwork class when Quentin was asked to go to the school office. He returned with a bag. Mr Gubby asked him if his bike had been found. Tearfully Quentin opened the bag to reveal the metallic green cycle frame cut into small pieces…' Friend **Ed Barnett**.

'There was a caravan selling food which was 'forbidden territory' to us on Mitcham Common. Quentin took me there. He bought a hamburger made of meat and potatoes and gave me a bite – and it tasted absolutely wonderful! When I went back a few days later and got one of my own it didn't taste the same at all. Quentin had a 'thing' about his mother's Flapjacks – but I didn't get a bite of those! He was very small, but very nice. Friend **David Randall**.

'I remember Quentin very well as we were class mates at Winterbourne School. He was a lovely lad. I would describe him as a young man with an old head on his shoulders. He was very well spoken and well mannered.' Junior school friend **Barry Bourne**.

'I remember Quentin as a thoroughly nice boy. A nice little chap. In fact I felt quite bad because one day he was helping me with the gears on my bicycle and he lent me a ratchet screwdriver to make adjustments. I later found that I still had it but I never got to return it. Sadly when we all moved on to our respective senior schools we lost touch and then to hear the dreadful news was just terrible. I have often thought about Quentin and have visited the cemetery a number of times. In my business I have travelled quite a bit and have flown to Stavanger and he has always been in my mind.' Junior School Friend **Alan Mayhew**.

Anthony Harrison – age 14

Howley Road, Croydon. Anthony's ambition was to play for Crystal Palace Football Club. He saved about £6 for pocket money for Norway by doing an early morning and evening paper round. He was also a Scout.

'Tony was an 'accident'. When dad went to register Tony after his birth the Registrar said 'What a lucky boy – born on the 7th of the 7th of the 47th! But he died when he was 14… He loved singing. He was a very happy boy but he was jealous of my husband and would sit between us! One day (when he was young) I came home from work to find he'd been experimenting with my make-up and what a mess he'd made! But Mum had cleaned him up before I got back. He really was a joy.' Sister **Judy Walker**.

'He was always smiling. He was quite quiet but a 'chirpy chappy' and quite smart. I can picture myself in the playground when our two groups met up, and Anthony was always smiling!' Friend **Dave King**.

'Anthony Harrison was in my Scout troop. We went to scout camp just before I returned to school and we had a memorial service for Anthony at the camp which was just outside Canterbury in Kent. Morris Brown, the scout master, broke down and couldn't finish the prayers.' Friend **Roger Culley**.

Peter Charles Milton Huggins – age 14

Gloucester Road, East Croydon. He wanted to be a sports writer, writing his own accounts of nearly all sports, and knew the subtler points of the games.

'Peter Huggins was the only son of Mr and Mrs Huggins who ran a sweet shop in Gloucester Road Croydon, and he and I were good mates. In those days many sweet shops sold cigarettes individually, and he on a few occasions would bring the odd one into school, so we could smoke it behind the bike sheds. So he and I started smoking age ten or eleven, but at that time we did not like it much. Lanfranc being close to Mitcham Common we often spent lunchtimes over the park having spent our pocket money at the local shop on Wagon Wheels and 'Jubbley's'. I think we got the cane a couple of times for getting back late.' Friend **Philip Rose**.

'Peter was quite detached and quiet, sometimes a bit isolated. He was a sweet boy, quiet and very pleasant. He was quietly spoken. He didn't look like he had the freedom to enjoy life.' Friend **Dave King**.

'Pete's parents ran a news agents shop in Gloucester Road, Croydon and I think Pete was the only child. He and I cycled to school together. If he was early, which was rare, he would cycle towards my house at Reeves Corner. If I was early I would cycle towards his house and quite often I would get as far as his house and wait outside for him. Pete liked his bed especially in the winter and sometimes his Dad, who would be putting stuff outside the shop when I arrived (remember when they used to hang newspapers outside the shops and nobody stole them) and he would say to me "I'll shout him for you son, I think he's only just got his backside out of bed" and I would hear him shouting "Pete, your mates here, don't keep him waiting". Pete would then arrive pushing his bike out of the shop, and you could tell he had just got out of bed, hair not combed, shirt not tucked in properly, probably not washed or cleaned his teeth, looked half a kip and his Dad would shout "Ta Ta son mind the roads, see you later". Pete was a nice guy who put a smile on my face every time I met him. One day in the school playground I grabbed Pete around the neck from behind, and in an attempt to shake me off we ran into one of the iron uprights on the rain shelter. I whacked my mouth on it and chipped the corner off of my front tooth and I only got my front teeth crowned about five years ago. So for forty odd years I was reminded of Pete every time I looked in a mirror.' **Friend Derek Meacher.**

Edwin Murray – age 14

Lakehall Road, Thornton Heath. Edwin was on his first holiday abroad. A tall boy with a pleasant manner, he would have taken his G.C.E. next year.

'Eddie Murray was the closest classmate of mine that went to Stavanger. We used to meet up on the way to school on our cycles and rode home together, parting at Thornton Heath Pond. We used to talk about girls and 45 records. My mother worked at Philips in Commerce Way and used to get records at a reduced price. I got Eddie a record once, something funny called 'Three Little Fishes' – a comedy recording I think. He said his girlfriend at the time thought it was very funny. I remember in a P.E. test at school Eddie shinned up a climbing rope using just his hands, much to our amazement.' Friend **John Braim.**

'As kids we would get together at weekends. We'd mooch around the area on our bikes, down the park and the shops. Then Ed had this wonderful idea to keep pigeons and we worked together making a coop.' Friend **Derek Meacher.**

John Peter Phelps – age 14

Ryefield Road, Upper Norwood. He was a tall, lively A-stream pupil and a member of Lanfranc's quiz team in the semi-final of the Croydon Civic Quiz.

'John was articulate and bright. He was lovely, probably older than his years. I felt he was quite sophisticated. Everyone liked him. We were a group of four but would always include whoever was around. John didn't take advantage with his intelligence.' Friend **Dave King**.

'John Phelps and I were firm friends and had been together on the two trips previous.' Friend **Ray Cattle**.

Lawrence Sims – age 14

Stanley Grove, West Croydon. He wanted to be a commercial artist. Bright and cheerful and full of 'Go' he would fill the house with modern music.

'Lawrence was a fellow art student at the Croydon College, Fairfield, during the early part of 1961. I was a member of the same evening class. He obviously showed promise as an artist of some degree otherwise he would not have achieved a place at the Croydon evening class. I cannot recall whether his flair was for design or illustration, but I do remember his fashionable dress. After evening class finished Lawrence and I would catch the bus and the first thing to do after boarding the bus was to go to the top, and whoever had a packet of cigarettes would share with the other; his would be a packet of Stuyvesant. We were both 14 at the time.' Friend **Ted Quelch**.

'Lawrence Sims was a fondly remembered fellow pupil in my year group at West Thornton Primary School where we worked hard and received a good primary education. We also played hard. We had sports and sports days and birthday parties at each other's houses. We put on shows to entertain each at the end of school terms. We even had school outings in later years; or at least those of us whose parents were able to find the money to let us go did. Lawrence was a part of all this.' Friend **Linda Arwood**.

'Lawrence Sims was my friend. I can remember his green boots, beetle boots, halfway up his ankle and knee. They had red toe caps and 'high' heels one and a half to two inches high. They were fashion boots and they went with him to Norway. He had mousy brown hair but he liked nice clothes. We played 'tracking' and 'four sticks' together. 'Tracking' was two teams running away and hiding in each other's gardens and then trying to get back to base. We played paper planes, bows and arrows, that type of thing.' Friend **Bill Tarbuck**.

Colin Leslie Smith – age 14

Natal Road, Thornton Heath. He wanted to be a commercial artist and his hobby was ice skating. He saved money from his paper-round for about a year for pocket money for his first school holiday.

'Colin was the life and soul of the family. He had a winning smile and he had a multitude of friends both in and out of school. Academic and also very artistic Colin was brilliant at drawing, especially cartoon characters which he kept in a drawing book. His main love was ice skating. He used to skate at Streatham Ice Rink on Saturdays where he'd go speed skating and barrel jumping. He made so many friends there and was loved by everyone. He took John his elder brother skating, and took him round a couple of times then led him into the centre and left him 'stranded' so he would get on with it! Two weeks before the Norway trip we all had a family holiday and now we treasure a photo of Colin sitting in a deckchair with a pint of beer held aloft saying 'Cheers!' Sister **Lesley Algar.**

'We lost a family friend in Colin Smith. He and I grew up together in the same street and being the same age went to primary and junior schools together. After the 11+ we went to different schools. His death affected us greatly. Some years before the tragedy, Colin gave my mother a rose plant (a cutting taken from the Smith family garden) which was planted in the garden just outside our front door. The blooms were magnificent red roses. As the plant grew, a visiting relative said it needed pruning and duly cut it back, obviously too much as it failed to bloom thereafter. However, shortly after Colin's death, a small blue flower appeared where the rose bush had been, which our next door neighbour identified as a Forget-Me-Not. None of the family knows how it got there and the event has been talked about over the years.' Friend **Terry Bryant.**

'Colin was a wonderful little boy who always had a smile on his face. He took a shine to my wife Grace and was always knocking on our door with flowers which we suspect he 'nicked' from his Mum's garden. He always called Grace 'Auntie'. The flowers were probably a bribe for her to push him in his home made trolley down the hill to the bottom of the road. Grace still can't talk about him without filling up with tears.' Neighbour **Nobby Bryant.**

'My best friend Colin died on the plane. I was due to go on the flight, but my mum could not afford the final instalment of five pounds – so I wasn't allowed to go on the holiday to Norway and five of my classmates died in it, and it still lives with me today.' Friend **Geoff Wood**.

'Colin Smith was another great friend. He had a brother John who I also knew. I remember getting sick around his house one day when we polished off a bottle of sherry....so sick that when his mum came home she said I had to stay the night!' Friend **Michael O'Rourke**.

Peter Derek Stacey – age 14
Keston Road, Thornton Heath. He had made himself almost an expert on the makes and types of aircraft, and where they operated.

'Peter was three and a half years older than me and I remember when we were smaller he used to tease me – a younger sister can be very irritating at times, but as we started getting older we argued less and Peter was very caring. Each year before Mothering Sunday he would take me to the florist at Thornton Heath Pond and we would buy a bunch of violets and primroses each with our pocket money, they cost 6d each bunch. When the day came we would each give a bunch of violets or primroses to my mother and maternal grandmother, so that both of them had one bunch of each type of flowers. Peter was worshipped by both my mother and maternal grandmother. My mother went to the cemetery every week after his death and on birthdays, Easter, Christmas, and anniversaries. When my parents retired to Dorset it was very difficult for her not going to the cemetery. As a boy he loved playing with his cars and we had a bald patch on the lawn where he always played with them. He loved Airfix kits and was always constructing something, buildings for his train set, (I still have the train set), and model planes which he used to hang from his bedroom ceiling. He had a crystal set radio set which he used to listen to in his bedroom. My mother used to let us both watch steam trains from the railway bridge at West Croydon on the way home from shopping trips. He always enjoyed watching the veteran car rally when the cars came through Croydon and we all went as a family. He used to say that when he left school he wanted to be a chef on an ocean liner. He loved being with people. On one occasion when my mother was cross with us he suggested we ran away to my grandmother's house.

We set off, he on his roller skates and me running beside him, finally reaching my grandmother's house about three or four miles away. Of course she was shocked to see us and we were taken with her to the local phone box so that she could phone my father at work and tell him we were there. We hadn't a phone, so she couldn't phone my mother. My father duly came and collected us, but I don't remember being in trouble for running away, and of course we gave no thought to the worry we had no doubt caused.' Sister **Linda Deeson**.

'He came to us on the 6th February 1947, a much wanted and much loved boy by all the family. I was one of his Godmothers. He was interested in all things, had a good sense of humour and enjoyed a good joke. He loved life and was not afraid to show affection – you had a bear hug when he arrived and another when he departed. He was very interested in model aircraft and desperately wanted to fly, and he achieved this ambition. For many years after we lost him I felt his presence with me, particularly if I was upset about anything and this was a great comfort to me. Memories fade as time passes but he still has a special place in my heart.' Godmother **Enid Jenkin**.

'I lived next door to Peter for just 6months in the summer before he died. Peter was like a childhood sweet heart. We used to play in each other's gardens and I remember exchanging Love Heart sweets. I was nine at the time and he would have been 13. He had a sister called Linda who was about the same age as me. I remember Peter was a very kind gentle, thoughtful boy. One day I had a bad headache and he went and got a cold cloth for my forehead. We were always playing together, he made me a periscope and we spied on his sister from my side of the fence. He also converted my sister's old pram trolley into a go kart. We used to trundle this go kart down an alley way through Croydon Cemetery to Mitcham Common where we used to have picnics and made tree houses. It seems ironic the alleyway where we walked is now where Peter rests with his other school friends. When Peter told me about this trip I was upset – what was I going to do for two weeks while he was away? You can imagine how devastated I was when I learnt of the tragedy. I didn't know Peter very long but I have fond memories of special summer days.' Friend **ShirleyAlford**.

John Leonard Wells – age 14
Barrow Road, Waddon. He was first class at games and was one of the school's outstanding characters. He won school cricket colours in both 1959 and 1960.

'John was a lovely person, always happy and good fun to be with. He was always good at sport and loved every minute of it. He loved cricket the best, – it was his true love. We were good friends and I sometimes played cricket with him as I was sporty too. We were always over in the playing fields on the Purley Way. John was always good fun with a good sense of humour. In 1961 my eldest son was 18 months old and John took him everywhere. John was always giggling and laughing, he was a happy child.' Sister **Shirley Harris**.

'My memories of John are of a good brother and a good friend, he is still missed. He was a great sportsman and a cheeky chap who took my girlfriend to the pictures before I went out with her. I still miss him.' Brother **Ken Wells**.

'John was younger than me but what drew us together was our love of sport and in John's case, his particular love of cricket. I witnessed a comprehensive 5 wicket victory for the Primary Schools Eleven, due in no small way to John who scored 17 runs out of the 73 required for the win, having already taken 2 wickets for a miserly 6 runs in the Selhurst Innings.' Cousin **Foster**.

'My friend John Wells reminded me of Tommy Steele.' Friend **Bill Tarbuck**.

'I was fairly close to John and in awe of him as an amazing fast bowler. We got to the Croydon schools final and batting first Lanfranc scored a healthy total. Then John set about bowling out the opposition for a humiliating total. John bowled like an athlete – everything in his body worked in harmony. John was a lovely chirpy guy as well, so he was easy to like.' Friend **Dave King**.

Martin Grenville White – age 14
Downsview Road, Upper Norwood. He was fond of animals. He had excellent reports from school and was top in two subjects.

'What do I recall of Martin? His smile and humour – that's what I remember. He was such a fun boy, everything he said and did, had humour in it. He always came out with a humorous comment, and things that I would get ticked off for,

Martin would come out with a witty comment and make my parents laugh and get away with! For example one day he came in from school and dropped his satchel on the floor. It burst open and its contents flew everywhere. My mother said 'pick it up' but Martin left it there with the comment 'It looks like a bomb's hit it! He was always very happy. Everything was to be enjoyed whether it was pushing his little sister Angela in her pushchair or cracking Brazil nuts! As little boys we enjoyed eating nuts but Brazil nuts were devilishly difficult to break until Martin instigated a fun method. Together we developed the art of putting a Brazil nut under the foot of a large armchair, and then we'd go across the other side of the room and run across together, jumping on the chair to crack the nut! Usually this worked very well, – but just sometimes there was a disaster. When I was eight and Martin was five there was a big difference between us but as we got older the three years meant less and less. By 1961 three years didn't make much difference at all and Martin wanted me to go on the trip to Norway too, but I didn't want to intrude on his space, so I declined. He was always very kind to his little sister Angela who was fascinated by the phases of the Moon and wanted to know what happened to the other bit of it, – when it was a half moon. Before he left for Norway he said to Angela 'I'm going away to look for the other bit of the moon for you.' When he didn't come back and little Angela kept asking where Martin was we told her 'He's still looking for the other half of the moon for you.' We were really good friends and good brothers. It makes me wonder how we'd get on now.' Brother **Bernard White**.

'Over the years, many people have said to me "You probably don't remember much of Martin, you were so young at the time". It was a remark that always made me bristle. Why would I not remember much of him? I idolised him, and I consider myself very fortunate that in the all-too-brief three and a half years that I had him as a lively, funny and thoroughly entertaining older brother, I amassed such a wealth of memories before he was taken away from all of us. Martin was indefatigably full of fun and laughter, the sunny spirit who was the family jester and entertainer as well as being loving, caring, gentle, and demonstrative in his affections. My brothers had adjoining bedrooms, the only access to Bernard's room being through Martin's, and I can clearly recall the delight I felt at weekends when they were not at school, and I used to prance into

Martin's room as soon as I was awake and climb into his bed for my cup of tea and biscuit, knowing that I cornered them to play with. I remember our house being swathed in scaffolding. To my squeals of laughter, Martin used to demonstrate the way you could squirt the hosepipe into the end of the scaffolding pipes to produce all sorts of fountains and waterfalls issuing from various points in the structure.' Sister **Angela Watson**.

Roger Philip White – age 14
Bradley Road, Upper Norwood. He was extremely fond of animals and bred rabbits and white mice. Before going on holiday he briefed a friend on how to look after the baby rabbits properly. It was his first holiday abroad.

'My brother Roger was football mad and often went with his father to see Crystal Palace matches.' Sister **Lorna Allen**.

'Regarding Roger White I recall he always sat next to Martin White in class and we all hung around together during school. Lanfranc was a good school and I enjoyed most of my time there. I remember Roger White, Martin White, myself and some others bought pea shooters to school once and I was the unlucky one to hit our technical drawing teacher in the face for which I got six of the best with a T-Square.' Friend **Philip Rose**.

'Roger and I were best friends from the age of five. My bedroom in my house in Woodend faced Roger's bedroom in Bradley Road and we were able to keep in touch long after bedtime by Morse code using our torches into the small hours. Roger and I worked together building and selling bikes from bits we found abandoned on bomb sites. We also built soap box carts and snow sledges. We made money where ever possible, including clearing snow from front garden paths. We caught voles on Mitcham Common after school and after converting Roger's dad's garage we bred voles very successfully, selling them at our schools and to all our friends. Roger went to Lanfranc and I went to Ingram School. I am sure that had Roger lived he and I would have been best friends now. I still remember the day I heard about the crash and went running over to Roger's house spending most of the day with Roger's Mum not really believing it to be true. I often visit Roger's resting place.' Friend **Graham Stanford**.

Second Year Lanfranc Boys

Gregory Paul Allen – age 13
Manor Road, South Norwood. Intelligent and clever with his hands, he made an electronic robot for the school Eisteddfod. He was an A-stream pupil.

'Gregory and his mother were a one parent family. His mother Rene was an only child and was a school teacher. She worked hard to be both mother and father to Gregory. I recall that she was an excellent artist.' Friend, **John White**.

'I grew up with Gregory Allen. He lived with his mother and grandparents. There was five years difference between Gregory and myself. Gregory was a frail child, having weak bones. I remember that he broke his collar bone, also a leg and an arm, at different times. I was very fond of both Gregory and his Mum. His grandfather was rather strict.' Friend Ms **C. V. Kent**.

'I knew Eggy as we both attended South Norwood Primary school, but just as a face in the crowd. He was in the year above us and at that age you don't mix with the younger boys. So he and another boy Clive (they called him "Carthorse") went up to Lanfranc the year before me. In the summer of 1960 after the school placements had been made, Eggy and Clive came to visit their old (and my current), form Master Mr Lapsley, and the three boys going to Lanfranc were introduced. As I was the cyclist they suggested that I joined them, they would show me the way and as it was a pretty tough school, they would look after me!' Friend **Len Dee**.

'Sometimes I cycled home via Thornton Heath pond and I remember having a race with Gregory 'Eggy' Allen. He had a heavy old bike with rod brakes but he managed to keep up with me on my newish racer. We were not really friends but we got on well, he was quite a laugh.' Friend, **John Cooke**.

'I treasure a red and white felt ram ten inches tall and covered in exquisite stitching. He was given to me by Gregory's mother who taught needlework. Gregory had fairish hair and was about my height. We didn't often socialise in each other's houses spending our time with other children on the street, riding bikes and roller-skating. The old golf course nearby provided a suburban wilderness in which to create our camps. When he wasn't cycling to school we'd meet on the bus coming home where he'd talk to me, quite openly, in front of his school friends ignoring their sniggering and exaggerated eye movements. My friend next door said he was my boyfriend. Gregory's mother wrote to me after the funeral saying simply: 'Gregory was very fond of you and I know he would want you to have something to remember him by. He always loved this ram so I would like you to have it.' Friend **Madeleine Urquhart**.

Alan James Lee – age 13

Rosecourt Road, West Croydon. He was top of his class in the second year A-stream. He shared a paper round with David Gore.

'Alan Lee and I were good playmates when we were at Elmwood Road School, being separated after the 11 plus exams. One day, he and I were involved in a war game when he 'took cover' behind some dustbins. I lobbed a stone in his direction, pretending it to be a hand grenade, and as he bobbed his head up to see where I was, the stone struck him above the right eye. Alan, I am sure, would have borne it without any grudge, taking it for the unintended accident that it was. Well, the day after the air crash, the Croydon Advertiser published Alan's picture with the other victims on its front page, and I was shocked to see that there, above his right eye, was the mark where my stone had hit him. I liked Alan dearly from the start. There wasn't an ounce of harm in the lad, though I seem to remember that he had a deliciously wicked sense of humour. We shared gobstoppers and one day we shared a stick of liquorice wood which one of us had found on the way in to school. When I painfully broke a tooth at school, and on another day banged my head really hard on the playground tarmac, Alan was there doing his best to make me laugh and forget the pain. He was a good friend. Shortly after the stone-throwing incident, I went on to Oval Primary, another school in Croydon, though Alan and I did stay in touch, meeting sometimes at the Saturday morning pictures (the ABC cinema at Broad Green), or in local swing parks. But then came the 11 plus exams. I went on to Archbishop Tenisons in Croydon, while Alan went to Lanfranc. After that we lost touch mostly until I heard of him being on that plane. I have carried the ache of losing him inside me for the past fifty years.' Friend **Bill Cooper.**

'Poor little Alan, he was such a sweet natured boy, very much loved by a very close family. My friend Joanie, his sister, was very fond of him. There was another brother who was older than them. I used to go to their house a lot. They were a lovely family.' Friend **Carol Thornton** nee **Brown**.

'I was at Lanfranc school for just two years before moving away the summer of the crash to attend the Ingram Secondary School. We caught tadpoles, frogs, and sticklebacks at Beddington Park. Having similar names, but of no relation, generated a sense of competition between us.' Friend **Barry Lee.**

'Alan Lee was my friend at junior school. I liked him because he was a bit of a rogue! I was surprised he was taken on the Norway trip because he was a rogue. We rode from Broad Green, with me on his saddle, to Mitcham Common. We got told off when we got home.' Friend **Barry Sturgess.**

We have not forgotten them.

EPILOGUE

On June 16th 1962 the 'Lanfranc Memorial' – a wooden sports pavilion was opened by Mrs Kettle, now no longer Croydon's mayor. Lanfranc school had survived an 'Annus horribilis'. From slow beginnings the school had begun to rise up again from the black memories of the air crash. Lanfranc's sporting prowess had suffered and it hadn't been triumphant in its matches against Croydon's other schools, but the 'Lanfranc grit' was still there and was being encouraged to fight again. Whilst the boys were slowly getting their vigour back, by comparison all could see that their headmaster remained badly affected by the tragedy. The bounce had gone from his step and his formerly bright eyes were sad. Little by little, however, Lanfranc returned to normal. The visit to Norway had helped lighten the school's atmosphere, whilst the opening of the memorial sports pavilion had helped to draw a line under what had happened.

The year had been gloomy but as the end of the summer term approached, senior boys talked of doing something funny on their last day. Teacher Ron Cox overheard John Martin suggesting some practical jokes and commented that the problem was that most pranks caused damage and showed no imagination. Challenged by this John and his friends decided to 'replace' a globe suspended from the ceiling in Ron's classroom. Inspired by the television programme 'It's a Square World', John painted a square box to look like a globe and substituted this, attaching a message – 'It's a square world Sir!' His second prank was more personal. Mr Patterson had always teased him about ballroom dancing, so during morning break he crept into the staff changing room and swapped Mr Patterson's clothes for feminine garb from the drama wardrobe. Mr Patterson had changed into his tracksuit for games, and on his return was annoyed to discover his clothes replaced by a woman's dress! By mid-afternoon Mr. Patterson, still in his tracksuit, was very short tempered. Eventually Mr Fowle announced (over the school loud speaker system), that leaving reports would be withheld unless the clothes were returned. John Martin was on his way to the headmaster's office to own up when the clothes were found. The mystery of the disappearance of Mr. Patterson's clothes amused everyone (except the man himself), and the school was lifted by a surge of high spirits. The boys thought it was a brilliant last day.

During their awful year, gaps in their ranks had been closed, and lost friends and masters had been commemorated. Lanfranc would go on, and now from being down, the only way to go was up. Many of Lanfranc's boys, who might have gone on the ill-fated trip, were now leaving school with a future ahead of them. These lucky boys were never to forget their friends who had perished – and many were inspired to live their lives better because of them.

At that time some wondered whether they would have lives to live because of the escalating Cold War which culminated with a frightening political and military stand-off between the United States and the Soviet Union over nuclear missiles based in Cuba. The situation worsened by October 27th to the point that nuclear catastrophe was hanging by a thread and was only averted when a secret deal was struck between President John F. Kennedy and Premier Nikita Khrushchev. The U.S. agreed to remove their missiles in Turkey in exchange for Soviet missiles being removed from Cuba. The world had been dangerously close to Nuclear War.

Resilient youngsters (not all of whom comprehended the dangers) were able to cope and move ahead. Contemplative adults, especially those coping with bereavement, found this a harsh climate in which to regenerate their broken lives. Women who shared their emotions with each other did better than men who bottled up their feelings. Many of the mothers of the Lanfranc Boys regularly visited the cemetery, often going together, or meeting in groups. They were largely able to move ahead. A group of parents met regularly at Elsie and Alan White's house and formed a self-help group, but some fathers kept a British 'stiff upper lip' and hid their pain as a means of self-preservation. Some dulled it in other ways. Mr Adams continued to 'lock' his son John away in order to be able to cope with life without him. He wasn't alone in doing so. These fathers suffered from deteriorating health.

At this time Eagle was fighting to remain viable. The last two remaining Vikings that remained in service on Eagle's 'Med-Air' contract flew until November 1962, but the partnership between the Cunard Steamship Company and Eagle had fallen apart. BOAC wanted to enjoy the lucrative partnership with Cunard and held secret negotiations to form BOAC-Cunard instead. Cunard stripped its assets from Eagle and transferred them to Eagle's government sponsored rival. The company's existence hung in the balance – but a fighting spirit existed in the 'Eagle family' and they clung on, presenting a 'business as usual' face.

Whilst Cunard Eagle changed its name to British Eagle a miracle happened for two mothers in Croydon. Both Eileen Adams and Mrs Benson found that they were unexpectedly pregnant. Eileen Adams found consolation in another son – David, 'a gift from God' – but as he grew up Eileen was forbidden by her husband to talk to him about John. Mrs Benson had a baby daughter and young Derek found he had a little sister, Sheila, filling Micky's place. Some older parents with adult children became grandparents and focused on these new arrivals to take the pain from their hearts. But those past childbearing age, and with no other children to focus upon, suffered deeply and never recovered. Their lives were empty and although they endeavoured to fill them by helping other youngsters, they were permanently blighted. Some siblings also suffered very badly, their lives were like buds checked by frost in May. They'd lost a vital family member and the trauma halted their development. Like nipped buds, they never fully opened. No one recognised them as victims of the Papa Mike crash, but they were.

In 1963 members of the Stavanger Red Cross, led by Sofus Tønnessen visited Croydon and they stayed with various families. It was an uplifting time for all concerned as families became acquainted with those who had rescued their sons and brothers. Tommy Fowle invited them all to Lanfranc and Sofus spoke to the boys who instantly liked him. He was made an honorary member of Lanfranc and presented with a badge from the school – which he sewed onto his jacket and treasured over the years. Many families had invited Red Cross members to stay, and some later returned to Norway to visit, establishing friendships which helped sustain them.

In 1963 both Mrs Catherine Kettle and Ernest Taberner sadly died before their 'three score years and ten'. Had the Lanfranc disaster taken its toll on them too?

The following year, 1964, started very badly for British Eagle. On February 29th, Leap Year's extra day, their Bristol 175 Britannia 312 (G-AOVO) flying to Austria, hit a mountain on its approach to Innsbruck's Kranebitten Airport. It seemed that the pilot had descended below the minimum safety level and the aircraft was destroyed on impact, with the loss of all 83 on board. It was Eagle's worst accident. At Lanfranc, Tommy Fowle was taken ill.

In 1965, the year that Croydon was swallowed up as part of Greater London, the Dean of Stavanger, Dr. Christian Svanholm, his wife, and the Stavanger Cathedral choir visited Croydon to lay a wreath at the Lanfranc Memorial Garden. The choir boys and men sang several Norwegian hymns, one sung by their leading tenor Tor Gilje, was the memorably beautiful *'I Himmelen'* – *'In Heaven Above'*. This visit helped continue Lanfranc's and the parent's connection with Stavanger. Tommy Fowle and his wife were present at the ceremony. He had recovered enough to continue to work tirelessly to restore his school to its former glory. Lanfranc and its pupils meant everything to him, and he carried on until another stroke, which happened in November, claimed his life. His pupils and colleagues mourned him. Everyone thought that he was the final victim of the Papa Mike tragedy.

Gradually Croydon's tragedy receded in significance as time passed. Life went on. Friends of those who had died were in apprenticeships or jobs. Families had closed ranks and were getting on with a changed life. British Eagle had its life as an airline company hanging in the balance – when disaster struck again.

A final fatal accident bizarrely occurred *seven years to the day* after the tragic Holtaheia disaster. On August 9th 1968, British Eagle Vickers Viscount (G-ATFN) crashed on the Munich-Nuremberg autobahn near Lagenbruck killing all 48 on board. An electrical system failure was thought to be the cause of the accident. Statistically the chances of a fatal crash in which all on board died occurring to the same airline on the same day separated by a time interval of seven years is infinitesimally small.

British Eagle was closed down in 1968. A vital licence held by Eagle was revoked by Labour Prime Minister Harold Wilson. It is said that Labour MP's cheered at the news of the company's downfall, preferring to protect their own state run airlines, BOAC and BEA. (Privatisation under Margaret Thatcher's Tory government occurred in 1987. This was too late for Harold Bamberg's airline.) In 1968 Eagle had landed, and would never take off again.

Eagle's Papa Mike crash was still claiming victims. When Jean Endicott lost her beloved Susan, half of her family had gone and so had the sparkle from her life. Jean died aged 53 in 1969, and was buried with her daughter Susan at Stoke Gabriel church.

The ashes of Tommy Fowle and two long serving masters from Lanfranc, Norman Cook and Sydney Gubby, are scattered with the Lanfranc Boys at the Lanfranc Memorial Garden. They wanted to be with 'their boys'.

Barry Crofts had wanted to go to Norway, along with all his best friends. He went on the Pilgrimage and to later remembrance services on Holtaheia. He kept a piece of wreckage of Papa Mike as a memento, visited Croydon Cemetery regularly, and his dying wish was to be buried near his friends.

Life changes as a result of the disaster

Unknown to anyone in Croydon there were 'victims' in Norway too. Many of those involved in the rescue had lives blighted by what they had experienced. Perhaps the worst case was the young Air Traffic Controller at Sola. Sverre Hodne was 35 years old in 1961 and despite being completely exonerated of any blame *whatsoever* he suffered very badly as a result of the air crash. Character-wise he was sensitive, studious, well informed, and always up to date. Somewhat of a loner, nevertheless, he had a good sense of humour and was considered by his colleagues and friends to be a very nice and dependable young man. The tragedy had a profound effect on him, from which he never fully recovered and which sadly, shortened his life. Although no journalist suggested any professional short-comings there were two letters sent to an Oslo newspaper that pointed the finger of blame at him. The letters were from members of the public who knew little about aviation, who possibly were so shocked by the tragedy that had happened in their country that they needed a scapegoat. Their misguided and untrue criticism hit Sverre very hard. There was no professional counselling in those days and his colleagues, aware of his innocence (and also aware that it could have been any of them facing unjust blame), tried their best to talk him out of it. They all went through a bad time at Sola ATC Tower following the disaster, but they all knew, absolutely, that they would have acted exactly the *same way* as Sverre. What they hadn't experienced, but Sverre had, was the lightning-bolt shock of discovering an aircraft he was guiding in to land – vanished! The agony of coping with this terrible situation, coupled with the enquiry and this destructive criticism that followed, psychologically afflicted him and affected his health. He was never the same again. In the words of Arne Helvik, former Chief ATC at Sola, *'Sverre Hodne was a nice fellow, calm, with a gentle sense of humour, professionally of very high standard. It was a heavy loss to the service and colleagues when he, broken in body and mind, died as a young man.'*

For Kaare N. Hidle, leader of the Red Cross Hjelpekorps in August 1961, the Holtaheia rescue made a deep and lasting impression, and the results were both bad and good. Queen Elizabeth II awarded the Stavanger Branch of the Red Cross an MBE (Member of the British Empire) for their work in rescuing the victims of Papa Mike. This was presented to Kaare as the leader of the Red Cross Hjelpekorps at that time. Being a man of few words, Kaare was loath to discuss the experience with anyone. He was a sensitive, gentle man, and the carnage he had seen at Holtaheia was so awful that he couldn't bear to be reminded of it. So he left his home in Stavanger and moved to Oslo. The move was life-changing again because in Oslo he met his future wife. Right from the start she asked him what he was running from – but he never wanted to talk about it. His son, Hans Juhl Hidle, believes that he owes the fact that he came into the world to the plane crash on Holtaheia. If it hadn't happened, his father would not have left Stavanger and met his mother, and so he would not have been born. Hans Juhl went on to become a competitive swimmer, and Kaare became a respected swimming judge, awarded a lifetime achievement award for his services to swimming. In the last months of Kaare Hidle's life he finally opened up and talked about his experience of Holtaheia. Hans wrote *'It was almost as if he knew his time was short and he needed to tell someone about the tragedy by relating to someone what he saw and experienced, and how he was affected by it all.'* (Kaare N. Hidle died November 17th 2007).

Kari Skuterud's future vocation was directed by the crash of Papa Mike. August 9th 1961 was her 17th birthday, and the tragedy hit her and her elder brother Rolf Ringe like a seismic shock. Kari was too young to help with the rescue, but when the Red Cross cleared away the wreckage, she was with them. Seeing the devastation on Holtaheia made her decide to become a nurse. She trained at Lovisenberg Hospital in Oslo, then as an Operation Theatre nurse, finally after 26 years at Stavanger Hospital (latterly as head nurse) in 1990 Kari joined the International Red Cross. Her humanitarian work took her to Somalia, Pakistan, Thailand, Angola, southern Sudan, Kenya, Afghanistan, Palestine, Eritrea, and Indonesia. Kari's husband of 42 years, Ola Skuterud, also a long term Red Cross member, worked with her in some of these countries. Their work called for a great deal of personal courage and altruism. Ola was kidnapped by a clan in Mogadishu whilst Kari was in Kandahar, Afghanistan. After that she joined her husband in Nairobi, and was the first white nurse to help after the bomb blast at the American Embassy in Nairobi in 1998, where 300 people died and 5000 were injured. Kari's selfless work as a Red Cross nurse is one example of a positive life change that resulted from the tragedy.

Everyone intimately involved had their lives changed in some way. Many friends and relatives of the Lanfranc Boys developed a phobia of flying which had to be overcome, but wasn't in some cases. Some Lanfranc boys were spurred to greater academic or sporting success – in memory of their friends. A few were also 'nipped in the bud' by the tragedy. All can trace their lives back to a turning point that happened because of the disaster. Young Angela White grew up having close Norwegian friends; went on to graduate in Scandinavian Studies, and has returned to Holtaheia many times.

I know that my life followed an entirely different route as a result of the disaster. Meeting Captain Endicott on Holtaheia and seeing the panorama from its summit changed my life. Having made a promise to my devastated father to work hard at school (at long last), and encouraged to think higher by Captain Endicott, I kept my word, worked very hard, passed my exams, and gained a place to study Zoology and Geology at London University – where I met my husband Nick. Although I organised an expedition to Arctic Norway in 1966 it wasn't until 1987 (a year after the 25th anniversary when a commemoration had occurred at the cross) that I revisited Holtaheia together with Nick and our son Chris and daughter Iona. It was a grey August day of low cloud that shrouded Holtaheia's summit. Whilst the others went down to read the plaque where Papa Mike had hit the mountain I stood alone by the monument (now encrusted with lichen growth and becoming submerged by stones brought by visitors), and I promised never to forget them. This book is the result of that promise.

Premonitions associated with the disaster

I had previously thought that I'd been the only one to have a premonition, but as people contacted me I discovered that several people also had deeply felt premonitions about the trip to Norway. This seemed strange but I found a possible explanation in the book 'The Power of Premonitions' by Dr. Larry Dossey M.D. He states that these premonitions are ones that occur to subconsciously inform a person to avoid a train or plane. Researcher William Cox, in the 1950's, compared the number of passengers of trains which had accidents to those same trains for the previous seven, 14, 21, and 28 days, over five years. He discovered that in every case where there was an accident, *fewer people* were on the trains that crashed, than were on similar trains that did not crash. The odds against this happening were more than 100:1. In one particular train disaster, only nine people were travelling on the train, whereas its normal average was 62 passengers. Dr. Larry Dossey believes that it isn't simply that people wake up on the morning, envisage a train (or plane) disaster, and decide not to go by that method of transport, it is that they experience a sense of unexplainable physical unease, depression, or distress. They cannot explain it but they feel that 'something bad is going to happen'. These people, if they can avoid it, do not travel. A premonition – from the Latin *prae*, 'before', and *monere*, 'warn', is a forewarning. It is simply a tragedy that in the case of the Papa Mike air crash no one could get out of their commitment to be on that ill-fated plane. Captain Watts was scheduled to go. First Officer Murray Smalley drew the short straw and had to stand in for someone who was off sick. It was to have been Susan Endicott's last flight. But why should it have been 'ill-fated'? Was it 'destined' to crash? Surely it wasn't. Yet why did so many of us have premonitions? There is no seemingly logical answer. One interesting story not included in the account came from Tom Danielsen, a young Norwegian from Stavanger who visited a shop in London's Oxford Street years later. On discovering he came from Stavanger the salesman (from Croydon) informed him that his son was on the list to go, but had taken a strangely strong feeling against the trip. He and his wife had tried hard to persuade him to go, but the boy insisted on withdrawing. Now they were eternally grateful. Tom Danielson was struck by the man's earnestness. This name of this boy is unknown.

New theories as to why Papa Mike may have crashed

On August 17th 2010 a meeting took place at Sola Aviation Museum, in the old German hangar close to the quarters of the RNoAF rescue team. Present were Sola Tower's retired Chief Air Traffic Controller Arne Helvik, retired Royal Norwegian Air Force Flight Engineer Karl Nilsen, and retired Royal Norwegian Air Force Pilot Bjørn N. Skogen, plus Nick and Rosalind Jones. The object of the meeting was to see if any new light could be cast upon the mystery. The lengthy discussion was recorded and transcribed and led to much correspondence with Bjørn, resulting in the drawing of a new flight path map. Some new information, plus reconsidered theories, emerged.

On the night of the crash and for some long time afterwards a question that vexed the airmen at Sola was that they believed Ground Control Assistance (GCA) was offered to Papa Mike but that it had been refused. Arne Helvik and Karl Nilsen both recalled, from conversations made at Sola at the time of the crash, that Papa Mike *was* offered GCA at some time before the aircraft was due to land. This assistance was declined. As a result Nils Abrahamsen, the Norwegian Air Force officer in charge, went home as normal at 1600 hours. (He could, however, have been called back and had GCA fully operational within 45 minutes.) If GCA *was* offered and declined, then this was *not* recorded in the Accident Report which stated instead that *'no request was made for this service by either the Pilot or Sola Tower.'* Was this statement recorded in the report because the offer of GCA happened *prior* to 1611 hours – after which time contact with Sola was fully listed in the report? There is no way of knowing. However the Accident Report stated again that *'No request for GCA service was made either by the Captain of G-AHPM or by the ATC Officer at Sola, presumably because it was not considered that the circumstances were such as to warrant this action.'* These two statements are at variance with the memories of those who were present at Sola Tower, and who have maintained that Papa Mike *was* asked, but refused. Their understanding being that it was declined due to envisaged 'extra costs' to Cunard Eagle Airways Ltd (which would not have been the case). Was it an oversight of the Commission to leave this offer of GCA from Sola out of the report? Was it left out deliberately? And if so why? Or could it be a case of wishful thinking on behalf of ATC officers at Sola Tower, *after* the event, which subsequently developed into well held beliefs? Unfortunately, all these years later, nothing can be proved either way.

It is interesting, nevertheless, to conjecture that an unrelated case of instrument failure that *might* have had some bearing on the case of Papa Mike wasn't mentioned. The Commission noted *'During the same afternoon and evening 8 other aircraft, – among them another Viking operated by Cunard Eagle Airways Ltd. landed at Sola without any problems of note.'* Technically this is correct because all 8 aircraft did land safely. However, when representatives of Cunard Eagle Airways Ltd flew in to Sola that night, they were not only talked down by GCA but just after landing the Viking inexplicably suffered *total electrical failure*. The ATC officer in the Tower lost radio contact and had to send Sola Airport's 'Follow Me' van out to lead the aircraft to the parking area. This was a 'problem of note' surely, but it was not included in the report. It begs the question as to whether some unknown cause might also have made Papa Mike's instruments to fail in the same way, and possibly at the same place.

Arne Helvik is a very well qualified expert who believes that the crash must have been due to total instrument failure. With 42 years experience in Civil Aviation he is convinced that total instrument failure is the only logical explanation. He can envisage no other reason why an experienced pilot could have flown completely off course, and instead of turning back around to fly *south* along the centre line back to Sola airport, instead flew *eastwards* and into the mountains. Arne Helvik is also adamant that the weather conditions were fair at Sola with good visibility, and that an ILS visible landing should have presented no difficulties. Total instrument failure not only would account for the gross deviation from the normal landing procedure, but also for lack of radio communication from the pilots, if they had realised they had not penetrated the localiser beam and were 'lost'. It would also account for Papa Mike flying at the low altitude of 1,500 feet when it had been cleared to fly at the safe height of 2,000 feet. Arne Helvik feels sure that two qualified pilots, of whom Captain Watts was very experienced, would have followed the exact procedure for landing. He has suggested that the reason for Papa Mike continuing its easterly approach, even if his electrics had failed, was because the pilot may have seen the sea below and believing that Talgjefjord was Hafrsfjord (near Sola), he may have been attempting a visual landing. He does not subscribe to other theories put forward, nor does he believe that Papa Mike flew over Stavanger. But how and why could a total instrument failure occur? And *if* this happened twice in the same day, at the same place, to the same type of plane, – a Viking, what could have caused it?

Bjørn N. Skogen, who was a radar operator at Møvik, near Kristiansand, at the time of the crash and was the airman who took the telephone call from Sola Tower on the night of August 9th, does not subscribe to Arne's theory of total instrument failure. Having qualified and worked as a pilot, over the years Bjørn N. Skogen has cogitated at length over what could have gone wrong with Papa Mike. Studying various reports, he has seen contradictions, but has been unable to draw firm conclusions. Nevertheless his theory is that a simple error, that of not flipping a switch, could have been responsible for the plane flying off course. Prior to Papa Mike approaching Sola Airport there had been no mistakes in procedure, but as it flew close, an error in naming the correct beacon was evident. *'Lima India'* was named instead of *'Zulu Oscar'*, and when the ATC emphasised *'Zulu Oscar'*, the reply from Papa Mike was simply *'Roger'*. (At this time ATC Sverre Hodne heard Papa Mike pass over the airfield.) The next transmission from Papa Mike came at 1620 hours. *'Eagle Papa Mike passed the ZO beacon, will call you on approach'* was said by First Officer Smalley. ZO was just north of the airfield. If the aircraft had now followed the correct procedure they would have turned 30 degrees to the left, (a course west, of 330 degrees on the compass). This would have taken them back briefly over the North Sea. The plane would have held this heading for two minutes, before starting a right (east) turn in order to intercept the localiser beam. After intercepting the beam Papa Mike should have continued turning for a southerly course, back along the centreline, its glide path inbound, for runway 18. It is at this procedural manoeuvre that Bjørn thinks an error may have occurred. Papa Mike's Instrument landing System (ILS), included a switch which controlled the localiser needle, and this had to be tuned correctly. *Approaching* a navigational beacon the switch would be in the 'To' position. *Departing* the same beacon the switch would be moved to the '**From**' position in order to fly *after* the directional needle, as opposed to flying *away* from it. The localiser needle itself would move automatically into three possible main positions during the final approach, informing the pilot if he was 'on course', or if he should 'fly right' or 'fly left', in order to line up with the runway. On turning and eventually crossing the centreline again, thereby intercepting the localiser beam from ZO, *if* the switch was *not* turned to the '**To**' position, but remained in the '**From**' position, then the aircraft would *not* have *completed* its turn, as the localiser needle would have been on the '*fly left*' side of the instrument. If this error had not been noticed then following this now misleading navigational guide would have resulted in the plane not turning south, but continuing heading *east* in a totally erroneous direction. Bjørn believes that the strong wind blowing from the south west only added to the difficulties, taking the aircraft further east and closer to the mountains where, in clouds, close to high ground, in an unfamiliar approach, it is possible that the pilot lost sense of direction and maybe even experienced vertigo, which could have led to fatal decisions. (When experienced by a pilot vertigo is very disorientating. In rare situations where this occurs the pilot must trust his instruments and not what his senses tell him.)

Bjorn N. Skogen subsequently wrote – 'It seems to me that Papa Mike never managed to intercept the ILS centreline, and in strong winds lost his bearings and ended up in the mountains. That he focused on the LII beacon (Lima India), and maybe pushed his attention on ZO (Zulu Oscar) down his priority list, might be of importance. The unusually strong winds would complicate the approach, but as Captain Watts declined the offer for a CGA, he cannot have regarded his ILS approach as hazardous. I have studied the map and comparing that with the radio communications, shows that when he reported at 1611 hours *'we are just coming up to Lima Echo Charlie at this time'*, and seven minutes later, at 1618 hours he said: *'we estimate Lima India in approximately two minutes'*, this gives 9 minutes from LEC to the beacon, if he meant LII, with a ground speed of 200 knots. If he meant ZO, then his ground speed was only 120 knots. The cruising speed of a Viking was 180 knots, and with a wind factor of +30 knots, would, under the given wind conditions (230 degrees at 60 knots) given him a speed in excess of 200 knots. This indicates to me that he was indeed concentrating on LII (Lima India), which was no part of the approved ILS procedure at all. If the 'To' and 'From' switch had not been corrected, then this might have caused the easterly route.' Bjørn states that this is only a theory, nevertheless one which could explain the deviant flight path. 'The To/From needle only indicates the aircraft's position right or left from the centreline, and has nothing to do with altitude. However, the same instrument (ILS) also has a horizontal needle which tells the pilot if the aircraft is above or below the glide path. The most comforting reading to the pilot is, therefore, when the two needles cross in the middle of the indicator.'

Although it sheds no light on why Papa Mike crashed on Holtaheia, it has been possible to draw a new reconstructed flight path of Papa Mike based upon witnessed sightings. This path lies further west and then north, than the Accident Commission's map, before its final easterly location. These sightings may not have been known to the Commission at the time.

Another map that was known to be incorrect has always concerned Mr. H.L. Frost (known as Jim), who was the retired Senior Servicing Engineer, Radio/Radar, of the European division of British Airways. Jim was based at London Airport in 1961. Now a nonagenarian he believes that the crash occurred primarily because First Officer Smalley wasn't given an up-to-date chart covering the Viking's flight, and that this would explain why he quoted the wrong beacon (Lima India) to the ATC at Sola. He believes that Papa Mikes' ADF (automatic direction finding system), was tuned for the *wrong beacon*, and that the vital correction from the ATC at Sola should have alerted the First Officer to his need to get the frequency and call sign of the correct beacon. Tragically, he didn't do so.

Bjørn N. Skogen had qualified this. 'ILS/VOR frequencies are fixed and the pilot will click the knob to the frequency number he seeks. VOR stands for Very High Frequency Omni Directional Range, and the NDB/ADF have a 'seeking turn knob' as a radio, and stands for Non Directional beacon/Automatic Direction Finding equipment, and is operated on a completely different frequency – and for these reasons it is impossible to inter-confuse these two systems.'

In his best-selling book 'The Air Crash Detective' (published in 1969) Stephen Barlay wrote about the Holtaheia plane crash. Chapter 1 of the book entitled 'Wasted Lives' investigated possibilities for the crash. Stephen Barlay knew the Royal Aircraft Establishment (RAE) Farnborough and its personnel well, and he had the opportunity to interview those who tested fragments of Papa Mike's radio. The question that needed to be solved being, 'was the radio actually working at the moment of impact?' A great deal hung on the answer. The RAE had two zealous investigators who tested (by destroying in various ways), dozens of radio valves under various conditions in order to discover, from oxidation of valve filaments, whether Papa Mike's radio was operational at the time of the crash. After exhaustive tests they established that the radio of Papa Mike *was* switched on at the time of impact and they assumed that it must have been working. But was it?

Stephen Barlay noted that investigators discovered, (as H.L. Frost has stated), that the type of route chart used by First Officer Smalley showed Lima India and other beacons – but not Zulu Oscar, and that this chart was mainly concerned with route facilities but *not landing aids*. He questions whether Papa Mike was really navigating towards the Zulu Oscar signal. At the crash site it was found that Papa Mike was still turning slightly to the left as if the pilots believed the aircraft to be on the *other* side. Was it possible that the pilots couldn't hear the ZO signal properly? Or was their set tuned to the wrong frequency?

Leading from this possibility, another line of investigation was to deduce the amount of interference that might have been caused by the radio beacon at Billum in Denmark. It was discovered that only a *small tuning error* could result in an 'overlapping signal' from the much stronger Danish radio beacon. This could have accounted for a misleading radio compass indication. But it would *not* account for the pilot's belief that Papa Mike was west of Zulu Oscar. It had to be an error with reading the ILS localiser needle, as Bjørn N. Skogen believes. Stephen Barlay records that the investigating Commission was finally *'unable to explain how the crew in a situation of this nature could continue on the heading indicated for the time stated unless they either did not note or were misinterpreting the ILS Indicator readings…'*

There is also one small added mystery that cannot be accounted for but should not be discounted either. Karl Nilsen and Egil Eriksson, both Royal Norwegian Air Force employees at Sola, accustomed to plane noises, heard a large propeller driven plane flying low over Stavanger at around the time Papa Mike went missing. Karl is absolutely adamant that the plane appeared to be flying low towards the north-east; and Egil stated that he heard the plane and wondered what it was doing there over the city. Arne Helvik is equally adamant that this simply cannot have been the case. Could it have been Papa Mike? Or could it have been one of the two Scandinavian Airline's flights, due to land shortly afterwards, that was diverted, or perhaps blown over the city in the strong prevailing wind conditions? Again there is no way of telling.

From deductions made from various responses recorded in the radiotelephony log, it appears that either radio contact was occasionally lost, or that First Officer Smalley didn't reply, or both. Although the Accident Investigation Commission chose to ignore these omissions in transmissions they may hold a clue. Perhaps something was going wrong with Papa Mike's radio.

The truth is that it is all simply academic today. Nothing was learnt from the Holtaheia plane crash. It is of no use pointing a finger of blame at anyone, nor any one thing, as nothing can be proved. The crash remains an unsolved mystery.

CONTRIBUTORS TO 'THE LANFRANC BOYS'

Piecing together so many contributions has been like constructing a giant jigsaw puzzle. I am indebted for the wealth of material entrusted to me by letter, email, telephone, and personal interview. Everyone who has contributed in any way deserves to be acknowledged because without their input of information, big or small, the content of this book could not have been written. Collectively they have supplied the untold story. I am deeply grateful to them all. I am also very grateful for all the photographic material which has been supplied.

From Norway

Helene Bjørntvedt, Jon Barstad (National Archives of Norway), Steinar Brandslet, Evelyn Clary, Tom Danielsen, Arild Drechsler, Egil Endresen, Egil Eriksson, Atle Faye (The Norwegian Archive, Library and Museum Authority), Jonas Friestad (Stavanger Aftenblad), Sigve Gramstad (State Archivist), Christine and Ola Helgesen, Arne Helvik, Hans Juhl Hidle, Målfrid Holta, Ragnvald Honganvik, Elinor Sandsmark Idsøe, Kjell Idsøe, Tor Inge Jøssang (Stavanger Aftenblad), Ingrid and Ola Lekvam, Asbjørn Løland, Åse Liv Ledaal Mæle, Else J. Meling, Karl Nilsen, Sven E. Omdal (Stavanger Aftenblad), Kjell Terje Osmundsen, Kåre Magnus Østerhus, Christian Øxnevad, Ludvig H. Øxnevad, Johan P. Petersen (Stavanger Red Cross), Ida Revang (Riksarkivet), Guro Skjæveland, Bjørn N. Skogen, Kari Skuterud, Kirsti Sydnes, Marianne Symes, Jan Magne Taarland, Per Tjetland, Sofus Tønnessen, and Reiden Wold (Stavanger Aftenblad Archives).

From Britain and elsewhere

Air Accidents Investigation Branch (AAIB), David Adams, Eileen Adams, Keith Alford, Lesley Algar, Lorna Allen, Dorothy Anstey, Linda Arwood, Ian Austen (Croydon Advertiser), Harold R. Bamberg, Miriam Barker, Rev. Clive Barlow,

Sue Barnes, Ed Barnett, Janis Barnett, Ethel Barr, Simon Barrett, Terry Barson, Shirley Bave, Ian Beacham, Peter Beacham, Ruth Beaven, Ian Bell, Derek Benson, Pam Benson, Chris Bennett (Croydon Local Studies Library), Leslie Bentley, Ivan Bignell, Sylvia Binelli, Terry Blackler, Barry Bourne, Jon Bowerman, Linda Bradbery, Shirley Bradbery, Raymond Bradley, John Braim, Mick Braim, David and Mary Brockett, Peggy Brookes, Terry Bryant, Nobby Bryant, Barbara Brown, Carol Brown, June Brown, Roy Brown, Zed Buckley, Michael Buckley, Geoff Budd, Tim Budd, Ray Cattle, Glennis Cavanagh, Paul Chapman, Juliette Chapple, Patricia Chase, Dave Clark (Headmaster The Archbishop Lanfranc School), Richard Clements, Jean Cook, John Cooke, Michael Cooke, Bill Cole, J. Collie, Michael Collin, Rev. Michael Cooper, Dr. William Cooper, Robin Cooper, Christine Corner (Croydon Local Studies Library), Mark Cottington, Dr. Ron Cox, Alice and Paul Crofts, Tony Crackett, Peter Crouch, Ray Croxton, Roger Culley, Faye Dawes, Joe Daws, Len Dee, Linda Deeson, Graham Edwards, Pat England, Mike Etheridge, Frances Evans, Paul Fairweather, Dennis Finch, Paula Flynn, Olga Fogwill, Alan Foster, D. L. Foster, Mary Foster, Myrtle Foster, Colin Francis, H.L. Frost, Terry Fry, Stella Garrett, David Gerrard, Julia Giles, Brian Gittins, Anthony Green, Martyn Green, Mike Green, Nigel Green, Reg Greenwood, Ian Greest, Martin Griffin, Clive Grumett, Bruce Guest, Clare Gulliver, William Hall, Peter Hamilton, Sue Harrington, Shirley Harris, Tony Hart, Lesley Haskins, Karen Haugh, Andrew Hawkins, Susan Hayes, Keith Hazell, Dave Heyden, Gina Hibberd, Celia Hoare, Pauline Hogan, Mel Holliday, Ted Holyoake, Betty Brownlie-Hughes, Martin Idale, Ray Ives, Mary Jamieson, Anthony Jenner, Diana Johnson, Marie Birketvedt-Jones and Chris Jones, Colin Jones, Iona Jones, Linda and Tim Jones, Michael Jones, Nick Jones, Phil Joyles, Dr. Simon Karginoff, Maureen Kay, David Keenan, Phil Kelly (British Eagle), Christine Kent, June Keep, Doug Kerr, Dave King, Jim Knight, Tove Lamb, Eileen Latter, Harry Lawrence, Barry Lee, Raymond LeRiche, Ann Lewis, David Lewsley, Peter Liversage, Laurence Kingston-Lynch, Janet Mann, Fiona Mantle, Colin Marlow, Lucy Marlow, Mary Marsh, John Martin, Lillian Martin, Robert Marston (Lanfranc Archives), Alison Martyn, Joan Matlock, Lisa Matthews, Derek Meacher, Chris Meyer, Chris Mitchell, Leslie Moorby, Peter J. Moore, Allan Mott, Peter Muncey, Michael Murphy, George Musgrove, Aline Nassif (Croydon Advertiser), Audrey Neale, Carol New,

Jonquil Nicol, Dorothy Oakley, B. Orford, Michael O'Rourke, Eddie Ottewell, Les Owen, Anthony Parsons, Graeme Paterson (The National Archives), Desiree Peacock, Keith Peck, Christine Phillips, Kathleen Phillips, Monica Porter (Daily Mail 'Missing and Found'), Jenny Powell, Stephen Prasher, Derek Page, Roger Page, Geoffrey Parr, Brenda Parry, Anthony K. Parsons, Sue Piner, Edward Quelch, Irene Raff, Rev. Susan Ramsaran, Dave Randall, Peggy Rest, Graham Reygate, Keith Rhodes, John Ridout, Suzy Rodrigues, Philip Rose, Tom Russell, Gareth Saunders, Janet Sawyer, Keith Scotchner, Joan Shannon, Diane Shepherd, Rev. Michael Percival Smith, William Smith, Robert Souter, Paul Sowan, Alan Spicer, John Sprake, Mike Spriggs, Graham Stanford, Angela Stanford, Barry Sturgess, Annette Tallon, Denise Tarling, Bill Tarbuck, Eric Tarrant (British Eagle Archivist), Chris Taylor, Eileen Taylor, Pat Taylor, Vicky Taylor, Jill Thomas, Christine Thorn, Colin Tinson, Jim Towers, Ann Turner, Mary Turner, Mervyn Twaits, Madeleine Urquhart, Derek Wade, Judy Walker, Sue Walker, Shirley Waller, Patricia Ward, Angela Watson, Ken and Maureen Wells, Brian West, Joan Williams, Davina Willis, Peter Willis, Tim Willis, Patrick Wilson, Bernard White, Graham White, John White, Gill Whiteley (Daily Mail 'Missing and Found'), Paul Whittam, Roger Worth, Don and Pat Wood, and Geoff Wood. Thank you all.

The boy who tossed the coin with my brother has, so far, not been found.

HOLTAHEIA

Holtaheia, a residual block of ancient metamorphic schist, was itself an innocent victim. Once vilified and hated for simply 'being in the way' of a lost plane, now it is a place of peace and tranquillity where people go to pay their respects to those who died and to add a stone to the cairn at the foot of the granite cross. Many sit there and are inspired by the beauty of the place and the melancholy of what happened. Ragnvald Honganvik was moved to write his Norwegian poem 'Runer i Stein', translated into English as 'Runics'. If you go to visit Holtaheia then choose a sunny, clear day, as mist often shrouds the summit. Admire the wonderful panorama but recall that at that spot, 34 teenage boys, two masters, two pilots, and one young stewardess, tragically lost their lives.

Runer i stein
by Ragnvald Honganvik

Eg står med ein bit i handa, av taggute plexi-glas,
Han låg her i røysa ved fjellet, der flyet vart
slat i knas.

Ein barneflokk hit ifrå England,
med feilkurs mot Holta fjell.
Sat trygge og glade i seta, og så var det
siste kveld...

Min glasbit er ikkje som kula, der framtid ein
kunne sjå.
Men den har fått riper og skraper, kan hende
frå desse små.

Varleg eg stryk desse "runer",
som talar om stein og om blod.
Men opp frå den brende røysa, ser eg nye
blomar gro – .

Runics by Ragnvald Honganvik
Translated by Else J. Meling

I am holding a piece in my hand
Of tagged, rough plexi-glass –
Laying among stones and sand
Where a plane crash happened, – alas.

Boys from Croydon were given a trip.
Marvellous of course – for them all,
But suddenly the plane had a slip
In the fog, at Holta-mountain's wall.

My piece of glass could never tell
About their fortune, sadness – joy,
It got some scratches as it fell. –
Remembrance from each little boy?

Prudently I touch this "runic" –
Telling about stone and blood.
Life – though – is always unique,
Burnt ground again gives flowers – wood.

Røde Kors Stavanger Hjelpekorps

STAVANGER RED CROSS TODAY

The Stavanger Branch of the Norwegian Red Cross has about 2,500 members, some 400 of whom are engaged in various volunteer activities. Although most of the relief work carried out by its members is of a local nature, Stavanger Red Cross also supports international humanitarian work in the Ukraine and Romania, and through financial donations, it supports Norwegian Red Cross relief work anywhere in the world.

Organised to provide rapid and efficient assistance to people requiring practical help or social contact, the Stavanger branch comprises a number of different activities – work with children, support to the adult population, organised youth activities and voluntary search and rescue. The local branch organisation today consists of three divisions: Search & Rescue (Hjelpekorps), Care, and Youth.

The Hjelpekorps (literally Relief Corps) maintains a year-round voluntary search and rescue stand-by service which may be called out by the local authorities including the Stavanger Rescue Coordination Centre. It participates in organised search for missing persons in and around the Stavanger area, would assist the local community in the event of a major disaster, and maintains a specialist avalanche and water rescue capability. This volunteer service also teaches first aid and mountain and sea safety. Besides, the young volunteers of the Hjelpekorps maintain a search and rescue capability at two points in the hills south-east of Stavanger through the winter week-ends and during ski holiday periods.

The Care Division of the Stavanger Red Cross provides a visitor service for lonely, sick and elderly people in need of social contact, social events, prison visits, court witness support, an aftercare network for psychiatric patients, assistance to newly arrived refugees, and support to political asylum seekers. Children's activities include arranging winter and summer holidays for the destitute, homework assistance to schoolchildren locally and through the Internet, a transport service for children caught in a parental conflict, and courses in non-violent parent-child communication. The Division also operates a child programme catering for 6 to 12-year-olds, with focus on Red Cross topics through play. Red Crossing is the name of a social arena for non-Norwegian and Norwegian residents including cooking and conversation groups, organised under the Care umbrella, as is "Buddy", a newly established service intended to bring Norwegian and newly arrived international students together.

Red Cross Youth welcomes young people from 13 to 30 years of age who wish to engage in local, national or international Red Cross work. Addressing issues which concern young people, the youth section focuses on such topics as rules of war, migration, and sexual health.

Young Stavanger Red Cross search and rescue volunteers on a mountain exercise. (Andreas Joergensen.)

SOLA AVIATION MUSEUM

Established in 1984, Sola Aviation Museum is a private foundation whose aims are to take care of historical aircraft, their equipment, and everything that can be connected to aviation history. Housed in the old German wartime hangar at Sola the museum has a very fine collection of old planes, both military and civil. For the 50th Anniversary of the Holtaheia air crash the museum have mounted an exhibition incorporating a piece of the wreckage of Papa Mike, brought down from the mountain, to commemorate the tragic event. www.flymuseum-sola.no

ADDENDUM

In tribute to his school friend 'Eggy' Allen and all the 'Lanfranc Boys' Len Dee has recorded a new version of 'Young Birds' as well as his own composition entitled 'That Bleak August Day'.

Chris Jones, nephew of Quentin Green lives in Norway and has visited Holtaheia several times, playing 'Amazing Grace' and 'Highland Cathedral' on his bagpipes by the cross. He has composed the bagpipe tune 'Holtaheia'.

Martyn Green, brother of Quentin, made a film of the 1962 Pilgrimage called 'Where the Wind Grieves'.

Details of all these and other additional material, including personal memories of Lanfranc School and what the 'other' Lanfranc boys went on to do with their lives can be found on the website – www.lanfranc-holtaheia.co.uk